Windows 10:

The Personal Trainer

Your personalized guide to Windows 10 from one of the world's
foremost Windows experts!

William R. Stanek

PUBLISHED BY

Stanek & Associates
PO Box 362
East Olympia, WA 98540-0362

Windows 10: The Personal Trainer

Cover Design: Creative Designs Ltd.
Editorial Development: Andover Publishing Solutions
Technical Review: L & L Technical Content Services

You can provide feedback related to this book by emailing the author at williamstanek@aol.com. Please use the name of the book as the subject line.

ISBN-13: 978-1515194316

Version: 1.0.1.9

> **Note**   I may periodically update this text and the version number shown above will let you know which version you are working with. If there's a specific feature you'd like me to write about in an update, message me on Facebook (http://facebook.com/williamstanekauthor). Please keep in mind readership of this book determines how much time I can dedicate to it.

Contents at a Glance

Table of Contents

Introduction

Windows 10: The Personal Trainer is the authoritative quick reference guide to Windows 10 and is designed to be a key resource you turn to whenever you have questions about Windows 10. To this end, the book zeroes in on the key aspects of Windows 10 that you'll use the most.

When you start working with Windows 10, you'll see at once that this operating system is visually different from earlier releases of Windows. What won't be readily apparent, however, is just how different—and that's because many of the most significant changes to the operating system are under the surface. These changes affect the underlying architecture, not just the interfaces—and they were some of the hardest for me to research and write about.

Inside this book's pages, you'll find comprehensive overviews, step-by-step procedures, frequently used tasks, documented examples, and much more. One of the goals is to keep the content so concise that the book remains compact and easy to navigate while at the same time ensuring that the book is packed with as much information as possible—making it a valuable resource.

What's This Book About?

Windows 10: The Personal Trainer covers all editions of Windows 10. In this book, I teach you how features work, why they work the way they do, and how to customize them to meet your needs. I also offer specific examples of how certain features can meet your needs, and how you can use other features to troubleshoot and resolve issues you might have. In addition, this book provides tips, best practices, and examples of how to fine-tune all major aspects of Windows 10. This book won't just teach you how to configure Windows 10; it will teach you how to squeeze every last bit of power out of it and make the most of the features and options it includes.

What Do I Need to Know?

This book is designed as a guide to what you need to know to get the most out of Windows 10. To get practical and useful information into your hands without the clutter of a ton of background material, I had to assume several things. If you are reading this book, I hope that you have basic networking skills and a basic understanding of Windows operating systems. I also assume that you are fairly familiar with Windows commands and procedures as well as the Windows user interface.

How Is This Book Organized?

Making this book easy to follow and understand was my number one goal! I really want anyone, skill level or work schedule aside, to be able to learn how to use Windows 10 effectively.

To make the book easy to use, I've divided it into chapters that take a progressively deeper look at Windows 10. Anyone who wants to learn how to use Windows 10 and its tools effectively should read this book. Because the approach used in this book is ideally suited to readers of all skill levels, you do not have to be a computer expert to understand and use the concepts examined in this book.

What Conventions Are Used in This Book?

I've used a variety of elements to help keep the text clear and easy to follow. You'll find code terms and listings in monospace type, except when I tell you to actually type a command. In that case, the command appears in bold type. When I introduce and define a new term, I put it in italics.

This book also has notes, tips and other sidebar elements that provide additional details on points that need emphasis.

Other Resources

Although some books are offered as all-in-one guides, there's simply no way one book can do it all. This book is intended to be used as a concise and easy-to-use resource. It covers everything you need to perform core tasks for Windows 10, but it is by no means exhaustive.

As you encounter new topics, take the time to practice what you've learned and read about. Seek additional information as necessary to get the practical experience and knowledge that you need.

I truly hope you find that *Windows 10: The Personal Trainer* helps you use Windows 10 successfully and effectively.

Thank you,

William R. Stanek

(williamstanek@aol.com)

Chapter 1. Getting to Know Windows 10

Ready to kick the tires and get to know Windows 10? Windows 10 isn't legacy Windows. It has an all new look and an interface that has some features of Windows 7, some features of Windows 8 and many new options. So much has changed, in fact, that from login to logout, you'll be required to work in new ways to get tasks done. Don't worry though, step-by-step in this chapter, I'll teach you the about:

- Input options
- The new login screen
- The new start menu
- The new desktop
- More

If you don't need help with the basics, jump ahead to Chapters 2 and 3, where I'll teach you all about customizing and personalizing Windows 10.

> **Note** Windows 10 runs on tablets, desktops, laptops, smartphones and other types of computing devices. Rather than mentioning all of these types of devices each time I talk about the operating system, I'll simply say your computer, your device or I may refer to your Windows 10 device. When I do this, I'm talking about all of the various types of devices Windows 10 runs on.

Using Touchscreens

Windows 10 supports two primary input types:

* Keyboard and mouse
* Touchscreen

While the keyboard and mouse are standard, a touchscreen allows you to manipulate on-screen elements in new ways. You can:

* **Tap**   Touch an on-screen element with your finger. A tap or double-tap of elements on the screen generally is the equivalent of a mouse click or double-click.
* **Press and hold**   Press your finger down on an on-screen element and leave it there for a few seconds. Pressing and holding elements on the screen generally is the equivalent of a right-click.
* **Pan (slide to scroll)**   Touch and drag across the screen with one or two fingers. Panning shows another part of a window that has scroll bars. Also referred to as sliding to scroll.
* **Pinch**   Touch an item with two or more fingers and then move the fingers toward each other. Pinching shows less information.
* **Rotate**   Touch two points on the screen and then twist. Rotating turns an item on screen in a clockwise or counter-clockwise direction.
* **Slide in from edge**   Starting from the edge of the screen, slide across the screen without lifting your finger. Sliding in from the left edge shows open apps and allows you to switch between them easily. Sliding in from the top or bottom edge shows commands for the active element.

- **Stretch**   Touch an item with two or more fingers and then move the fingers away from each other. Stretching shows more information.
- **Swipe to select**   Slide an item a short distance in the opposite direction compared to how the page scrolls. Swiping in this way selects the item and also may bring up related commands. If press and hold doesn't display commands and options for an item, try using swipe to select instead.

Keep in mind that throughout this guide, where I have used click, right-click and double-click, you can also use touch equivalents, tap, press and hold, and double tap. Also, when your Windows 10 device doesn't have a physical keyboard, you are able to enter text by using the onscreen keyboard. If a device has no physical keyboard, simply touch an input area on the screen, such as the Search box, to display the onscreen keyboard.

Installation Notes

Installing and setting up Windows 10 is a breeze. Just follow the prompts. During setup, you create a user account for administration of the computer. By default, this account is created as an Internet-connected local account synced to a Microsoft account. You don't have to accept this option and can instead create a standard local account that you can later choose to connect to a Microsoft account. Connecting your account syncs settings, documents, apps and more across your devices.

The only issue I had with setup was that the network connection was created with the Public profile and there's no direct way to change this to a Private profile. This is important because Windows Firewall is enabled by default and places more restrictions on the Public connection than a Private connection. These restrictions made it impossible to connect the computer to a domain. The fix was to run the Network Adapter troubleshooter, which detected that the network connection was set to Public and allowed me to set the network connection to Private.

You also could use PowerShell to make this change. The default alias for the first network connection on a device typically is "Ethernet". If so, you can use an elevated, administrator PowerShell console and the following code to change the "Ethernet" connection from public to private:

```
Get-NetConnectionProfile -InterfaceAlias "Ethernet" |
Set-NetConnectionProfile -NetworkCategory Private
```

Getting Signed In

Windows 10 has a new sign-in process that works with touchscreens as well as a keyboard and mouse. When you start or wake Windows 10, you'll see a preview screen. With a touch screen, swipe up to reveal the login screen. With a keyboard and mouse, simply press a key on the keyboard or click a mouse button to reveal the login screen.

By default, login is always required when you start or wake your Windows 10 device. The way login works depends on whether your computer is part of a business network. For computers that aren't joined to a business network, you have many login options, including:

- **Password**   A password is a mix of upper and lowercase letters, numbers and special characters, usually 8 or more characters in length. To login with a password, click your user name on the login screen, type your password and then press Enter on the keyboard or click the sign-in button (which shows a right-facing arrow).

- **Pin**   A pin is a sequence of 4 or more numbers. To login with a pin, click your user name on the login screen, type your pin and then press Enter on the keyboard or click the sign-in button (which shows a right-facing arrow).

- **Picture password**   A picture password is a unique series of movements on a previously-selected photo, such as a line drawn between two flowers and a circle drawn around a specific flower. To login with a picture password, click your user name on the login screen and then use the touch interface to make the required movements.

> **Tip**   If you're having trouble logging in using a password or pin, click the reveal icon (which has a symbol representing an eye) to display the exact text you typed.

User name and password are the default login technique. You can add a pin, picture password or both using Settings. As discussed in Chapter 3, Settings has replaced Control Panel as the go to resource for most configuration options. In Chapter 3, you'll learn techniques for working with Settings as well as other interface elements that can help you personalize Windows 10.

In business networks, the domain settings control whether you can use pins and picture passwords. In a domain, if your user name isn't displayed on the login screen, click Other User, type your user name, type your password and then press Enter on the keyboard or click the sign-in button.

Local Accounts, Domain Accounts, Microsoft Accounts, Oh My!

Windows 10 supports:

- Local accounts
- Domain accounts

The account types available depend on whether your computer is part of a business network. If your computer isn't part of a business network, your computer has only local accounts. As the designator implies, local accounts are created on your computer. Otherwise, if your computer is part of a business network, your computer has both local accounts and domain accounts.

Real World   Domain accounts exist on the business network, as part of either an Active Directory domain or an Azure-based Active Directory domain. The difference between the two has to do with whether your organization hosts its own servers. If your organization hosts its own servers, you connect to a business network that is part of a standard Active Directory domain. If your organization doesn't host its own servers, you connect to a business network that is serviced via Internet-hosted servers that are part of an Azure AD domain.

Local and Domain Accounts

Local accounts and domain accounts can be Internet-connected to sync settings, documents and purchases across devices. Two types of Internet-connected accounts are supported:

* Microsoft accounts
* School or work accounts

You can connect Microsoft accounts and school or work accounts to both local and domain accounts to get the Internet-connected benefits of syncing settings, documents, purchases and more. With a non-business computer or device, you simply use the Microsoft account for first sign in to create a local account that uses Microsoft account for login. You also can add accounts using the Microsoft account information to create additional local accounts that use Microsoft accounts for login. From then on, the local accounts and the Microsoft accounts are synced and you login using the Microsoft account.

With a non-business computer or device, you can add a school or work account as well to get the get the Internet-connected benefits of syncing settings, documents and more with Office 365 or other Microsoft business services. Here, you use Settings to connect to the account. Thereafter, whenever you login with your local account or Microsoft account, you receive the additional connected benefits of the business service.

Note Determining whether you are using a local account or a Microsoft account is easy. Local accounts use a name string,

such as TedG or SaraH. Microsoft accounts use email
addresses, such as williams@imaginedlands.com.

Accessing Business Networks

When your computer is part of a business network, you can login
using a local account or a domain account, either of which can be
connected to a Microsoft account, a school or work account or both.
As before, when you connect a local account to a Microsoft account,
settings, documents, purchases and more are synced across devices.
When you add a school or work account to a local account or a
Microsoft account, the accounts similarly become connected and
synced.

When you connect a Microsoft account or a school or work account
to a domain account, the accounts are synced but you continue to
login using the domain account. Switching between local accounts
and domain accounts requires using the Other Account option on
the login screen.

On the Other Accounts screen, you specify the account name to use
in *Node\name* format where *Node* is the location for login and *name*
is the user name. The Node can be a domain name, the name of the
device, or "." which refers to the local device. For example, if you want
to log in to the ImaginedLands domain as WilliamS, you'd specify the
account name as imaginedlands\williams. If the local device is named
Computer14 and you want to log in as TedG, you can specify the
account name as either Computer14\TedG or .\TedG.

Getting Around the New Desktops

No, that's not a typo in the heading. With Windows 10, you can have many desktops and each desktop is its own virtual space that can span multiple displays. This means the days when Windows was fixed with a single desktop are gone—finally!

Figure 1-1 shows a desktop with the default configuration. As you can see from the figure, Microsoft revised and refined the taskbar. The Start button opens the Start Menu. For ease of reference, I may sometimes refer to this button simply as Start, as in click Start to open the Start menu.

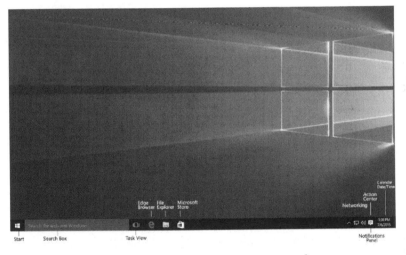

Figure 1-1 Use the desktop to organize your work.

While clicking Start opens the Start Menu, right-clicking Start displays the shortcut menu shown in Figure 1-2. Click any of the options on the shortcut menu to open the related tool. Click Shut Down Or Sign Out to display additional options for shutting down the computer, entering sleep mode and signing out.

> **Tip** An even quicker way to log out? Press Windows logo key + L.

```
Programs and Features
Power Options
Event Viewer
System
Device Manager
Network Connections
Disk Management
Computer Management
Command Prompt
Command Prompt (Admin)

Task Manager
Control Panel
File Explorer
Search
Run

Shut down or sign out          >
Desktop
```

Figure 1-2 Get quick access to commonly used options and features.

> **Tip** You can also display the shortcut menu by pressing the Windows logo key + X.

In the default configuration, the shortcut menu has options for opening the Command Prompt as a standard user or as an administrator. You can modify Start Menu properties to replace these menu items with options for working with Windows PowerShell by following these steps:

1. Right-click an open area on the taskbar and then select Properties.

2. In the Properties dialog box, select the Navigation tab.

3. On the Navigation tab, select the Replace Command Prompt with Windows PowerShell... option and then click OK.

Cortana & Search

The Search box allows you to quickly and easily search Settings, Control Panel, personal files, apps and the web. To use the search feature, simply start typing when the Start menu is open or click in the Search box and then start typing.

As Figure 1-3 shows, the first time you use search, you'll have the option of configuring Cortana as your virtual assistant. If you want to set up Cortana, click Next and follow the prompts. Otherwise, click Not Interested and proceed with your search.

> **Note** If you don't configure Cortana and want to use this feature later, simply click in the Search box, click the Gear icon to access Search Settings and then set Cortana Can Give You Suggestions... to Off by clicking it. This will take you back to the prompt shown in Figure 1-3, allowing you to configure Cortana.

Figure 1-3 Use Cortana to assist you and provide helpful reminders.

Whether you use Cortana or not, search with Windows 10 is much more intelligent than with Windows 8. Windows 8 was a mess, often showing web results when you really only wanted results from the local computer and not being clear about where results were coming from. Windows 10 fixes this (mostly). In Figure 1-4, I entered "display" as my search. Here, the standard search results show related utilities first, settings next and then apps in the Microsoft Store. If you subsequently wanted to search your personal documents, you'd

then click My Stuff. Or if you wanted to search the Web instead,
you'd then click Web.

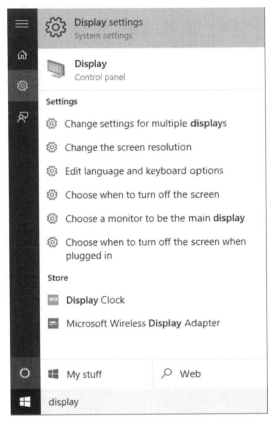

Figure 1-4 Get smarter, better search results with Windows 10.

Although online and web results are included by default in search
results, you can easily change this option so that results only come
from Settings, Control Panel, personal files, and apps. Simply click in
the Search box, click the Gear icon to access Search Settings and then
set Search Online... to Off by clicking it.

As you might expect, there are many more options for search and many powerful parameters you can use to tailor your searches. These options and more are discussed in Chapter 5 "Organizing, Searching, and Indexing." Chapter 5 also tells you how to fix search when things go wrong.

Real World   The first time you sign in Windows will prepare your environment and there'll be a slight delay before you can start working. Once you can access the desktop, Windows keeps working in the background to set up your environment and part of this process include creating the search indexes for Settings, Control Panel, personal files, and apps.

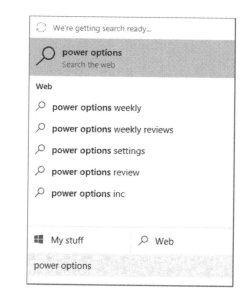

As the graphic shows, while the indexes are being created, you won't get the expected search results and Windows will display a message about getting search ready.

Task View & Changing Desktops

Click the Task View button to display the Task View panel or press the Windows logo key + Tab. As Figure 1-5 shows, the Task View panel shows a preview of each desktop and allows you to easily add, remove or switch between desktops. With this panel open, you can:

- Add a desktop simply by clicking the New Desktop option. Although you can have many desktops, the desktop space is more manageable when you have between one and nine desktops.
- Switch between desktops simply by clicking the desktop you want to open.
- Delete a desktop simply by right-clicking it and then selecting the Delete button (an X in the upper right corner of the desktop preview).

Figure 1-5 Use the Task View panel to switch between and manage your desktops.

Getting Around the New Start Menu

The Start Menu in Windows 10 combines the best features of the Start Menu used in Windows 7 with the best features of the Start menu used in Windows 8. As Figure 1-6 shows, the Start Menu features two columns of options. In the first column, you have quick access to the most used apps.

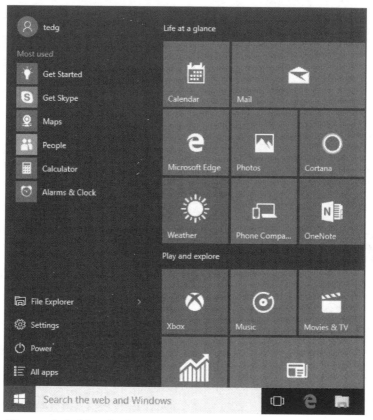

Figure 1-6 Use the Start Menu to access your apps and options.

Tip "Life at a Glance" and "Play and Explore" are editable headings for the two primary tile regions. To change these headings, simply click the heading to enable editing, make the appropriate changes and then click somewhere else on the Start menu. For example, you can delete "Life at a Glance" and enter "Now Playing" as the heading.

In the upper left corner of the Start menu, the user name for the currently logged on user is displayed. Click the name to display an options menu that allows you to change account settings, lock the account or sign out.

In the lower left corner of the Start menu, you'll find additional options, including

- **File Explorer** Opens File Explorer, which replaces Windows Explorer as the utility for exploring your computer. You can open File Explorer quickly by pressing Windows logo key + E.
- **Settings** Opens the Settings panel. Settings replaces Control Panel for managing most configuration settings. Open Settings quickly by pressing Windows logo key + I.
- **Power** Displays the power options.

> **Tip** By default, File Explorer opens with Quick Access selected in the main pane. If you'd rather have File Explorer open with This PC selected, click Options on the View toolbar and then select Change Folder And Search Options. Next, in the Folder Options dialog box, select This PC as the option for the Open File Explorer To list.

The available power options depend on how you are logged in. When you are logged in directly, you can select:

- **Restart**   Shuts down and then restarts the computer
- **Sleep**   Puts the computer in sleep mode, if possible given the system configuration and state.
- **Shut Down**   Shuts down the computer.

> **Note**   If you want to lock the computer or log out instead, click Start, click your user name on the Start menu and then click Lock or Sign Out as appropriate.

If you are logged in remotely, such as when you are accessing a home computer from work, you only have the option to disconnect. Keep in mind your computer's power configuration determines how sleep mode works. When working with sleep mode, it is important to remember that the computer is still drawing power and that you should never open the case or back cover when a Windows 10 device is in the sleep state. Always power off the device before poking around inside the cover.

In the lower left corner, you'll also find the All Apps button which displays the All Apps list. As shown in Figure 1-7, the All Apps list contains a 0-9 A-Z list of available apps. When shown, the list replaces the items in the first column, allowing you to click any entry to open the related app or to click Back to go back to the standard view. Slide or scroll to see the entire list.

Figure 1-7 Use the All Apps list to find apps you want to open.

The second column on the Start menu shows tiles for apps pinned to Start. Any app on the computer can have a tile on the Start menu. Clicking a tile runs the app. When you right-click a tile, you display configuration options. As shown in Figure 1-8, you can use these options to:

* Unpin the app from Start
* Change the size of the tile on the Start menu
* Turn live tiles on or off
* Pin the app to the taskbar

Figure 1-8 Use the options to manage the tile.

Although the previous examples, show the tiles with the live feature turned off, just about any tile can have its live featured turned on, which then displays current information from the app, such as the current weather for the Weather app, the current news heading for the News app or a stock market report for the Stock app.

Entering and Exiting Tablet Mode

When you're using Windows 10 on a tablet PC, tablet mode usually is what you want to use. However, tablet mode changes the way Windows works and you may either love or hate it.

In tablet mode, the Start Menu is replaced with a Start screen, as shown in Figure 1-9. The standard Start screen options include:

- **Options button**   Shown in the upper left corner, you must click this button to display the Start options panel (or when working with Start, by swiping in from the left).
- **Power button**   Provides access to power options, which can include: sleep, shutdown and restart.

- **Apps button**   Displays the All Apps list, which you can use to start programs not shown on the Start screen.
- **Start button**   Switches between Start and the desktop.

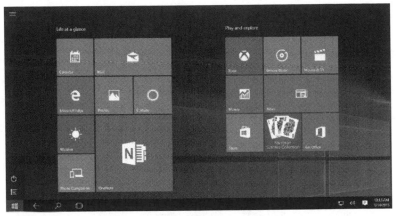

Figure 1-9 Accessing Start in tablet mode.

When you click an app on Start, the app opens on the desktop in full-screen mode. The Task View button provides one way to switch between apps. Click the Task View button to see a preview of open apps and then click the app you want to open.

In Tablet mode, app icons on the taskbar are hidden by default. This means you won't see any items pinned to the taskbar or icons for open windows or running apps.

All of these snap behaviors are configurable and controlled with System Settings by following these steps:

1.   Click Start and then click Settings.
2.   In the Settings dialog box, click System. On the System page, click Tablet Mode.

3. In the main pane, use these options to manage the way tablet mode works:

- If you don't want to use tablet mode, you can disable the feature by toggling the Make Windows More Touch-Friendly... option to the Off position.
- If you want Windows 10 to go to the desktop instead of Start when you login, set When I Sign In to Go To The Desktop.
- If you want access to pinned items, open windows and running apps via the taskbar, you can disable by setting Hide App Icons... to the Off position by clicking it.

> **Tip** Not used to toggle switches? Toggles have On/Off positions. You change the position from On to Off or Off to On simply by clicking the toggle.

Customizing User Accounts

User accounts have many properties, including a password, a picture, an account name, and an account type designation. You can manage the properties for local accounts, as long as you have an administrator account or the user name and password of an administrator account.

Changing Account Pictures

Your account picture is displayed on the logon screen and on the Start menu. When you use a picture, Windows 10 automatically optimizes the picture and saves the optimized copy as part of your personal Contact entry in Windows Contacts. Although it may seem strange to save the picture as part of your personal .contact file, doing so is a quick and easy shortcut for the operating system. Most pictures are optimized to a file size of 50 KB or less—even high-resolution pictures.

To change your account picture, follow these steps:

1. Click Start and then click Settings. Next, in Settings, click Accounts.

2. As Figure 1-10 shows, your current account picture (if any) is shown. Click Browse.

3. Use the Open dialog box to choose the picture you want to use. The picture must be in a standard picture format, such as BMP, GIF, JPEG, PNG, DIB, or TIFF.

> **Note** If your computer has a camera, you also can create a picture. Click Camera and follow the prompts.

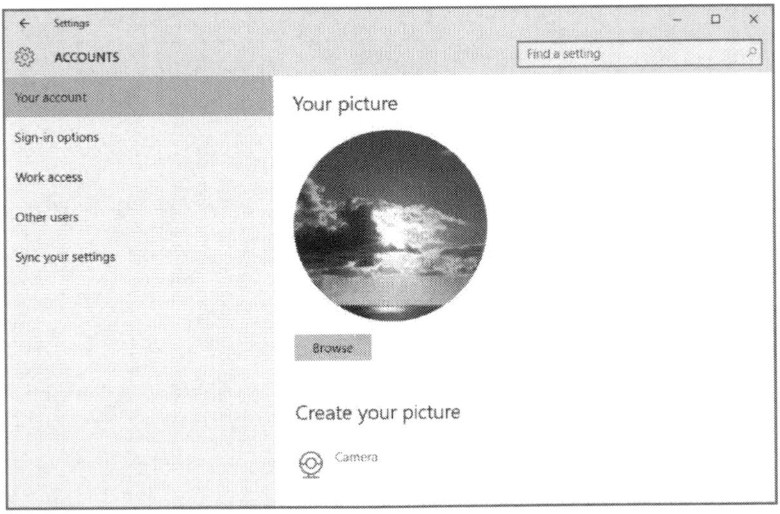

Figure 1-10 Choosing a picture for your user account

Changing Account Types

User accounts are either standard user accounts with limited privileges or administrator user accounts with full privileges. As a safety precaution, you might want to use a standard account for web browsing and other online activities and the administrator account only when you need to manage or maintain your computer.

It's common for computers to have multiple users, resulting in several user accounts created on it, and at least one of these must be an administrator account. If you are logged on with a standard user account, you can change the account type to Administrator. If you are logged on with an administrator account, you can change the account type to Standard User (as long as it's not the last administrator account on the computer).

Real World   Ideally, you should create at least two administrator accounts on your computer—with passwords. If you forget the password for one account, you can simply log on with the other account and use the User Accounts options in Control Panel to change your password. But only do this if you've truly lost your password. Why? When you change an account password via another account, you'll lose all EFS-encrypted files, personal certificates, and stored passwords for both websites and network resources.

You can change the account type by following these steps:

1. Type **User Accounts** in the Search box and press Enter. This opens the User Accounts page in Control Panel.

2. Click Manage User Accounts. If you are logged on as a standard user, provide the account name and password of an administrator when prompted and then click Yes.

3. In the User Accounts dialog, double-click the account you want to modify.

4. In the Properties dialog box for the user, on the Group Membership tab, select either Standard User or Administrator and then click OK.

Changing and Recovering Your Password

Periodically, you should change your account password or PIN. This makes it more difficult for someone to gain access to your computer. You can change the standard password, PIN or picture password associated with your user account by following these steps:

1. Click Start and then click Settings. Next, in Settings, click Accounts.

2. On the Accounts page, click Sign-In Options in the left pane.

3. Under Password, PIN or Picture, click Change and then follow the prompts.

If you are using a local account and you've lost or forgotten your password, you can recover and reset your password by following these steps:

1. Using another computer, open a browser window and access https://account.live.com/password/reset.

2. Specify why you can't login as I Forgot My Password, click Next and then follow the prompts.

If you are using a local account and you've lost or forgotten your password, you can use another account to recover (but only if you followed my earlier advice about creating another administrator account). To do so, follow these steps:

1. Type **User Accounts** in the Search box and press Enter. This opens the User Accounts page in Control Panel.

2. Click Manage User Accounts. If you are logged on as a standard user, provide the account name and password of an administrator when prompted and then click Yes.

3. In the User Accounts dialog, click the account you want to modify and then click Reset Password.

4. After you enter and then confirm the new password, click OK. You'll then be able to login using this password.

> **Note**   When you change an account password via another account, you'll lose all EFS-encrypted files, personal certificates, and stored passwords for both websites and network resources.

Chapter 2. Customizing the Windows 10 Interface

Windows 10 is more customizable than any earlier release of the Microsoft Windows operating system. Powerful features and options combined with traditional favorites allow you to work in new ways. You can perform tasks more efficiently, and you can optimize and customize the operating system in many ways.

Teaching you how to make Windows 10 work the way you want it to is what this book is all about. If you were moving in to a house, apartment, or dorm room, you would want to make the space your own. We do the same with just about everything in our lives, yet surprisingly few people take the time to make their virtual space their own, which can make using a computer a frustrating experience.

One of the ways to make Windows 10 your own is to customize the interface. In any operating system, the interface is everything that connects you to your computer and its basic elements, including the desktop, the menu system, and the taskbar. The way these basic elements look depends on appearance settings. The way they behave depends on customization settings saved in the user profile associated with a particular user account. Because your user account and its associated profile are separate from the profiles associated with other user accounts on a computer, you can customize the interface without affecting other users, and your preferred settings will be remembered and restored each time you log on.

Boosting Your Desktop IQ

The desktop is what you see after you start your computer and log on. It's your virtual workspace, and you must master it to begin using your computer faster and smarter. If you skipped Chapter 1 because you already know the basics, you may want to take a peek at "Getting Around the New Desktops" in Chapter 1 anyway as this will teach you how to create new desktops and navigate between them.

Optimizing Interface Performance

Windows 10 supports visual effects animations, fades and translucent selection rectangles. The Windows 10 desktop with these features enabled is pretty, but like any cosmetic, their value depends on many factors.

On older or less powerful devices, you will want to use less of the pretty stuff; using fewer system resources makes Windows more responsive. The same is likely to be true for that new netbook or tablet PC you just bought.

You can optimize the desktop for the way you want to work by following these steps:

1. Type **SystemPropertiesAdvanced** in the Search box, and then press Enter to open the System Properties dialog box with the Advanced tab selected. (You can get to the same dialog box through Control Panel as well. Click System And Security and then click System. In the left pane, click Advanced System Settings.)

Tip Although there are many shortcuts you can use to access the various tabs and options of the System Properties dialog box, you need not know or remember them all. Instead, pick one technique you like, put it to memory, and use it. The technique I like most is the one mentioned in this step. If the Advanced tab isn't the one I want to work with after I've opened the dialog box, I simply click the tab I want to use, rather than trying to remember that SystemPropertiesComputerName opens the Computer Name tab, SystemPropertiesHardware opens the Hardware tab, SystemPropertiesProtection opens the System Protection tab, and SystemPropertiesRemote opens the Remote tab.

Real World If command memorization isn't your thing but you'd still like a quick and easy way to access System Properties, try this: Type **SystemPropertiesAdvanced** in the Search box. Right-click SystemPropertiesAdvanced in the results, and then click Open File Location. In File Explorer, right-click SystemPropertiesAdvanced and then select Pin To Taskbar. Now the System Properties | Advanced Tab shortcut is available on the taskbar. Whenever you want to access it, simply click the related icon on the taskbar.

2. In the Performance section, click Settings to open the Performance Options dialog box, shown in Figure 2-1. You can now:

- Select Adjust For Best Performance to get rid of all the pretty stuff, or select Adjust For Best Appearance to enable all the pretty stuff.
- Select or clear individual visual effects.

3. Save your changes by clicking OK twice to close both dialog boxes.

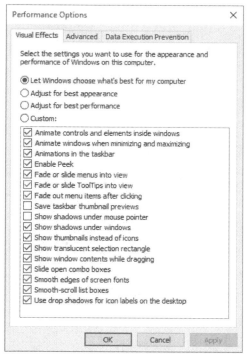

Figure 2-1 Configuring visual effects to optimize the desktop for the way you want to use it.

The visual add-ons that have the biggest effect on performance include:

* **Animate Controls And Elements Inside Windows**
  Controls the slow-fade effect on buttons and tabs in dialog boxes. When off, buttons glow and tabs open without animation.

* **Animate Windows When Minimizing And Maximizing**
  Determines whether squeezing or stretching animation is used

when minimizing or maximizing windows. When off, Windows pop into position.

- **Animations In the Taskbar**   Controls animations associated with jump lists, thumbnail previews, and sliding taskbar buttons. When off, no animations are used.
- **Fade Or Slide Menus Into View**   Controls whether menus fade or slide into view. When off, menus snap open without delay.
- **Fade Or Slide ToolTips Into View**   Controls whether tooltips fade or slide into view. When off, tooltips snap open without delay.
- **Fade Out Menu Items After Clicking**   Controls whether menu items fade out after clicking. When off, the item selected opens without delay.
- **Slide Open Combo Boxes**   Controls the animations associated with drop-down list boxes. When off, drop-down lists snap open.

Mastering Desktop Essentials

Like a real workspace, the desktop can get cluttered. Programs that you run and folders that you open appear on the desktop in separate windows, and all these open windows can quickly make it difficult to get to the desktop itself. To quickly declutter, you can rearrange open program and folder windows by right-clicking an empty area of the taskbar and then clicking one of the following viewing options:

- **Cascade Windows**   Arranges the open windows so that they overlap, with the title bar remaining visible.
- **Show Windows Stacked**   Resizes the open windows and arranges them on top of each other, in one or more columns.

- **Show Windows Side by Side**   Resizes the open windows and stacks them side by side.

To get to the desktop without decluttering, use the small, blank button on the far right of the taskbar. This button is called the Show Desktop button. You can temporarily hide all open windows by clicking the Show Desktop button. Click the button again to unhide the windows and restore them to their previous state. Alternatively, right-click the taskbar and select Show The Desktop or Show Open Windows as appropriate.

> **Tip**   Another way to hide or show open windows is to press the Windows logo key+D.

The Task View is also handy for working with the desktop. As I told you earlier, you use Task View to add, remove and switch between desktops. When you click the Task View button, you see a preview of each open window on the active desktop, as shown in Figure 2-2.

In the Task View preview mode, you can:

- Bring any window to the front simply by clicking on it.
- Close any window by hovering over it and then clicking the close button in the upper right corner of the window.

> **Note**   You hover by moving the mouse pointer over a screen element. If you must hover and click, you move the mouse over the element and then click the button or option. With a touch screen, you simply need to tap the element and then tap the button or option.

Figure 2-2 The Task View shows a preview of windows open on the active desktop.

You can store files, folders, and shortcuts on the desktop for quick and easy access. Any file or folder that you drag from a File Explorer window to the desktop stays on the desktop. Rather than placing files or folders on the desktop, you can add a shortcut to a file or folder to the desktop by following these steps:

1. Click the File Explorer icon on the taskbar to use File Explorer to locate the file or folder that you want to add to the desktop.

2. Right-click the file or folder. On the shortcut menu, point to Send To, and then click Desktop (Create Shortcut).

You can also add system icons to the desktop. By default, the only system icon on the desktop is the Recycle Bin. You can add or remove system icons by completing the following steps:

1. Right-click an empty area of the desktop, and then click Personalize.

2. In the left pane of the Personalization window, click Themes and then in the main pane under Related Settings, click Desktop Icon Settings. This opens the Desktop Icon Settings dialog box, as shown in Figure 2-3.

3. Add or remove icons by selecting or clearing their related check boxes and then clicking OK to save your changes.

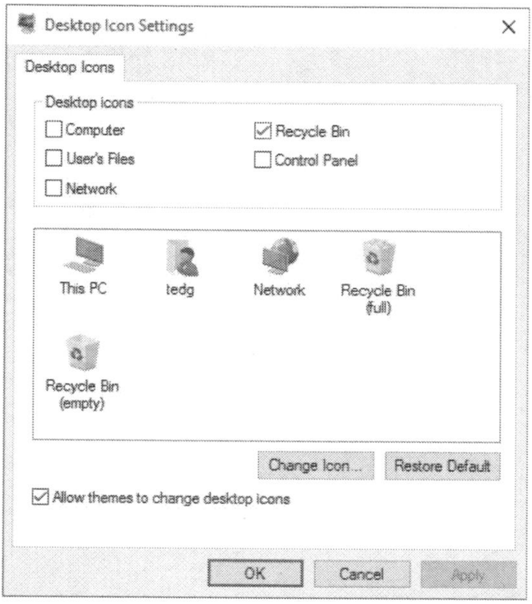

Figure 2-3 Add or remove desktop icons.

Some of the desktop icons can be renamed by right-clicking the icon, clicking Rename, typing the desired name, and then pressing Enter. For example, you could rename Recycle Bin as Trash Barrel by right-clicking Recycle Bin, clicking Rename, typing Trash Barrel, and then pressing Enter.

If you no longer want an icon or shortcut on the desktop, right-click it, and then click Delete. When prompted, confirm the action by clicking Yes. Each icon has special options and uses:

- **Accessing computers and devices on your network** Double-clicking the Network icon opens a window where you can access the computers and devices on your network.
- **Accessing Control Panel** Double-clicking the Control Panel icon opens the Control Panel, which provides access to system configuration and management tools.
- **Accessing hard disks and devices** Double-clicking the This PC icon opens a window from which you can access hard disk drives and devices with removable storage.
- **Accessing the System page in Control Panel** Right-clicking the This PC icon and clicking Properties displays the System page in Control Panel.
- **Accessing File Explorer** Double-clicking the folder icon for the user's files opens your user profile folder in File Explorer.
- **Connecting to network drives** Right-clicking the This PC icon (or the Network icon) and selecting Map Network Drive allows you to connect to shared network folders.
- **Managing your computer** Right-clicking the This PC icon and clicking Manage opens the Computer Management console.
- **Removing deleted items** Right-clicking the Recycle Bin icon and clicking Empty Recycle Bin permanently removes all items in the Recycle Bin.
- **Restoring deleted items** Double-clicking the Recycle Bin icon opens the Recycle Bin, which you can use to view or restore deleted items.

Now that you know how to add items to the desktop, try this:

1. Create a custom Show Desktop button that you can place anywhere on the desktop, open Notepad.exe, type the commands below, and then save the file on the desktop as Show.scf.

```
[Shell]
Command=2
IconFile=Explorer.exe,3
[Taskbar]
Command=ToggleDesktop
```

2. Now double-click the related icon to display or hide windows on the active desktop.

Stretching the Desktop

Increasingly, desktop PCs and laptops support multiple display devices, allowing you to add a monitor to increase your desktop space. Not only is this a relatively inexpensive way to make your computer more useful, it can also boost your productivity.

Here's an example: You connect two monitors to your computer, or add a monitor as an additional output for your laptop. By placing the screens side by side and enabling multiple displays, you effectively stretch your desktop space and make it possible to view programs and files open on both screens at the same time. This allows you to have multiple windows open all the time—some on your primary screen and some on your secondary screen.

As Windows 10 supports multiple desktops, each of these multiple desktops would also then stretch across the multiple displays. Here, the desktops provide the virtual space and the displays provide the physical space.

Typically, if a computer supports multiple displays, it has multiple display adapter connectors. For example, if a desktop PC has three display adapter connectors (two digital and one analog), it likely supports at least two monitors; if a laptop has additional display adapter connectors (digital or analog), it likely supports at least two monitors.

You can confirm the number of supported displays by checking the technical specifications for your display adapter on the manufacturer's website. To determine the type of display adapter on your computer, right-click an empty area of the desktop, and then click Screen Resolution. On the Screen Resolution page, click the Advanced Settings link. The adapter type listed for your display adapter shows the manufacturer name and model information, such as NVIDIA GeForce GTX 980.

Getting a computer that supports multiple monitors to stretch the desktop across two monitors is best handled as follows:

1. With the computer shut down (and not in the sleep or hibernate state), connect the monitors to the computer, and then turn on the monitors.

2. Next, start your computer and log on.

> **Troubleshooting** The logon screen should appear on one of the monitors (although not necessarily on the one directly in front of you). If the logon screen doesn't appear, turn off both monitors in turn, and then turn the monitors back on. If a

monitor has multiple modes, such as analog and digital, wait
for the monitor to switch to the appropriate mode or
manually configure the mode by using the monitor's
configuration settings. You may need to wiggle the mouse or
press keys on the keyboard to get the monitor to sense the
appropriate mode.

3.   Right-click an open area on the desktop, and then click
     Display Settings to open the Display page in Settings, as
     shown in Figure 2-4.

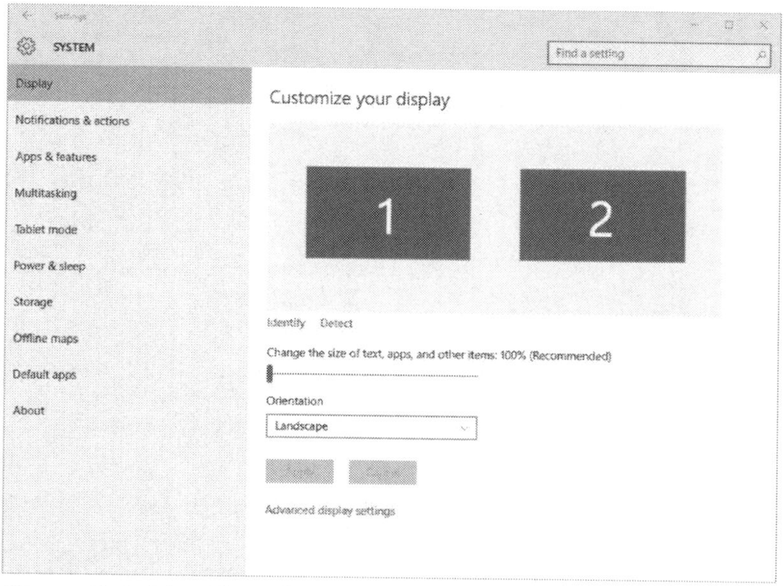

Figure 2-4 Identify and orient the displays

4.   Click Detect to have Windows display the identity number of
     each monitor. With two monitors, the displays are numbered
     1 and 2. By default, Display 1 always includes the Start menu,
     taskbar, and notification tray, but you can change this as
     discussed in the "Making the Taskbar Dance" section, later in
     this chapter.

5. Confirm the display order. Windows doesn't know how you've placed the monitors on your desktop. Instead, it assumes that the primary display device is the first one connected and the secondary display device is the second one connected. It also assumes that the second display is to the right of the first display, which allows you to move the mouse pointer to the right to go from the desktop on the first display to the desktop stretched to the second display.

6. You can tell windows how your monitors are oriented in several ways. If Display 2 is on the left side of Display 1, click the representation of the Display 2 desktop on the Screen Resolution page, drag it to the left past the Display 1 desktop, release the mouse button, and then click Apply. The orientation should now show Display 1 on the left and Display 2 on the right; you can confirm proper configuration by clicking the Identify button. To reverse this procedure, perform the same steps, but drag to right instead of to the left.

Real World   If you identify and orient the displays incorrectly, moving from the desktop on one monitor to the stretched desktop on the other monitor won't be logical. For example, if Display 2 is physically located to the right of Display 1, but you've incorrectly configured the displays, you may not be able to access the stretched desktop on Display 2 by moving the pointer to the right. Instead, you may need to move the pointer to the left, past the edge of Display 1's desktop, and vice versa.

After you've connected an additional monitor and oriented it properly, working with multiple monitors is fairly straightforward. When you stretch the desktop across two displays, the resolution setting of both displays determines how large the desktop is. If

Display 1's resolution is 1920 x 1080 and Display 2's resolution is 1920 x 1080, the effective resolution is 3840 x 1080.

When you maximize windows, they fill their current display from edge to edge. You can click on windows and drag them from the desktop on one display to the stretched desktop on another display. After you click and drag a window, size it as appropriate for the way you want to use it. For many programs, Windows remembers where you've positioned a window when you close it; the next time you open the window, it appears positioned on the appropriate display, as you last worked with it. However, some programs won't remember your preferred monitor, either by design or because the program isn't appropriate for multiple displays.

Any wallpaper you've selected as the background for your desktop will appear on all your displays. Whether you choose a picture position of Fill, Fit, Stretch, or Center, you see a duplicate of the background on each display.

If you want different pictures to appear on each display, you must create pictures at the appropriate resolution, store them in an appropriate folder (such as a subfolder of C:\Windows\Web\Wallpaper), select them as your desktop background, and use the Span or Tile option of the Choose A Fit list. For example, if Display 1's resolution is 1920 x 1080 and Display 2's resolution is 1920 x 1080, using an art program such as Photoshop, you could combine two 1920 x 1080 images to create one 3840 x 1080 image. You would then store this image in an appropriate folder and select it as your tiled or spanned wallpaper.

The standard screensavers that come with Windows also stretch across your displays automatically. There's no need to do anything special to make this happen.

Ready to Ditch Snap?

Theoretically, you use snap to arrange windows side by side. Here is how snap is supposed to work:

1. If you want two windows to appear side by side on the desktop, you drag the title bar of the first window to the left or right side of the screen until an outline of the expanded window appears, then release the mouse to expand the window.

2. Afterward, you drag the title bar of the second window to the opposite side of the screen until an outline of the expanded window appears, then release the mouse to expand the second window.

3. To return the window to its original size, you simply drag the title bar away from the top of the desktop and then release.

Personally though, snap is always doing what I don't want it to when I use that technique. The only technique that actually works reliably for me is when I snap windows using the keyboard. To snap the active window to the side of the desktop using the keyboard, press either Windows logo key + Left Arrow or Windows logo key + Right Arrow. After you do this, you'll be in Task View and can snap the second window to the opposite side of the screen simply by clicking it.

For easy reference, the keyboard shortcuts for snap are as follows:

- **Windows key + Left Arrow or Right Arrow**   Toggles the screen snap position of the app. Snap splits the screen, so if the app is being displayed normally, Windows key + Left Arrow snaps it to the left and Windows key + Right Arrow snaps it to the right.
- **Windows key + Up Arrow**   Displays the app in Full Screen mode.
- **Windows key + Down Arrow**   Exits Full Screen mode and returns the app to its original window state.

All of these snap behaviors are configurable and controlled with System Settings by following these steps:

1. Click Start and then click Settings.
2. In the Settings dialog box, click System. On the System page, click Multitasking.
3. In the main pane, under Snap, use these options to manage the way snap works:

- If you don't want to use snap, you can disable the feature by toggling the Arrange Windows Automatically... option to the Off position.
- If you don't want to use snap to display two windows side by side, you can disable the feature by toggling the When I Snap More Than One Window... option to the Off position.
- If you don't want snap to show what window you can snap next after you snap a window, you can disable the feature by toggling the When I Snap A Window, Show... option to the Off position.

Making the Start Menu Work for You

The Start button provides access to your computer's menu system. You open the Start menu simply by clicking the Start button. You also can display the Start menu by pressing the Windows logo key on your keyboard, or by pressing Control+Esc.

As you probably know, the Start menu allows you to run apps, open folders, search your computer, get help, and more. What you may not know is how to customize the Start menu so that it works the way you want it to.

> **Tip** Use Search to quickly run any installed program, system utility or get to system settings. Simply type the program, utility or option name in the Search box. Results for programs, system utilities and system settings are displayed before other types of search results.

By default, the Start menu looks similar to the example shown in Figure 2-5. Here, you have two columns of entries, with settings and options on the left and apps on the right. In the lower left corner, note the following options:

* File Explorer
* Settings
* All Apps

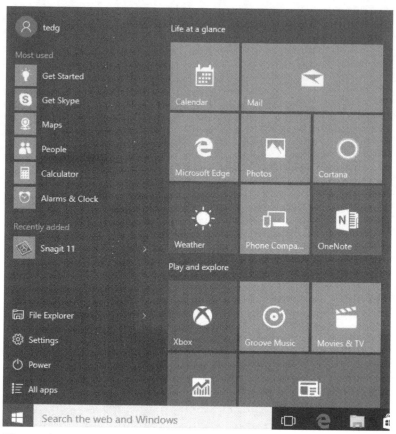

Figure 2-5 Make the most of Start by customizing it.

File Explorer and Settings are two of many options that can appear in this area of the menu. While these options are enabled by default, many other options, including those for Documents, Downloads, Music and Pictures, are disabled by default. To control which of these options are displayed, follow these steps:

1. Click Start and then click Settings. In the Settings dialog box, click Personalization.

2. On the Personalization page, select Start in the left column.

3. In the main pane, click the Choose Which Folders Appear on Start link. This opens the Choose Which Folders page, as shown in Figure 2-6.

4. Enable or disable specific options by clicking the related On/Off switch. For example, if the Music switch is off, click the toggle under Music to set the switch to the On position.

Figure 2-6 Enable or disable folders on the Start menu

Keep in mind that All Apps isn't an option you can turn on or off. If you click All Apps when you are working with Start, you see a scrollable list of all the apps installed on the device in the leftmost column of the Start menu.

Scroll through the list and you'll see folders that store lists of related tools, including folders for Windows Accessories, Windows Administrative Tools, Windows System and more. Click the folder to expand or hide its contents.

Pinning Apps and Using Full-Screen Mode

You can pin an app to Start by following these steps:

1. On the Start menu, click the All Apps option, and then locate the app in the list.

2. Right-click the app in the list and select Pin To Start.

> **Real World**   Sometimes the program you want to pin is not readily accessed in the menu system. In this case, locate the application's executable file (.exe) in File Explorer. Right-click the file, and then click Pin To Start.

By default, as shown in Figure 2-7, apps you pin are added to a third section under the "Life At a Glance" and "Play And Explore" sections. You can customize the apps lists by pinning items to the Start menu, resizing Start, creating new sections and more. The first customization trick you need to learn is the art of creating sections.

As an alternative to using the popup Start menu, you can use Start in full-screen mode, which is similar to the Start screen in Windows 8. In full-screen mode, items in the left hand column are hidden until you click one of the available buttons. Specifically, you must click the button in the upper left corner to view the standard sidebar and its options.

Figure 2-7 Pin apps to the Start menu for quick access.

To enable or disable full-screen mode for Start, follow these steps:

1. Click Start and then click Settings. In the Settings dialog box, click Personalization.

2. On the Personalization page, select Start in the left column.

3. Enable or disable full-screen mode by clicking the related On/Off switch.

Creating Sections

As mentioned previously, when you pin apps to Start, they are added to a new section by default. Windows 10 will in fact let you create many new sections. You create a new section simply by dragging a tile into an empty area. When you drag the tile to a new area, Windows will highlight the area to let you know you a new section will be created.

As with the default sections, each new section can be named. To name a section, complete these steps:

1. Move the mouse cursor over an empty area above the tiles in the section to display the Name Group option and then click. (With a touch screen, simply tap this area)
2. The cursor changes to an insertion point. Type the desired heading and then press Enter or click elsewhere.

If you want an app you've pinned to appear in one of the two standard sections, simply click and drag the app tile to the section you want it to be in. Windows 10 will resize the section automatically to accommodate the addition or removal of tiles. You can use the same click and drag technique to move tiles from one section to another.

Resizing and Reorganizing Tiles

Often after you move tiles around, you'll want to optimize the tile size. To resize a tile, right-click it, point to Resize and then select the desired size. Standard tiles can be set to small or medium size. Tiles capable of displaying live contents, live tiles, can be set:

- Small—70x70 pixels, four small tiles fill the same space as one medium.
- Medium—150x150 pixels, the standard tile size
- Wide—310x150 pixels, a tile that is two medium tiles wide.
- Large—310x310 pixels, one large tile fills the same space as four mediums.

See Figure 2-8 for examples. The default tile size is medium, which is standard block size.

Figure 2-8 Size tiles to personalize the available space on the Start menu.

While you are adding tiles and moving them around Start, you may want to resize the menu. To change the default height of Start, click and drag the top edge. Drag up to increase the height; drag down to decrease the height. To change the default width of Start, click and drag the right edge. Drag right to increase the width; drag left to decrease the width.

Customizing the Most Used and Recently Added Lists

On the Start menu, the most used and recently added apps are listed in the upper left. You can remove a program from the most used list by right-clicking it and then clicking Don't Show In This List. However, this won't prevent the program from being added to the list in the future.

You can turn the most used and recently added lists on or off by completing the following steps:

1. Click Start and then click Settings.
2. In the Settings dialog box, click Personalization. On the Personalization page, select Start in the left column. This displays the Personalization page shown in Figure 2-9.
3. Enable or disable the Show Most Used Apps list by clicking the related On/Off switch.
4. Enable or disable the Show Recently Added Apps list by clicking the related On/Off switch.

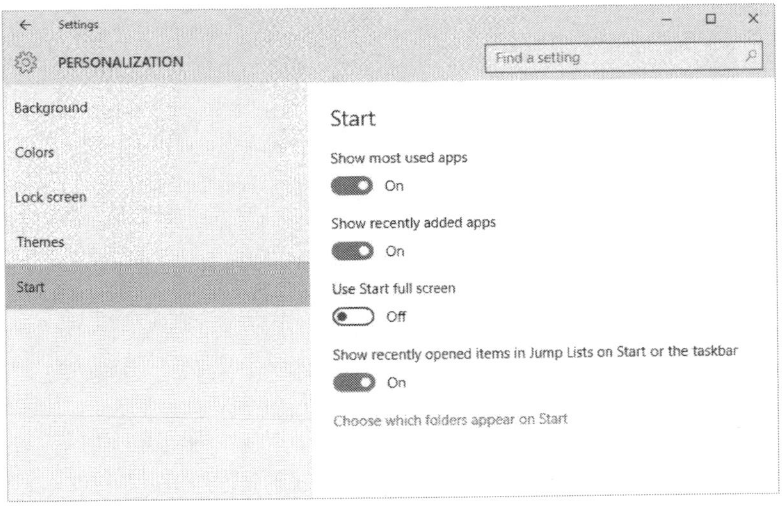

Figure 2-9 Use Personalization settings to customize start.

Making the Taskbar Dance

You use the taskbar to manage your apps and open windows. The taskbar displays buttons for pinned and open items that allow you to quickly access items you've opened and start applications.

Putting the Taskbar Where You Want It

By default, the taskbar is always displayed along the bottom of the desktop on your primary monitor. If you want to move the taskbar to another location, first make sure it's not locked. To do this, right-click the taskbar to display the taskbar options shown in Figure 2-10.

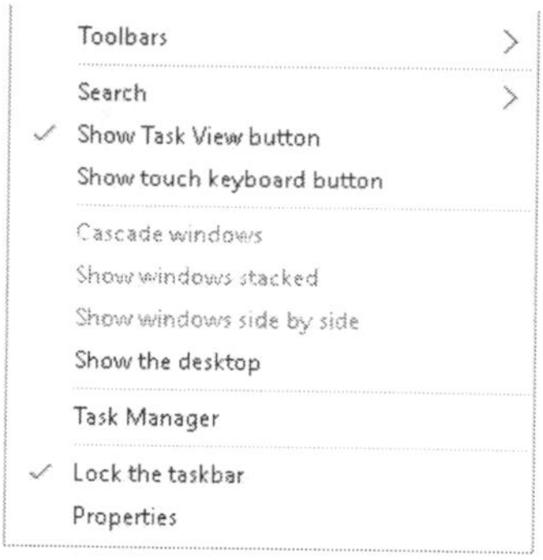

Toolbars	>
Search	>
✓ Show Task View button	
Show touch keyboard button	
Cascade windows	
Show windows stacked	
Show windows side by side	
Show the desktop	
Task Manager	
✓ Lock the taskbar	
Properties	

Figure 2-10 Use the Taskbar options to control basic settings.

> **Note**   If you're using Windows 10 on a tablet PC, see "Entering and Exiting Tablet Mode" in Chapter 1 for details on change the way the taskbar works in tablet mode.

A checkmark beside the Lock The Taskbar option indicates the taskbar is locked and can't be moved. To unlock the taskbar, right-click it and clear the Lock The Taskbar option by clicking it (which should remove the checkmark).

After you unlock the taskbar, you can position it wherever you want by clicking on it and dragging. You can:

- Drag the taskbar to the left or right to dock it on the left or right side of the primary desktop. Drag up to dock the taskbar to the top of the primary desktop.
- Dock the taskbar to a location on another monitor. Simply drag the taskbar to the desired left, right, top, or bottom location on the stretched desktop.

After you position the taskbar where you want it, you should lock it in position. To do this, right-click an open area of the taskbar, and then select the Lock The Taskbar option. A check mark indicates that it is locked.

Real World   On stretched desktops, you create a desktop that stretches across multiple displays, such as when your computer has two monitors, and the taskbar only appears on your primary monitor. If you'd like the taskbar to appear on the primary monitor and secondary monitors, follow these steps:

1. Click Start and then click Settings.

2. In the Settings dialog box, click System. On the System page, click Multitasking.

3. In the main pane, under Virtual Desktops, select All Desktops as the option for On The Taskbar, Show...

Customizing Taskbar Appearance

You can customize the taskbar in several other ways. The first, by right-clicking it and using the options available, including:

- **Show Task View Button**   Controls the display of the Task View button. If you clear this option, you'll hide the Task View button and won't be able to use Task View or add, remove or switch between desktops.
- **Toolbars**   Controls the display of the toolbars that can be added to the taskbar. The standard toolbars are Address, Links and Desktop. You also can select New Toolbar to choose a folder to add as a toolbar.

You can customize other aspects of the taskbar by using the Taskbar And Start Menu Properties dialog box, shown in Figure 2-11. To access this dialog box, right-click an open area of the taskbar, and then click Properties. Select or clear options as desired and click OK to save your changes.

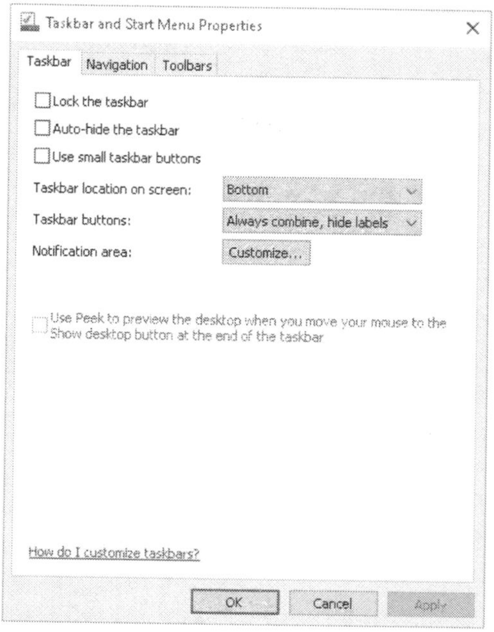

Figure 2-11 Use the Properties dialog box to customize the taskbar appearance.

The available options include:

- **Lock The Taskbar**   Locks the taskbar in place to prevent accidental moving or resizing. You must clear this option to move or resize the taskbar.
- **Auto-Hide The Taskbar**   Hides the taskbar when you aren't using it and displays the taskbar only when you move the cursor over it. If you clear this option, the taskbar is always displayed

(although not always on top), which you may prefer, especially if you move the taskbar around a stretched desktop.

> **Tip** If the taskbar is hidden and you forget where it is docked, you can quickly display the taskbar and Start menu by pressing the Windows logo key.

- **Use Small Taskbar Buttons** Reduces the size of taskbar buttons, allowing more buttons to fit on the taskbar. On my desktop PC, I prefer large icons, which makes them easier to click, but on my tablet PC, I prefer small icons so they take up less screen space.
- **Taskbar Location On Screen** Sets the relative location of the taskbar on the currently targeted display. As we discussed previously, you can move the taskbar manually as well when it is unlocked.
- **Taskbar Buttons** Specifies whether taskbar buttons are always combined, combined only when the taskbar is full, or never combined.

See the next section for more information on combining buttons and using related options.

> **Note** Typically, you'll want to combine similar items to reduce taskbar clutter. Rather than displaying a button for each program, the taskbar groups similar buttons by default. Grouping buttons saves room on the taskbar and helps reduce the likelihood that you'll need to expand the taskbar to find the buttons for open programs.

Pinning Programs to the Taskbar

You can pin items that you work with frequently to the taskbar. Pinning an item to the taskbar creates a shortcut that allows you to quickly open a program, folder, or related window.

Pinning items is easy. If you know the name of the program you want to pin to the taskbar, start typing the program name into the Search box. When you see the program in the results list, right-click it, and then click Pin To Taskbar. From this point on, whenever you want to access the program, simply click the related icon on the taskbar.

Another way to find items to pin is to access the Start menu, and then click the All Apps button. When you find the program you want to pin, right-click the program's menu item, and then click Pin To Taskbar.

To remove a pinned program from the taskbar, right-click its icon, and then click Unpin This Program From The Taskbar. This removes the program's button from the taskbar.

You can set the order of buttons for all opened and pinned programs. To do this, click the button on the taskbar and drag it left or right to the desired position.

When buttons are combined on the taskbar, clicking an item with multiple windows displays a thumbnail with a representation of each open window. You can hover over a window to peek at it on the desktop (as long as the appropriate Aero features are enabled) or click a window that you want to work with to open it. For example, if you open three different folders in File Explorer, these items are grouped together in one taskbar button. Hovering over the taskbar button displays a thumbnail with an entry for each window, allowing you to select the grouped window to open by clicking it.

Taskbar buttons make it easy to close windows as well. To close a window, whether grouped or not, move the pointer over the related taskbar button. When the thumbnail appears, move the mouse pointer to the right, and then click the close button for the window you want to close.

Using Flip Views and Jump Lists

Flip views and jump lists are some of the most powerful features of Windows 10. Why? They allow you to quickly get to items that you want to work with.

Display the standard flip view by pressing Alt+Tab. As shown in Figure 2-12, the flip view contains live thumbnails of all open windows, which are continuously updated to reflect their current state. You can work with a flip view in a variety of ways. Here are a few techniques:

- Press Alt+Tab, and then hold Alt to keep the flip view open.
- Press Tab while you hold the Alt key to cycle through the windows.
- Release the Alt key to bring the currently selected window to the front.
- Select a window and bring it to the front by clicking it.

Figure 2-12 Using the flip view.

By default, flip view shows windows are open only on the active desktop. If you're like me and use several desktops all the time, you may want flip view to show windows that are open on any desktop. To configure this option, follow these steps:

1. Click Start and then click Settings.

2. In the Settings dialog box, click System. On the System page, click Multitasking.

3. In the main pane, under Virtual Desktops, select All Desktops as the option for Pressing Alt + Tab Shows Windows That Are Open On.

If you think flip views are cool, wait until you try jump lists. Jump lists are displayed after a short delay whenever you right-click an item that has been pinned to the taskbar. When a program's jump list is displayed, you can select a file to open or task to perform simply by clicking it.

Most applications display recently used items or frequently used items. Some applications have enhanced jump lists that also provide quick access to tasks that you can perform with the application.

Windows 10 also allows you to pin items to a program's jump list. To do this, drag an item associated with a program to the program's button pinned on the taskbar and release when the Pin To option appears. Consider the following real-world scenario:

- You want to pin Microsoft Word to the taskbar and pin important documents to its jump list. To pin Word to the taskbar, you access the Start menu, type **Word.exe** in the Search box, right-click Word.exe in the results, and then click Pin To Taskbar.
- After pinning Word to the taskbar, you want to add important documents to its jump list. You open File Explorer, locate the first document, drag the document file from the Explorer window to the Word button on the taskbar. When the Pin To Word option appears, you release the mouse button to add the first document to the jump list. You repeat this process to build your list.

Other ways to use jump lists include the following:

- Simply open File Explorer and locate and then drag an important folder from this window to the pinned File Explorer on the taskbar. When the Pin To File Explorer option appears, release the mouse button to add the folder to the jump list. Repeat this process to build your list.
- If you pin Control Panel to the taskbar, you can add frequently used tasks to its jump list. To pin Control Panel to the taskbar, access the Start menu, type **Control Panel** in the Search box, right-click Control Panel in the results, and then click Pin To Taskbar. After you've pinned Control Panel to the taskbar, simply open Control Panel, locate an important task, and then

drag the address link for the task to the pinned Control Panel on the taskbar. When the Pin To Control Panel option appears, release the mouse button to add the task to the jump list. Repeat this process to build your list.

Real World   Sometimes, you'll want to run programs pinned to the taskbar with administrator privileges. To do this, right-click the shortcut on the taskbar to display the options menu for the program and then in the options list, right-click the program name. If you can run the program with administrator privileges, the second options menu will have a Run As Administrator option which you can select.

Chapter 3. Personalizing the Appearance of Windows 10

You can make Windows 10 yours by personalizing its appearance. From fine-tuning your window colors to choosing your desktop backgrounds, screen savers, sounds, mouse pointers, themes, and display settings, you can personalize Windows 10 in many ways. Navigating this maze of options can be tricky, however, especially when you want to achieve robust performance while maintaining a desired look and feel.

Many factors can affect your computer's appearance and performance, including hardware components and account controls. You achieve a balance between appearance and performance by making trade-offs when applying personalization settings, yet personalization settings largely determine the quality of your experience.

Of the many interconnected appearance and performance features, you have the most control over the following:

- Basic interfaces and account controls
- Desktop themes, screen savers, and backgrounds
- Personal account settings

In this chapter, you'll learn how to fine-tune these features while maintaining the balance between appearance and performance.

Customizing Basic Interfaces

Windows has many customizable interface features. You can customize your computer's control panels, prompts, and more. This section shows you how.

Personalizing Control Panel

Control Panel provides quick access to important system utilities and tasks. You can display the Control Panel from any File Explorer view by clicking the leftmost arrow button on the Address bar and then clicking Control Panel (see Figure 3-1).

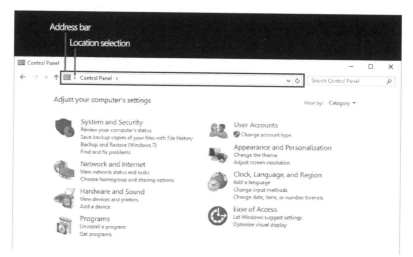

Figure 3-1 Using the address bar in File Explorer select Control panel as the location.

Tip   Did you know that Control Panel is simply a File Explorer view panel? This PC, Network, Libraries and other view panels are accessible as well using the address bar, and when you are working with any of these views, you can switch to other views using the address bar.

When you are working with Control Panel, Control Panel has several different views available. You can change views in Control Panel by using the options on the View By list. Category view, accessed by clicking Category in the View By list, shows system utilities by category, utility name, and key tasks. All Control Panel Items view, accessed by clicking Large Icons or Small Icons in the View By list, lists all items in the Control Panel alphabetically by name.

In Category view, all utilities and tasks are accessed with a single click, as with options and programs on the Start menu. You might want to configure your computer to use the more efficient single-click option to open documents, pictures and other items as well. Configuring single-click open on all items may also help you avoid confusion as to whether you need to click or double-click something.

When you have single-click open configured, pointing to an item selects it and clicking opens it. To configure single-click open, follow these steps:

1.   In Control Panel, click Appearance And Personalization.
2.   Under File Explorer Options, click Specify Single- Or Double-Click To Open.
3.   In the File Explorer Options dialog box, on the General tab, select Single-Click To Open An Item (Point To Select), and then click OK.

With everything set to open with one click, you might find that working with Control Panel and File Explorer is much more intuitive.

Fine-Tuning Control Prompts

In Chapter 1, I introduced you to local and domain user accounts, both of which can be Internet connected. When you are working with local user accounts, the account can either be a standard user account or an administrator account.

Standard users can perform any general computing tasks, such as starting programs, opening documents, and creating folders, as well as any support tasks that do not affect other users or the security of the computer. Administrators, on the other hand, have complete access to the computer and can make changes that affect other users and the security of the computer.

In Windows 10, regardless of whether you are logged on as a standard user or an administrator, you see a User Account Control (UAC) prompt by default when programs try to make changes to your computer and when you try to run certain privileged applications. UAC is a collection of features designed to help protect your computer from malicious programs by improving security.

Generally, when you are logged on as a standard user, you are prompted to provide administrator credentials. On most personal or small office computers, each local computer administrator account is listed by name on the prompt, and you must click an account, type the account's password, and then click OK to proceed. If you log on to a domain, the prompt shows the logon domain and provides user name and password boxes. In this case, you must enter the name of an administrator account, type the account's password, and then click OK to proceed.

When you are logged on with an administrator account, you are prompted for consent to continue. The consent prompt works the same regardless of whether you are connected to a domain, and you must simply click OK to proceed.

The process of getting approval, prior to running an application in administrator mode and performing actions that change system-wide settings, is known as elevation. Elevation enhances security by providing notification when you are about to perform an action that could affect system settings, such as installing an application, and eliminating the ability for malicious programs to invoke administrator privileges without your knowledge and consent.

Windows 10 performs several tasks before elevating the privileges and displaying the UAC prompt, but there is just one that you need to know about: Windows switches to a secure, isolated desktop before displaying the consent prompt, which prevents other processes or applications from providing the required permissions or consent.

> **Note**   Only the prompt itself runs on the secure desktop. All other running programs and processes continue to run on the interactive user desktop.

Elevation, consent prompts, and the secure desktop are the key aspects of UAC that affect you and how you use your computer. To reduce the number of prompts you see, UAC can differentiate between changes to Windows settings and changes to the operating system made by programs and devices. Most of the time, for example, you'll only want to know when programs are trying to install themselves or make changes to the operating system; you won't want to be prompted every time you try to change Windows settings. You also can configure UAC so that the secure desktop is not used.

Real World   UAC can prevent you from installing certain types of programs on your computer. Sometimes you can get around this by right-clicking the program's .exe or other installer file and selecting Run As Administrator. Keep in mind, however, that after the program is installed, it might need to always run with administrator privileges. Instead of right-clicking the program and selecting Run As Administrator every time you want to use it, make the change permanent by right-clicking the program's shortcut or installed .exe file and selecting Properties. On the Compatibility tab, in the Settings section, select Run This Program As An Administrator, and then click OK.

To fine-tune UAC, follow these steps:

1. In Control Panel with Category view, click the Review Your Computer's Status link under System And Security.

2. In the left pane, click Change User Account Control Settings.

Tip   Alternatively, type **wscui.cpl** in the Search box and then press Enter. In Action Center, click Change User Account Control Settings.

3. On the User Account Control Settings page, shown in Figure 3-2, use the slider to choose when to be notified about changes

to the computer, and then click OK to save your settings. The available options are:

- **Always Notify Me When**   Always notifies you when programs try to install software or make changes to the computer and when you change Windows settings. You should choose this option if your computer requires the highest security possible and you frequently install software and visit unfamiliar websites.
- **Notify Me Only When Apps Try To Make Changes To My Computer (Default)**   Notifies you only when programs try to make changes to the computer but not when you change Windows settings. You should choose this option if your computer requires high security but you want to reduce the number of notification prompts.
- **Notify Me Only When Apps Try To Make Changes To My Computer (Do Not Dim My Desktop)**   Works the same as Default but also prevents UAC from switching to the secure desktop. You should choose this option if you work in a trusted environment with familiar applications and you do not visit unfamiliar websites. You may also want to use this option if it takes a long time for your computer to switch to the secure desktop.
- **Never Notify Me When**   Turns off all UAC notification prompts. You should choose this option if security is not a priority and you work in a trusted environment. If you select this option, you must restart your computer for this change to take effect.

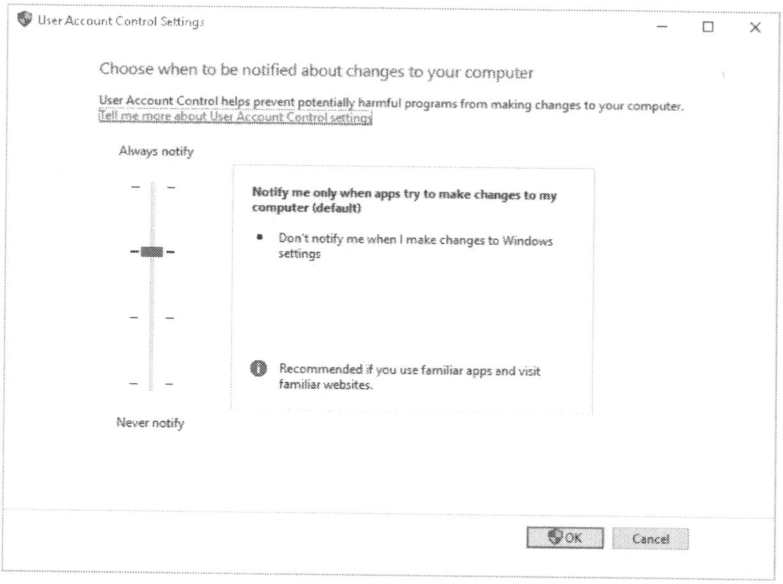

Figure 3-2 Optimize UAC for the way you work.

> **Note**   Depending on the current configuration of UAC, you may be prompted for permissions or consent. In a domain, you might not be able to manage UAC by using this technique, although you may be able to configure individual UAC features in Local Security Policy, accessible from the All Apps\Windows Administrative Tools menu. When you are working with Local Security Policy, expand Local Policies under Security Settings, and then click Security Options. Next scroll until you see the UAC policies.

Creating an Alternate Control Panel View

You may have heard about an alternate view for Control Panel that I've been calling the Ultimate Control Panel. To create an alternate view for Control Panel, you simply open File Explorer and create a new folder, preferably on the desktop. Give the folder any name you like, followed by a period and the globally unique identifier (GUID) for the alternate Control Panel view.

The GUID is: {ED7BA470-8E54-465E-825C-99712043E01C}. For example, you could name your folder:

```
MyStuff.{ED7BA470-8E54-465E-825C-
99712043E01C}
```

Or

```
ViewPanel.{ED7BA470-8E54-465E-825C-
99712043E01C}
```

Or

```
JustCool.{ED7BA470-8E54-465E-825C-
99712043E01C}
```

Ultimate Control Panel is shown in Figure 3-3. Remember, it's the GUID, not the text string, that does the magic. The GUID is a registered value in the operating system, and it identifies the alternate Control Panel view. When you create and name the folder in this way, you'll have an Ultimate Control Panel that helps you quickly perform common tasks, by allowing easy navigation of many Control Panel options.

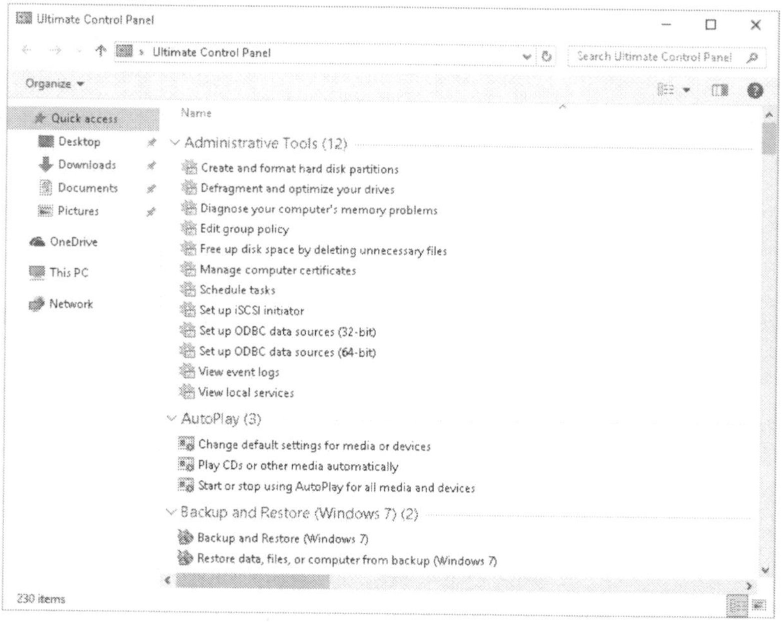

Figure 3-3 Use Ultimate Control Panel to access lists of settings grouped by category.

Creating a Dedicated Administrator Command Prompt

You use the command prompt to access the Windows 10 command-line interface. If you're a seasoned computer pro, you know this, and you also know that you must elevate the command prompt to perform any administrator tasks. Normally, you do this by accessing Command Prompt by right-clicking the Windows logo, and then clicking Command Prompt (Admin). You also can do this by accessing the Start screen, typing cmd.exe, right-clicking Command Prompt in the results list, and clicking Run As Administrator. The result is the same either way: a command prompt that allows you to run tasks that require administrator privileges.

If you pinned Command Prompt to the taskbar, getting an administrator command prompt is a bit more difficult. More difficult, really? Yes, really. To elevate, you must right-click the pinned Command Prompt, right-click Command Prompt again in the jump list, and then click Run As Administrator.

You may be wondering if there is a workaround, and there is. Cmd.exe is stored in the %WinDir%\System32 folder, where %WinDir% is an environment variable that points to the base installation folder for Windows such as C:\Windows. After you locate the file, create a copy by right-clicking Cmd.exe and clicking Copy, and then paste the copy to another folder by accessing the folder, right-clicking, and then clicking Paste. It's a good idea to paste the copy into one of your personal folders, such as Documents.

Next, right-click the copy of Cmd.exe and click Properties. On the Compatibility tab, in the Settings section, select Run This Program As An Administrator, and then click OK. Finally, right-click the copy of Cmd.exe again and click Pin To Start Menu or Pin To Taskbar. Now the pinned copy of Cmd.exe will always run with administrator privileges.

Optimizing Backgrounds, Themes and More

You can access personalization settings at any time by using the Personalization page in Settings. To access this page, simply right-click on the desktop and click Personalize. Personalization settings control the backgrounds used on the desktop and lock screen, the window colors, the themes and more. Before you work with

Windows 10 backgrounds and themes, it's important to note that by default Windows 10 automatically picks an accent color for graphics and window edges from the background. Although this can be a beautiful effect, it can also be rather jarring if you have different backgrounds on different desktops or rapidly shift through backgrounds using the slideshow option. Don't worry, you can turn this feature off and I'll show you how.

Customizing and Creating Your Own Desktop Backgrounds

If you really want to express your true self, the desktop background can help you do it. The Windows desktop can display a solid background color or a picture as its wallpaper. Windows 10 provides a starter set of background images that you can use as wallpaper.

To access the Background page, shown in Figure 3-4, simply right-click on the desktop and click Personalize.

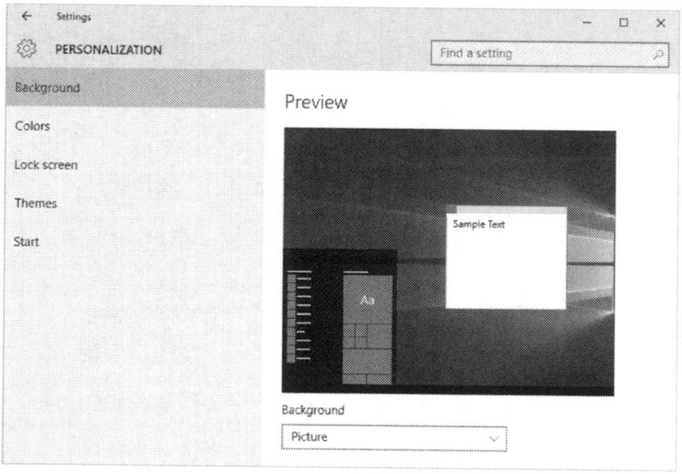

Figure 3-4 Customizing the desktop background.

The default wallpaper images are stored in subfolders of the %WinDir%\Web\Wallpaper folder, where %WinDir% is an environment variable that points to the base installation folder for Windows such as C:\Windows. For the most part, these images are sized for either widescreen viewing at 1920 x 1200, but there may also be images sized for widescreen viewing on stretched desktops at 3840 x 1200. If you select an image at one of these sizes and your computer monitor has a different display resolution size, Windows resizes the image automatically every time the image is used.

Note The best pictures for stretched desktops are panoramas, as panoramas are very wide, and when you are working with backgrounds and themes, you'll find backgrounds and themes designed for stretched desktops are often referred to as panoramic backgrounds or panoramic themes.

Tip To remove the overhead associated with background resizing, you can size your background images so that they are the same size as your preferred display resolution. If you do this, however, make sure that you save the re-sized images to a new location and then choose this new location. Don't overwrite the existing images.

You can also create background images to use as wallpaper. To do so, simply create appropriately sized images as .bmp, .gif, .jpg, .jpg, .jpeg, .dib, .png, .tif, or .tiff files, and then add these files to the appropriate subfolders of the %WinDir%\Web\Wallpaper folder. If you do not have access to that folder, or if you would prefer to not make changes to that folder, you can also use pictures from your Pictures Library or elsewhere.

> **Note** You should optimize every background image you use. If you don't do this, you risk affecting your computer's performance because Windows will need to resize the image every time it is used.

Windows 10 allows you to use three different types of backgrounds:

- Pictures
- Solid Colors
- Slideshows

Using Pictures for Backgrounds

You can set the picture background for the desktop by completing the following steps:

1. Right-click an open area of the desktop, and then click Personalize. In the left column, Background is selected by default, as shown previously in Figure 3-4.

2. On the Background list, choose Picture. Next, click the picture you want to use, or click Browse to select a picture in another location, such as your personal Documents or Pictures folder.

3. When you are using a background image, you must also use the Choose A Fit option to select a display option for the background. The positioning options are:

- **Fill**   Fills the desktop background with the image. Generally, the fill is accomplished by zooming in, which may result in the sides of the image being cropped.

- **Fit**   Fits the image to the desktop background. Because current proportions are maintained in most cases, this is a good option for photos and large images that you want to see without stretching or expanding.

- **Stretch**   Stretches the image to fill the desktop background. The proportions are maintained as closely as possible, and then the height is stretched to fill any remaining gaps.

- **Tile**   Repeats the image so that it covers the entire screen. This is a good option for small images and icons (and also to get a single image to fill two screens, as discussed in Chapter 2, "Customizing the Windows 10 Interface").

- **Center**   Centers the image on the desktop background. Any area that the image doesn't fill uses the current desktop background color. Click Change Background Color to set the background color for the area the image doesn't fill.

- **Span**   Allows the image to fill a stretched desktop by spanning the space from one desktop to the other.

Using Solid Colors for Backgrounds

You can set a solid color for the desktop background by completing the following steps:

1. Right-click an open area of the desktop, and then click Personalize. In the left column, Background is selected by default, as shown previously in Figure 3-4.

2. On the Background list, choose Solid Color.

3. Under Background Colors, click the background color that you want to use.

Using Slideshow Backgrounds

With a slideshow, the background image changes automatically based on a specific schedule, such as every 30 minutes or daily. Before you can use a slideshow, however, you need to create a picture album containing the pictures you want to display in the background.

The default picture album is the Pictures library in your personal folders. As pictures in your library likely aren't sized or optimized for the desktop, displaying the images may be rather inefficient in terms of system resource usage. If you want to reduce resource usage, you should optimize the size of images and then copy these to a new folder that you then use as your photo album.

> **Tip** The optimum size of images for your device depends on the display settings. To check the display settings for you device, click Start and then click Settings. In the Settings dialog box, click System. With Display selected in the left pane, scroll down in the main pane and then select Advanced Display Settings. Under Resolution, you'll see the current resolution for the device's display, such as 1280 x 1024 or 1920 x 1200. If you've stretched the desktop on your device and want to create a stretched background, the background size should be 2 times the width of the display. Thus, if the display is 1920 pixels wide, the image should be 3840 pixels wide.

You configure the slideshow for the background by completing the following steps:

1. Right-click an open area of the desktop, and then click Personalize. In the left column, Background is selected by default.

2. On the Background list, choose Slideshow, as shown in Figure 3-5.

3. By default, your Pictures library is used as the source album for the slideshow. To use a different source, click Browse to select a picture in another location, such as your personal Documents or Pictures folder.

> **Tip** If you have administrator access to the device, you can set one of the Windows wallpaper folders as the source. Click Browse, navigate to the base folder for wallpaper, such as C:\Windows\Web and then choose the folder to use.

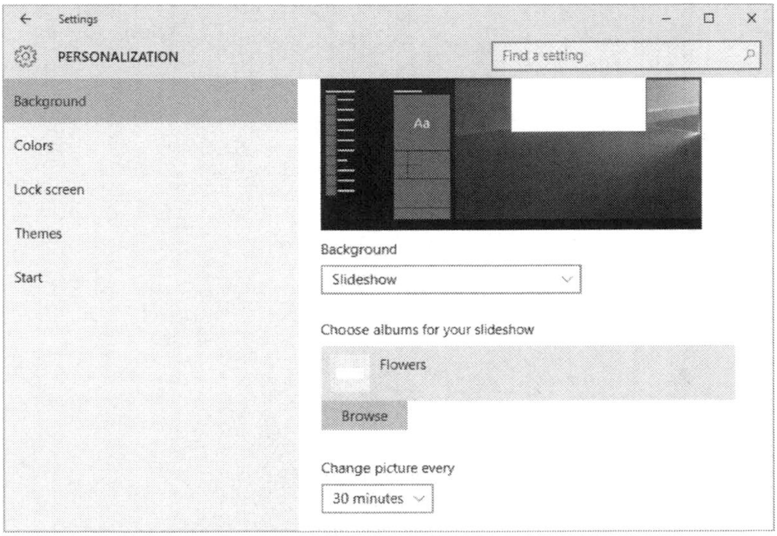

Figure 3-5 Creating a change schedule.

4. Use the Change Picture Every list to specify how often pictures should be rotated, such as every 30 minutes, every hour, every 6 hours or every day.

5. You must also select a display option for the background. The positioning options are:

- **Center** Centers the image on the desktop background. Any area that the image doesn't fill uses the current desktop background color. Click Change Background Color to set the background color for the area the image doesn't fill.
- **Fill** Fills the desktop background with the image. Generally, the fill is accomplished by zooming in, which may result in the sides of the image being cropped.
- **Fit** Fits the image to the desktop background. Because current proportions are maintained in most cases, this is a good option for photos and large images that you want to see without stretching or expanding.
- **Stretch** Stretches the image to fill the desktop background. The proportions are maintained as closely as possible, and then the height is stretched to fill any remaining gaps.
- **Tile** Repeats the image so that it covers the entire screen. This is a good option for small images and icons (and also to get a single image to fill two screens, as discussed in Chapter 2, "Customizing the Windows 10 Interface").
- **Span** Allows the image to fill a stretched desktop by spanning the space from one desktop to the other.

Customizing the Lock Screen

Like the desktop, the lock screen can have a picture or slideshow background. Windows 10 provides a starter set of background images for the lock screen. The default lock screen images are stored in subfolders of the %WinDir%\Web\Screen folder, where %WinDir% is an environment variable that points to the base installation folder for Windows such as C:\Windows.

For the most part, the default images are sized for either widescreen viewing at 1920 x 1200, but there may also be images sized for widescreen viewing on stretched desktops at 3840 x 1200 or larger. If you select an image at one of these sizes and your computer monitor has a different display resolution size, Windows resizes the image automatically every time the image is used.

To access the Lock Screen page, shown in Figure 3-6, simply right-click on the desktop and click Personalize. Next, on the Personalization page, click Lock Screen in the left column.

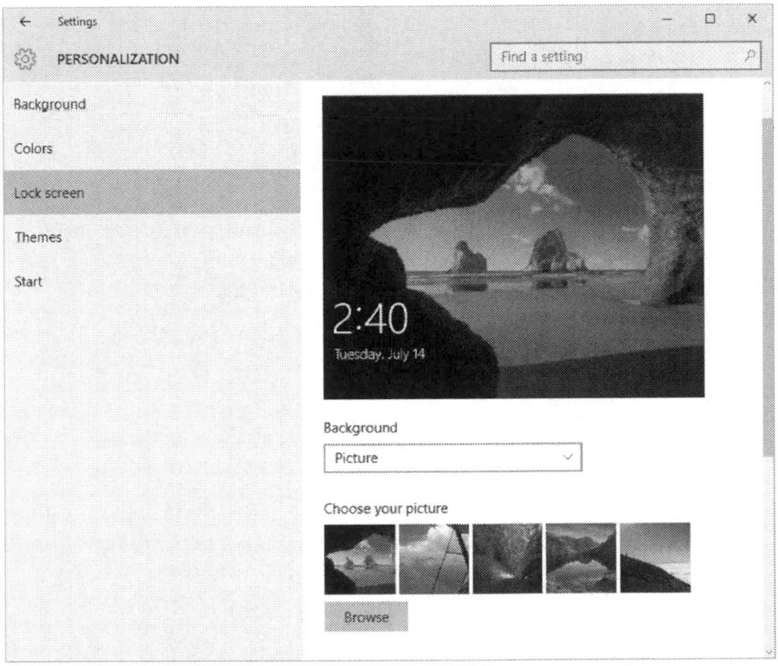

Figure 3-6 Customizing the lock screen.

Just as you can create background images to use as wallpaper, you can create background images for the lock screen. To do so, simply create appropriately sized images as .bmp, .gif, .jpg, .jpg, .jpeg, .dib, .png, .tif, or .tiff files, and then add these files to the %WinDir%\Web\Screen folder. If you do not have access to that folder, or if you would prefer to not make changes to that folder, you can also use pictures from your Pictures Library or elsewhere.

Windows 10 allows you to use two different types of backgrounds on the lock screen:

- Pictures
- Slideshows

You also can specify apps that can display their status on the lock screen, such as Alarms & Clock, Mail, Weather and Calendar.

Using Pictures on the Lock Screen

You can set the picture for the lock screen by completing the following steps:

1. Right-click an open area of the desktop, and then click Personalize. Next, on the Personalization page, click Lock Screen in the left column.
2. On the Background list, choose Picture. Next, click the picture you want to use, or click Browse to select a picture in another location, such as your personal Documents or Pictures folder.

By default, the picture fills the screen. Generally, the fill is accomplished by zooming in. If you want the picture to fill a stretched desktop by spanning the space from one desktop to the other, you'll need to create a picture that is 2 times the width of the display. Thus, if the display is 1920 pixels wide, the image should be 3840 pixels wide.

Using Slideshows on the Lock Screen

With a slideshow, the image on the lock screen changes automatically every few minutes. Before you can use a slideshow, however, you need to create a picture album containing the pictures you want to display in the background.

The default picture album is the Pictures library in your personal folders. As pictures in your library likely aren't sized or optimized for the lock screen, only pictures that fit the screen are displayed by default. Also by default, when you are using Windows on a desktop or laptop computer, Windows shows the lock screen when the computer is inactive rather than turning off the screen.

> **Tip** The optimum size of images for your device depends on the display settings. To check the display settings for you device, click Start and then click Settings. In the Settings dialog box, click System. With Display selected in the left pane, scroll down in the main pane and then select Advanced Display Settings. Under Resolution, you'll see the current resolution for the device's display, such as 1280 x 1024 or 1920 x 1200. If you've stretched the desktop on your device and want to create a stretched background, the background size should be 2 times the width of the display. Thus, if the display is 1920 pixels wide, the image should be 3840 pixels wide.

You configure the slideshow for the lock screen by completing the following steps:

1. Right-click an open area of the desktop, and then click Personalize. Next, on the Personalization page, click Lock Screen in the left column.

2. On the Background list, choose Slideshow. By default, your Pictures library is used as the source album for the slideshow. You can now add and remove source albums. If you don't want the Pictures library to be used as a source album (perhaps due to it containing embarrassing photos), click Pictures under Choose Albums... and then click Remove.

3. The photos in each selected album will be used in the slideshow. To use add a source album, click Add A Folder and then select the source folder. To use remove a source album, click the folder under Choose Albums... and then select Remove.

While you're working with slideshows on the lock screen, you may want to configure advanced settings to optimize the way the slideshows work. If so, click the Advanced Slideshow Settings link and then use these options for optimization:

■ **Include Camera Roll Folders...** By default, this option is Off and camera roll folders from your Pictures library and OneDrive aren't included in slideshows. If you want these folders included automatically, click the related toggle to switch it to the On position.

■ **Use Only Pictures That Fit My Screen** By default, this option is On and only pictures that are sized appropriately are displayed on the lock screen. If you want to include images regardless of whether they are sized appropriately, click the related toggle to switch it to the Off position.

- **When My PC Is Inactive, Show Lock Screen** By default, this option for desktop and laptop computers is On. This means the lock screen is displayed when the computer is inactive instead of turning off the display. If you want the display to turn off, click the related toggle to switch it to the Off position.

By default, the screen doesn't turn off while the slideshow is playing. To change this behavior, click the Turn Off Screen After... list and then choose a specific turn off time, such as after 30 minutes or after 1 hour.

Configuring Notifications on the Lock Screen

Getting notifications on the lock screen is handy so that you don't have to login to get information you may be looking for, such as whether you have new messages, what the weather is like or what the stock market is doing. Apps that can run in the background and show notifications on the lock screen include:

- Alarms & Clocks
- Calendar
- Mail
- People
- Store
- Weather
- Xbox

While all of these apps can display short notifications, referred to as quick statuses, only a few apps can display longer, detailed status updates, which for the out-of-the-box apps, includes Weather, Calendar and Xbox.

You can specify apps that can display status updates on the lock screen by completing the following steps:

1. Right-click an open area of the desktop, and then click Personalize. Next, on the Personalization page, click Lock Screen in the left column.

2. In the main pane, scroll down, until you see the status settings shown in Figure 3-7.

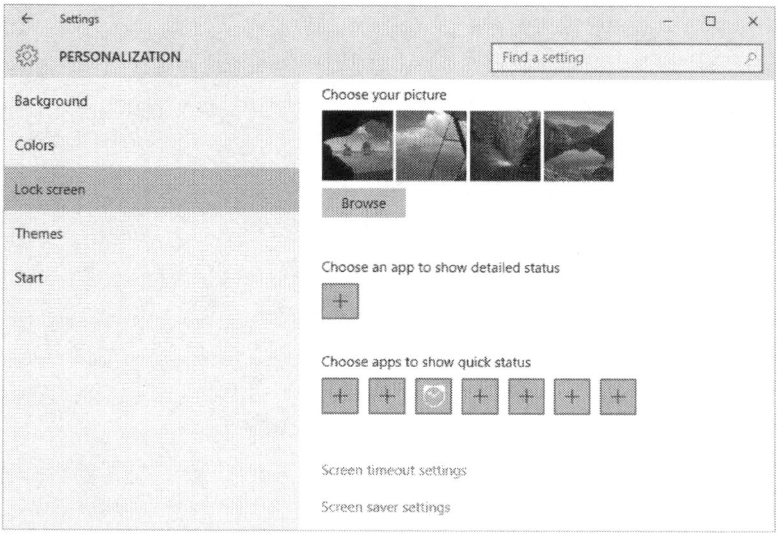

Figure 3-7 Specify apps that can display status updates on the lock screen.

3. You can configure one app to show detailed status updates on the lock screen. Click Choose An App To Show Detailed Status and then select one of the available apps. If you don't want any app to show a detailed status, select None.

4. Using the Choose Apps To Show Quick Status options, you can configure up to seven apps to show quick status updates on the lock screen. Click one of the available slots and then select an app to display updates in this slow. If you don't want any app to show a quick status in a particular slot, select None.

Selecting and Tuning Themes

Desktop themes are combinations of the visual and audio elements that set the appearance of menus, icons, backgrounds, screen savers, system sounds, and mouse pointers. Whenever you switch between themes or modify certain aspects of a theme, you set the user experience level and color scheme for your computer.

Choosing a Theme

In addition to any custom themes you create, several default themes are available. You can apply a default or saved theme by completing these steps:

1. Right-click an open area of the desktop, and then click Personalize. Next, on the Personalization page, click Themes.

2. In the main pane under Themes, click the Theme Settings link. This opens Control Panel, as shown in Figure 3-8.

3. Use the Theme list to select the theme you want to use. If you want to use a saved theme from the Microsoft website, click Get More Themes Online and select the theme or themes to download and install.

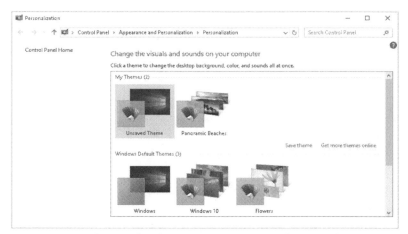

Figure 3-8 Choose the theme to use or get a theme online.

As you've seen, you can switch to any available theme by simply selecting it on the Personalization page in Control Panel. The High Contrast themes are special themes that allow you to forego the pretty stuff to improve performance and readability. High Contrast themes use only the most basic elements and are designed for people with vision disabilities.

With all other themes, Windows automatically adjusts the accent color for graphics and window edges based on the colors used in the background image. The accent color can also be extended to Start, the taskbar, window links and more.

Setting the Accent Color

You can customize the way accent colors are used by following these steps:

1. Right-click an open area of the desktop, and then click Personalize. Next, on the Personalization page, click Colors in the left column.

2. To pick an accent color rather than have Windows pick the color, set Automatically Pick An Accent Color... to Off. As shown in Figure 3-9, you can then choose the accent color. Simply click the color to use.

3. To extend the accent color to Start, the taskbar, window links and more, scroll down and then set Show Color On Start... to On.

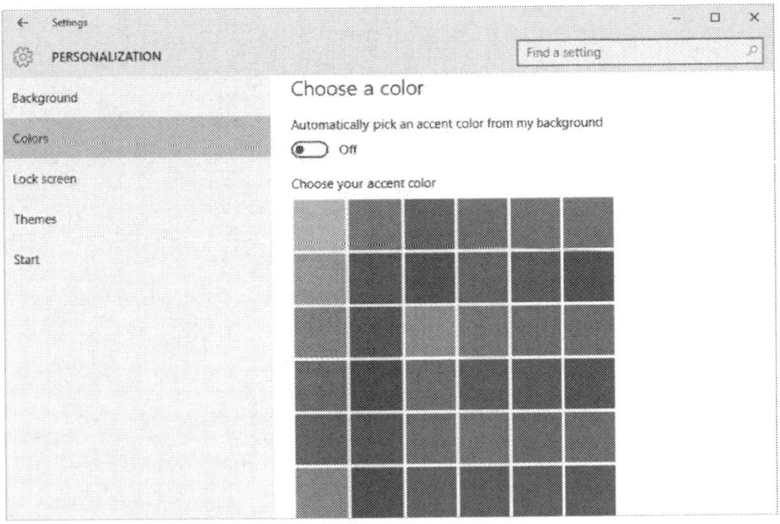

Figure 3-9 Choose the accent color to use.

Real World   By default, Start, taskbar and action center have transparent backgrounds, meaning you can see what's open behind them. Personally, I don't like this effect and always disable it so that these screen elements have a solid background. Disabling this feature has an added benefit: It reduces resource usage and can actually make your computer slightly more responsive. To disable transparent backgrounds, set Make Start, Taskbar... to Off. This options is also on the Colors panel under Settings > Personalization. If your device has an older processor or doesn't have a lot of physical memory, you also want to use the standard Windows theme rather than any of the fancy themes.

Configuring Screen Timeout and Screen Savers

You also can express yourself by using screen savers. Screen savers can be configured to turn on when a computer has been idle for a specified period. Screen savers were originally designed to prevent image burn-in by displaying a continually changing image. With today's monitors, burn-in is not really a problem, but screen savers stuck still around because they offered the ability to password-lock your computer automatically when the screen saver turned on.

Beginning with Windows 8, Microsoft separated the locking functionality from the screensaver functionality, creating a true lock screen. Because of this Windows 10 doesn't use a screensaver by default and you only need to configure one if you like the feature. Instead of using a screensaver, Windows 10 displays the lock screen until the display is turned off, which happens automatically based on the settings in the active power plan. For example, the default power plan, called Balanced, tells Windows 10 to turn off the display after 10 minutes when the computer is plugged in or after 5 minutes when running on battery. These default settings do depend on the type of device, such as whether you are working with a Surface tablet or a desktop computer.

Configuring When the Screen Turns Off

You can set the screen timeout value by performing the following steps:

1. Right-click an open area of the desktop, and then click Personalize. Next, on the Personalization page, click Lock Screen in the left column.

2. In the main pane, scroll down and click the Screen Timeout Settings link.

3. Use the selection list provided under the Screen heading to specify when the screen should turn off, such as after 15 minutes of inactivity. If you are working with a device that has a battery, you'll have two selection lists, one for when the device is plugged in and the other for when the device is running on battery.

4. Optionally, use the selection lists under the Sleep heading to specify when the device should enter sleep mode, such as after 30 minutes of inactivity. Again, if you are working with a device that has a battery, you'll have two selection lists, one for when the device is plugged in and the other for when the device is running on battery.

> **Real World**   Keep in mind, Windows 10 performs many housekeeping tasks in the background when your computer is idle, such as creating indexes, defragmenting hard disks, creating whole computer backups, and setting system restore points. Thus, you want to consider carefully when to have the device enter sleep mode. Wait too long and you'll use power. Wait not long enough and Windows may have to run housekeeping tasks when you're trying to work.

Configuring a Screen Saver

If you want Windows to use a screen saver, you can configure one by following these steps:

1. Right-click an open area of the desktop, and then click Personalize. Next, on the Personalization page, click Lock Screen in the left column.

2. In the main pane, scroll down and click the Screen Saver Settings link to open the Screen Saver Settings dialog box.

3. Use the Screen Saver list, shown in Figure 3-10, to select a screen saver. Although you can install additional screen savers, the standard options are as follows:

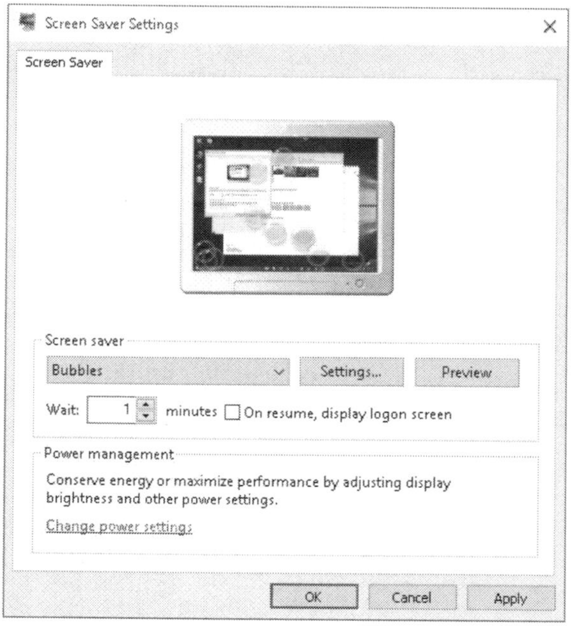

Figure 3-10 Choosing a screen saver

- **(None)**   Turns off the screen saver.

- **3D Text** Displays the system time or custom text as a 3D message against a black background. (Uses the file %WinDir%\System32\SsText3d.scr)

- **Blank** Displays a blank screen (a black background with no text or images). (Uses the file %WinDir%\System32\Scrnsave.scr)

- **Bubbles** Displays multicolored bubbles floating across your desktop while the open windows and documents on the desktop remain visible. (Uses the file %WinDir%\System32\Bubbles.scr)

- **Mystify** Displays arcing bands of lines in various geometric patterns against a black background. (Uses the file %WinDir%\System32\Mystify.scr)

- **Photos** Displays photos and videos from a selected folder as a slideshow. Make sure you know what images will be shown before you set this up to avoid potential embarrassment. (Uses the file %WinDir%\System32\PhotoScreensaver.scr)

- **Ribbons** Displays ribbons of various thicknesses and changing lines against a black background. (Uses the file %WinDir%\System32\Ribbons.scr)

4. Password-protect the screen saver by selecting On Resume, Display Logon Screen. Clear this option only if you do not want to use password protection.

5. Use the Wait control to specify how long the computer must be idle before the screen saver is activated. At home, a reasonable value is between 10 and 15 minutes. At the office, you might want to set this to between 5 and 7 minutes. In many offices, the Wait setting is set by corporate policy and cannot be changed.

6. Click OK.

The Photos and 3D Text screen savers have additional options (as will just about any custom screen savers you install). The Photos screen saver displays a slideshow of photos, such as your portfolio or family pictures.

To customize the Photos screen saver, follow these steps:

1. In the Screen Saver Settings dialog box, select Photos, and then click Settings to display the Photos Screen Saver dialog box shown in Figure 3-11.

2. By default, this screen saver displays the images in your Pictures library, which is a combination of your My Pictures folder and the Public Pictures folder. To use photos from a different folder, click Browse, and then select the folder you want to use.

3. Use Slide Show Speed list to set the speed of the slideshow. The options are Slow, Medium, and Fast.

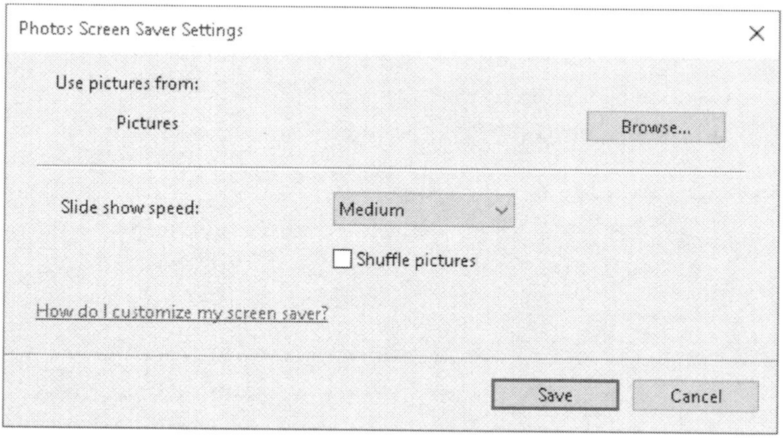

Figure 3-11 Fine-tuning the photos screen saver

4. Photos are displayed in alphanumeric order by default. If you want to shuffle the photos and display them in random order, select the Shuffle Pictures check box.

5. Click Save, and then click OK.

To customize the 3D Text screen saver, follow these steps:

1. In the Screen Saver Settings dialog box, select 3D Text, and then click Settings to display the 3D Text Settings dialog box shown in Figure 3-12.

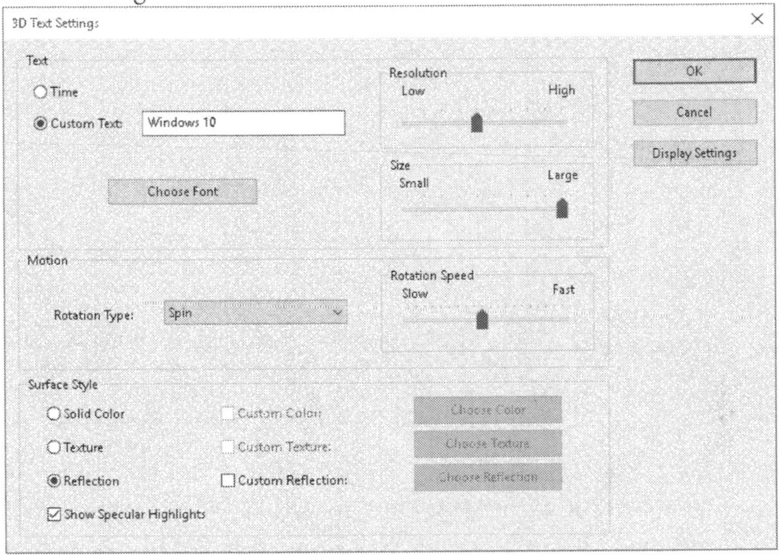

Figure 3-12 Fine-tuning the 3D text screen saver

2. Display the current time or a custom message as 3D text. To display the current time as 3D text, select Time. To display a custom message as 3D text, select Custom Text and type your message.

3. Click Choose Font, and then use the Font dialog box to set the font for the 3D text. The default font is Tahoma.

4. Use the Resolution slider to control the display resolution of the text and the Size slider to control the size of the text. The higher the resolution and larger the text, the more processing power required to draw and move the message.

5. Use the Rotation Speed slider to control the speed at which the text moves and rotates on the screen. The faster the rotation, the more processing power required to draw and move the message.

6. Use the Rotation Type list to select the type of rotation to use, such as tumble or spin. Set the rotation type to None to turn off rotation and reduce the amount of processing power required to draw and move the message.

7. Use the Surface Style options to configure the way the 3D text looks. For example, Solid Color displays the text in a solid color. Click Custom Color and then click Choose Color to display the Color dialog box. Choose the color to use, and click then OK.

8. Click OK twice to save your settings.

Configuring and Creating Your System Sounds

A sound scheme is a set of sounds that you use together. Windows 10 plays sounds in response to a wide variety of events, such as when you log on, when you open or close programs, and when you log off. Programs you install can have their own sounds as well. You manage all of these sounds collectively by using sound schemes.

> **Tip** Want your computer to play a snippet from a particular song when you log on or log off? You can do this! When you're configuring sounds for your computer, Windows Logon and Windows Logoff are listed under program events. Simply use any sound editor to create a .wav snippet from the original song files and configure the resulting .wav files for each related event in the Program Events list.

You can configure your system to use an existing sound scheme by completing the following steps:

1. Right-click an open area of the desktop, and then click Personalize. Next, on the Personalization page, click Themes in the left column.

2. In the main pane, click the Advanced Sound Settings link to display the Sound dialog box with the Sounds tab selected, as shown in Figure 3-13.

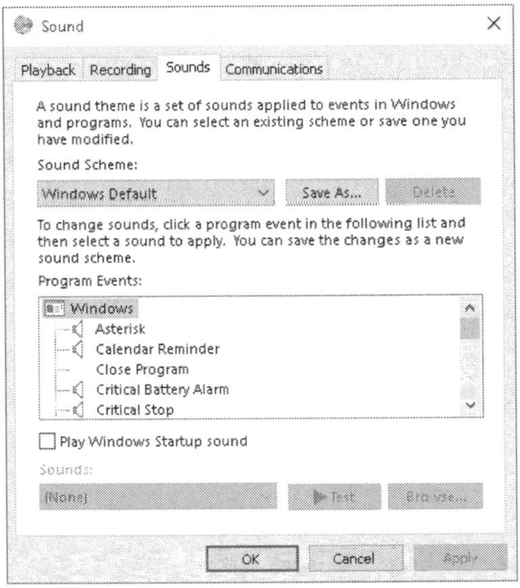

Figure 3-13 Selecting your system sounds

3. Use the Sound Scheme list to choose the sound scheme to use. Windows 10 has two standard sound schemes:

■   No Sounds, which turns off all program sounds except the Windows Startup sound played when you log on.

■   Windows Default, which is configured to use the standard Windows sounds.

> **Note** Other sound schemes available typically depend on the edition of Windows 10 installed on your device, the device manufacturer, and the extras you've installed. Some of the available sound schemes you might see include Afternoon, Calligraphy, Characters, Cityscape, Delta, Festival, Garden, Heritage, Landscape, Quirky, Raga, Savanna, and Sonata.

4. In the Program Events list, sounds are organized according to the program to which they relate and the related event that triggers the sound. To preview a sound for a particular event, select the event in the program list and then click Test.

5. To change the sound for an event, select the event in the Program Events list and then use the Sounds list to choose an available sound. You can also click Browse to select other sounds available on the system. The sound files must be in Microsoft .wav format.

6. If you changed the default sounds for a scheme and want to save the changes, click Save As, type a name for the scheme in the field provided, and then click OK.

7. Save your sound settings by clicking OK.

> **Tip** Want to access the Sound dialog box directly? In the Search box, type **Mmsys.cpl,** and then press Enter.

Customizing Your Mouse Pointers

A pointer scheme is a set of mouse pointers that you use together. The three types of mouse pointers you see the most are the Normal Select pointer, the Text Select pointer, and the Link Select pointer. You can configure the appearance of these and other types of mouse pointers and manage them collectively by using pointer schemes.

The available pointer schemes include:

- **(None)** This doesn't turn mouse pointers off. Instead, it uses nondescript pointers.
- **Windows Black** Inverts the pointer colors so that black backgrounds are used instead of white backgrounds. Also comes in large and extra-large options.
- **Windows Standard** The standard pointers used with Windows Standard settings. Also comes in large and extra-large options.
- **Magnified** Gives the standard pointers a bold edge so they are easier to see.
- **Windows Inverted** Inverts the pointer colors so that black backgrounds are used and gives them bold edges so they are easier to see. Also comes in large and extra-large options.

You can configure your system to use an existing pointer scheme by completing the following steps:

1. Right-click an open area of the desktop, and then click Personalize. Next, on the Personalization page, click Themes in the left column.

2. In the main pane, click the Mouse Pointer Settings link to display the Mouse Properties dialog box with the Pointers tab selected, as shown in Figure 3-14.

> **Note** Drop shadows for pointers are disabled by default, which is generally a good thing as it makes the pointer look clearer on the screen. If you like the drop shadow effect, however, you can enable them by selecting Enable Pointer Shadow.

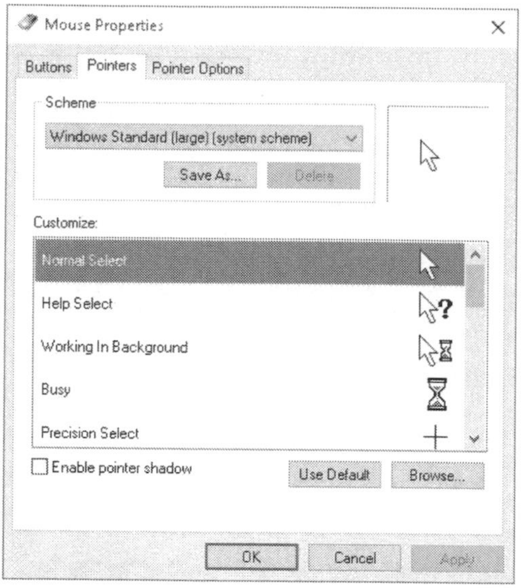

Figure 3-14 Selecting your mouse pointers

3. Use the Scheme list to choose the pointer scheme to use.

4. In the Customize list, pointers are organized according to
    their type. To change a pointer, select the pointer and then
    click Browse. This opens the Browse dialog box with the
    Cursors folder selected. Choose the cursor pointer to use, and
    then click Open.

5. If you changed the default pointers for a scheme and want to
    save the changes, click Save As, type a name for the scheme in
    the field provided, and then click OK.

6. Save your pointer settings by clicking OK.

> **Tip**   To manage mouse settings as well as pointers, In the
> Search box, type **Main.cpl,** and then press Enter. You can now
> configure mouse buttons, pointers, scrolling, and more.

Saving Your Custom Themes and Creating Theme Packs

So far you have tuned and tweaked window colors, backgrounds, sounds, pointers, and screen savers. Now you'll want to save your settings as a unified theme so you can be sure that you can use it again and again. To do this, follow these steps:

1. Right-click an open area of the desktop, and then click Personalize. Next, on the Personalization page, click Themes.

2. In the main pane under Themes, click the Theme Settings link. This opens Control Panel.

3. On the Personalization page, under the My Themes heading, you'll see Unsaved Theme. Right-click this theme, and then click Save Theme. Or simply click the Save Theme link with this theme selected.

4. In the Save Theme As dialog box, enter a name for your custom theme and then click Save. Theme definition files end with the .theme file extension.

5. Unless deleted in the future, the custom theme will appear as a My Themes option. You'll then be able to load the theme simply by clicking it.

A theme you save in this way will only be available to you. That's because the theme is saved in your user profile (%UserProfile%\AppData\Local\Microsoft\Windows\Themes). If you want to be able to share a theme with others, you must create a theme pack by following these steps:

1. Right-click an open area of the desktop, and then click Personalize. Next, on the Personalization page, click Themes.

2. In the main pane under Themes, click the Theme Settings link. This opens Control Panel.

3. On the Personalization page, under the My Themes heading, you'll see Unsaved Theme. Right-click this theme, and then click Save Theme For Sharing.

4. In the Save Theme Pack As dialog box, enter a name for your custom theme pack and then click Save. Theme pack definition files end with the .themepack file extension and are saved in your Documents folder by default. Saved theme packs can be several megabytes in size.

5. Copy the theme pack to a folder accessible to the person you are sharing with. Have the person double-click the theme pack file to load it as a theme and save it to his or her own My Themes list.

Tip You might be wondering how you delete a custom theme that you no longer want. Well, to do this, select a different theme, right-click the theme you no longer want in the My Themes list, and then click Delete Theme.

Customizing Your Displays

In Chapter 2, you learned how to configure multiple displays. Now let's take a closer look at customizing display settings.

Adjusting Display Size and Orientation

With some devices, you may want to change the display size of text, apps and other screen elements to make them larger or smaller. Sometimes, you may want each of your monitors to have a different orientation. For example, you may want your primary monitor to show landscape view while using portrait view on your secondary monitor. Portrait view does make reading and editing documents easier, but isn't necessarily a good choice otherwise.

You can adjust size and orientation by following these steps:

1. Right-click an open area of the desktop, and then click Display Settings. This opens Settings to the System > Display page.

2. Use the Change... slider to modify the size of screen elements. The default size is 100%. You can increase size by sliding to the right and decrease size by sliding to the left.

3. Optionally, use the Orientation list to specify an alternate orientation for a monitor, such as portrait. The default orientation is landscape.

4. Click Apply.

Windows 10 automatically optimizes display settings for each of your monitors by selecting a screen resolution, refresh rate, and color bitness that seem most appropriate based on its testing. Normally, the settings Windows selects work well, but they might not be the optimal settings for your device.

You can adjust display settings by completing the following steps:

1. Right-click an open area of the desktop, and then click Display Settings. This opens Settings to the System > Display page.

2. Click the Advanced Display Settings link.

3. Display 1 is selected by default. If you want to configure the second monitor, click 2 to select it.

4. Use the Resolution list to set the display size, such as 1920 × 1200 pixels.

5. Scroll down and click Display Adapter Properties. Set the color quality or refresh rate using one of the following options:

- On the Adapter tab, click List All Modes. The List All Modes dialog box shows the color qualities and refresh rates supported by the selected monitor. Click OK.
- On the Monitor tab, use the Screen Refresh Rate list to set the desired refresh rate. If different color bitness is available, use the Colors list to select a color quality, such as True Color (32 bit).

6. Click OK to save your settings.

As discussed in Chapter 2, if multiple monitors are connected to your computer, you can designate one monitor as the primary and the other as the secondary monitor. You can also extend the desktop onto your second monitor. After you've configured your monitors, you'll find that pressing the Windows logo key+P is a convenient way to quickly change the monitor configuration. After pressing the Windows log key+P, you can:

- Select PC Screen Only to use only the main computer monitor or the built-in screen on a laptop.
- Select Duplicate to display the main computer monitor or the built-in screen on a laptop on a second monitor.
- Select Extend to extend the display across two monitors.
- Select Second Screen Only to display only on an external monitor or projector.

Managing Monitor and Graphics Card Properties

If the monitor or graphics card shown in the display Properties dialog box does not match the one you are using, you should visit your computer, monitor, or graphics card manufacturer's website and obtain the proper driver. Typically, you can do this by accessing the manufacturer's support page and entering the model of your computer, monitor, or graphics card.

Most manufacturers maintain drivers for several years and provide updates for these drivers as they become available. Typically, the update is delivered in a zipped file containing the drivers you need and an executable installer. To extract the files from a ZIP, right-click the .zip file and then click Extract All. After you select a destination folder, click Extract.

You install monitor drives and graphics card drivers using separate procedures. To specify the monitor driver to use, follow these steps:

1. Right-click an open area of the desktop, and then click Display Settings. This opens Settings to the System > Display page.

2. Scroll down and click the Advanced Display Settings link.

3. Display 1 is selected by default. If you want to configure the second monitor, click 2 to select it.

4. Click Display Adapter Properties. On the Monitor tab, click Properties.

5. On the Driver tab, click Update Driver to start the Update Driver Software wizard. Click Browse My Computer For Driver Software.

6. Select a search location by clicking Browse, using the Browse For Folder dialog box to select the start folder for the search, and then clicking OK. Windows 10 searches all subfolders of the selected folder automatically, and you can select the drive root path, such as C, to search an entire drive.

7. Click Next. Click Close when the driver installation is completed.

Typically, graphics drivers are installed using an executable installer. Run the installer and reboot if the installer asks you to do so. Otherwise, manually specify the graphics card driver to use by following these steps:

1. Right-click an open area of the desktop, and then click Display Settings. This opens Settings to the System > Display page.

2. Scroll down and click the Advanced Display Settings link.

3. Display 1 is selected by default. If you want to configure the second monitor, click 2 to select it.

4. Click Display Adapter Properties. On the Adapter tab, click Properties.

5. On the Driver tab, click Update Driver to start the Update Driver Software wizard. Click Browse My Computer For Driver Software.

6. Select a search location by clicking Browse, using the Browse For Folder dialog box to select the start folder for the search, and then clicking OK. Windows 10 searches all subfolders of the selected folder automatically, and you can select the drive root path, such as C, to search an entire drive.

7. Click Next. Click Close when the driver installation is completed.

Calibrating Color and Using Color Profiles

Color calibration allows you to improve the way color is used on your display and to make sure that colors are displayed as accurately as possible. To calibrate the color, follow these steps:

1. Right-click an open area of the desktop, and then click Display Settings. This opens Settings to the System > Display page.

2. Scroll down and click the Advanced Display Settings link.

3. Display 1 is selected by default. If you want to configure the second monitor, click 2 to select it.

4. Under Related Settings, click Color Calibration to start the Display Color Calibration wizard and then follow the prompts.

Color profiles allow you to get truer colors for specific uses. For example, you may need to more accurately match on-screen colors to print colors, and a color profile designed for this purpose can help you do that. After you obtain the color profile, you must install it on each monitor separately by following these steps:

1. Right-click an open area of the desktop, and then click Display Settings. This opens Settings to the System > Display page.

2. Scroll down and click the Advanced Display Settings link.

3. Display 1 is selected by default. If you want to configure the second monitor, click 2 to select it.

4. Click Display Adapter Properties. On the Color Management tab, click Color Management.

5. In the Color Management dialog box, select the All Profiles tab to get information about currently installed color profiles. Click Add.

6. In the Install Profile dialog box, find the color profile you want to use and then click Add.

7. In the Color Management dialog box, select the Devices tab. Click the new profile, and then click Set As Default Profile.

> **Tip** Want to get to the Color Management dialog box directly? In the Search box, type **Colorcpl.exe,** and then press Enter. When you access color management in this way, be sure to use the Device list to choose the display you want to work with.

Real World   If you don't have a color profile and still would like the benefits of one, use the Display Color Calibration tool to fine-tune display colors to your liking.

Chapter 4. Customizing Boot, Startup, and Power Options

If you really want to know how a car works, you need to open the hood and take a look at the parts that make it go. The same is true for a desktop computer. Open the case of a desktop computer and you'll see the actual parts that make your computer go: drives and controllers, central processing units, memory modules, and more, all connected via wires or circuitry to the computer's motherboard.

But attaching a myriad of devices with wires and circuitry to a motherboard isn't what makes them work together. What makes them work together is your computer's firmware interface, which acts as the intermediary among devices, their internal code, if present, and higher-level processes.

Customizing Your Computer's Firmware Interface

The way a firmware interface operates and the tasks it performs depend on the type of firmware interface and the type of central processing unit (CPU). Most computers built today have CPUs with 64-bit instruction sets and Unified Extensible Firmware Interface (UEFI) for firmware.

UEFI can be wrapped around either BIOS or EFI. For our purposes, a computer that uses UEFI wrapped around BIOS is BIOS-based, as is a computer that uses BIOS by itself, and a computer that uses UEFI wrapped around EFI is EFI-based.

> **Caution**   Only change firmware interface settings when you fully understand the possible repercussions of doing so. Improperly configuring a computer's firmware interface may prevent it from booting and staring the operating system. You should document every change you make to your computer's firmware interface in a notebook. If you get into trouble, you may be able to restore your computer's factory default settings by using an option in the firmware interface. Keep in mind, however, that the factory default settings may not be the same as the settings configured when your computer was delivered to you.

Getting to Know Your Computer's Firmware Interface

Firmware interfaces know little about the operating system your computer is running. Windows 10 initializes itself by loading a pre-operating system boot environment prior to loading the operating system. This boot environment helps your computer validate the integrity of startup processes and the operating system itself before actually running the operating system.

The boot environment also acts as an abstraction layer between the firmware interface and the operating system. By abstracting the underlying interfaces, the boot environment allows Windows 10 to work with BIOS, EFI, and any other underlying interface framework in the same way.

Your computer's firmware interface manages the preboot data flow between the operating system and attached devices. When the firmware interface initializes your computer, it first determines whether all attached devices are available and functioning, and then it activates all the hardware required by the computer to boot, including:

- Graphics and audio controllers
- Internal drives and controllers
- Internal expansion cards
- Motherboard chipsets or System on a Chip (SoC)
- Processors and processor caches
- System memory

> **Real World** Most devices running Windows 10 have either a motherboard chipset or a System on a Chip (SoC). Generally, desktop and laptop computers running Intel or AMD X64-based processors have motherboard chipsets and Surface or other tablets have Intel Atom processors. Atom processors replace the ARM processors that were used previously for tablets. Rather than refer to both types of chipsets here, I've generalized and will simply refer to motherboard chipsets.

After the firmware interface completes this process, it transfers control of the computer to the operating system. The firmware interface implementation determines what happens next. With BIOS-based computers, Windows Boot Manager and Windows Boot Loader are used to boot into the operating system. Windows Boot Manager initializes the operating system by starting the Windows Boot Loader, which in turn starts the operating system using information in the boot configuration data (BCD) store.

Entries in the BCD store identify the boot manager to use during startup and the specific boot applications available on your computer. Windows Boot Manager controls the boot experience and lets you choose the boot application to run. Boot applications load a specific operating system or operating system version. For example, Windows 10 is loaded by a Windows Boot Loader application.

Through BCD parameters, you can add options that control the way the operating system starts, the way computer components are used, and the way operating system features are used.

> **Note** With UEFI, UEFI boot services provide an abstraction layer wrapped around BIOS or EFI. A computer with BIOS in its underlying architecture uses a BIOS-based approach to booting into the operating system. A computer with EFI in its underlying architecture uses an EFI-based approach to booting into the operating system.

Accessing and Setting Your Computer's Firmware Interface

When you turn on most computers, you access the firmware interface by pressing the button shown for Setup in the initial display. For example, you might press F2 during the first few seconds of startup to enter the firmware interface. Firmware interfaces have control options that allow you to adjust the functionality of hardware. You can use these controls to perform basic tasks, including:

- Accessing firmware event logs for troubleshooting information
- Adjusting display brightness (on laptop computers)
- Adjusting the hard disk noise level

- Adjusting the number of cores the processor uses and their speed
- Changing the boot sequence for devices
- Changing the motherboard clock's date and time
- Obtaining configuration information for memory, processors, and more
- Restoring the firmware interface to its default (factory) configuration
- Turning on or off modular add-on devices

While you are working with the firmware interface, you may also be able to create supervisor, user, and general passwords that are not accessible from the operating system. When a supervisor password is set, you must provide the password before you can modify the firmware configuration. When a user password is set, you must enter the password during startup before the computer will load the operating system. If you forget these passwords, you might not be able to operate the computer or change firmware settings until you clear the forgotten passwords, which generally also clears any customization you have made to the firmware interface.

The way the firmware interface works depends on the computer you are working with, the type of firmware interface, and the version of the firmware interface. Desktop computers typically have more firmware configuration options than portable computers do.

Most firmware interfaces have several menu pages that provide information and controls. Two important controls you'll see are network boot and boot order. When network booting is enabled, the computer boots from the network. This is something you might want at the office, but you generally don't want this enabled at home. Boot order sets the priority order for your computer's bootable devices. Your computer tries to start the operating system using the highest-priority device first. If this fails, your computer tries the device with the second-highest priority, and so on. Generally, you'll want your computer to look to its primary removable media device first, and its primary hard drive next, before looking to other bootable devices.

Because configuring boot options in firmware isn't necessarily intuitive, I'll provide two examples using computers from different manufacturers. On a Dell desktop computer that I have, you manage boot settings on the Boot Sequence submenu under System in the firmware interface. The boot order is listed as follows (based on the device present in my computer):

1. Onboard or USB DVD-ROM Drive
2. Onboard SATA Hard Drive
3. Onboard or USB Floppy Drive (not present)
4. Onboard IDE Hard Drive (not present)
5. Add-in Hard Drive (not present)
6. USB Device (not present)
7. Add-in Hard Drive (not present)

In this example, internal devices are listed as "Onboard." Because you generally want the computer to check its primary DVD-ROM drive for bootable media first and then check its primary hard drive, the computer's primary DVD-ROM drive has the highest boot order, and the computer's primary hard drive is listed with the second-highest boot order.

Several options are available for navigating the list. You can use the Up and Down arrow keys to select a device, and then press the U or D key to move the device up or down in the boot order list. You can press the Spacebar to exclude or include a device from the boot list. Press Delete to permanently delete the device if it is not physically present and you no longer want it in the list.

Other important menus in the interface include the following:

- Under Drives in the firmware interface, submenus allow you to enable, disable, and configure drives. Diskette Drive configures floppy drives. Drive 0: SATA-0 enables or disables this specific device. Drive 1: SATA-1 enables or disables this device. SATA Operation sets the hardware RAID configuration.
- Under Onboard Devices, you can use the options on the USB Controller submenu to enable or disable booting from USB storage devices.

For comparison, on an HP laptop of mine, the boot settings are found on the Boot Order and Boot Options submenus on the firmware interface's System Configuration page. On the Boot Order submenu, the boot order is listed as follows:

1. USB Floppy
2. ATAPI CD/DVD ROM Drive
3. Notebook Hard Drive
4. USB Diskette on Key
5. USB Hard Drive
6. Network Adapter

On this computer, you use the Up and Down arrow keys to select a device, and then press F5 or F6 to move the device up or down in the list. The computer distinguishes between USB flash keys (referred to as USB diskettes on keys) and USB drives (referred to as USB hard drives). However, you won't really see a difference between the two.

The Boot Options submenu has these options:

- **F10 and F12 Delay (sec)**   Specifies the amount of time you have to press F10 or F12 before startup begins.
- **DVD-ROM Boot**   Controls whether DVD-ROM boot during startup is enabled or disabled.
- **Floppy Boot**   Controls whether floppy boot during startup is enabled or disabled.
- **Internal Network Adapter Boot**   Controls whether network boot during startup is enabled or disabled.

Here, the main options for navigating the list are the Up and Down arrow keys. You use these keys to select an option, and then press Enter to view and set the option.

Every firmware interface has an Exit option. The Exit page allows you to exit the firmware interface and resume startup of the computer. Pay particular attention to the related options. Generally, you can either exit the firmware interface and discard your changes, or exit the firmware interface and save your changes. Save only when you are certain that you've correctly modified the firmware interface. Incorrectly configuring the firmware interface can make your computer unbootable.

Desktop computers can have a dizzying array of options and suboptions. And because there are few standards and conventions among firmware interface manufacturers, firmware interface options with similar purposes can have very different labels. Read the descriptions of the options to help you as you may want to customize these options for the way in which you want your computer to work.

Real World   Your computer's firmware interface is updatable, and you may need to update the firmware to resolve problems or improve efficiency. However, if you are not experiencing problems on a computer and are not aware of any additional functionality in the firmware interface that you need, you might not need to update a computer to the latest version of the firmware interface. Remember that an improper update can harm the computer and prevent it from starting. That said, when you are trying to install a new operating system on your computer and you are getting a strange error, firmware may be to blame. For example, when I was trying to install Windows 10, one of my laptops wasn't able to find the drivers for its internal controls and drives—even when I provided them—and sometimes also got a media error. When I updated the firmware to the latest version these problems went away and I was able to install Windows 10.

Tracking and Configuring Power On and Resume

Knowing the sequence of events for a cold start of a computer from power on through log on can help you understand exactly how your computer works. When you press the power button to turn on your computer, many events happen in the background:

1. The firmware interface performs a Power On Self Test (POST) to preliminarily configure the computer and then performs setup to initialize the computer.

> **Note** A cold start is the initial power on of a computer. The sequence of events varies if the computer is resuming from sleep, standby, or hibernation, as well as if you are starting an operating system other than Windows or a Windows operating system other than Windows 10, Windows 10, or Windows Server 2012.

2. The firmware interface passes control to the operating system loader, which in this case is the boot manager. The boot manager starts the boot loader. The boot loader uses the firmware interface's boot services to complete operating system boot and then load the operating system.

3. The operating system loads, which involves the following:

    a. Loading (but not running) the operating system kernel, Ntoskrnl.exe

    b. Loading (but not running) the hardware abstraction layer (HAL), Hal.dll

    c. Loading the HKEY_LOCAL_MACHINE\SYSTEM registry hive into memory (from %SystemRoot%\System32\Config\System)

    d. Scanning the HKEY_LOCAL_MACHINE\SYSTEM\Services key for device drivers and then loading (but not initializing) the drivers that are configured for the boot class into memory

> **Note** In this context, drivers are also services. This means that both device drivers and system services are prepared.

    e. Enabling memory paging

4. The boot loader passes control to the operating system kernel. The kernel and the HAL initialize the Windows executive, which in turn processes the configuration information stored in the HKEY_LOCAL_MACHINE\SYSTEM\ CurrentControlSet hive and then starts device drivers and system services.

5. The kernel starts the Session Manager (Smss.exe). The session manager:

    a. Initializes the system environment by creating system environment variables.

    b. Starts the Win32 subsystem (Csrss.exe). Here, Windows switches the display output from text mode to graphics mode.

    c. Starts the Windows Logon Manager (Winlogon.exe), which in turn starts the Services Control Manager (Services.exe) and the Local Security Authority (Lsass.exe) and waits for a user to logon.

    d. Creates any additional paging files that are required.

    e. As necessary, performs delayed renaming of in-use files that were updated in the previous session.

6. The Windows Logon Manager waits for a user to logon. The logon user interface and the default credential provider collect the user name and password and pass this information to the Local Security Authority for authentication.

7. The Windows Logon Manager runs Userinit.exe and the File Explorer shell. Userinit.exe initializes the user environment by creating user environment variables, running startup programs, and performing other essential tasks.

Knowing this event sequence can help you identify the source of startup problems. Keep the following in mind:

* If your computer fails during the Power On Self Test's preliminary configuration, the likely cause of the problem is hardware failure or a missing device.
* If your computer fails during the setup initialization, the likely cause of the problem is the firmware configuration, the disk subsystem, or the file system.
* If your computer fails during the boot loader process, BCD data, improper OS selection for loading, or an invalid boot loader are the likely cause of the problem.
* If your computer fails during kernel and HAL initialization, driver or service configuration or service dependencies are the likely cause of the problem.
* If your computer fails before logon and during Session Manager setup, the graphics display mode, system environment, or component configuration are the likely cause of the problem.

Understanding how your computer resumes is equally important. During a resume from sleep, standby, or hibernation, your computer's advanced power settings determine how the computer turns itself back on. A computer's motherboard chipset, firmware, and operating system must support the Advanced Configuration and Power Interface (ACPI) version that implements the advanced power state feature you are trying to use. ACPI-aware components track the power state of the computer. An ACPI-aware operating system can generate a request that the system be switched to a different power state, and the firmware interface responds by enabling the requested power state.

There are six different power states, ranging from S0 (completely powered on and fully operational) to S5 (completely powered off). Everything in between is a sleep state. S1, S2, and S3 are low-power consumption states in which some or all contexts are maintained in memory. S4 is the no-power hibernate state in which context data is written to disk.

Motherboard chipsets support specific power states. One motherboard might support the S0, S1, S4, and S5 states, whereas another might support the S0, S1, S3, S4, and S5 states. As a computer user, you don't need to know the exact specifics of each state. Just remember this:

- S0 means the computer is on.
- S1, S2, and S3 mean the computer is a sleep state but still using some power.
- S4 means the computer is hibernating and not using power.
- S5 means the computer is off.

Your computer's firmware interface has related power management settings. You can use After Power Failure, AC Recovery, or a similar setting to specify what the computer does after a power failure. If you want the computer to remain off after power is restored, set the computer to stay off. If you want the computer to go back to the state it was in before power failed, set the computer to use the last state. If you want the computer to turn itself on after a power failure, set the computer to power on.

Another power option you may see is Wake On LAN From S5 or Auto Power On. This type of option determines the action taken when the system power is off and a power management wake event occurs. If you configure this option, you'll be able to specify whether the computer stays off or powers on.

You may also have control over whether S1 or S3 suspend mode is used. From a user perspective, it really doesn't matter whether S1 or S3 is used. However, from a computer perspective it matters a lot, and you'll only want to switch modes if you are trying to correct a resume problem. For example, if your computer is having problems resuming from a sleep state, a troubleshooting option may involve changing the suspend mode.

If you encounter startup problems just prior to or after logon, the issue is probably related to a misconfigured service or startup application. To temporarily resolve this so you can log on, you can disable services and startup applications, as discussed later in this chapter.

Getting Firmware and Power Management Information

You can use the PowerCfg utility to get information about your computer's firmware and power management configuration. When you run PowerCfg and create a utilization report, the utility performs a detailed diagnostics of your system that analyzes the computer's configuration and identifies any power efficiency issues. As Figure 4-1 shows, the report is generated in HTML and displayed using a web browser, such as Microsoft Edge. The report:

* Specifies the type of firmware, the firmware date and version.
* Identifies services and devices with power management issues, if any.

- Specifies whether your battery is failing or becoming inefficient, if applicable.
- Identifies the specific sleep states supported. (These details are in the Information section.)

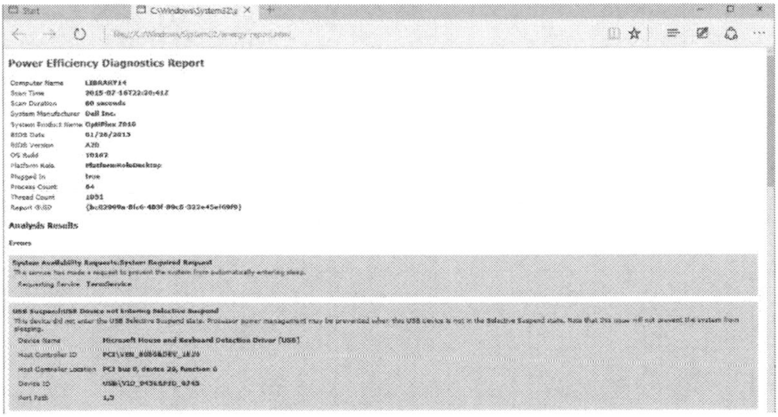

Figure 4-1 A power efficiency diagnostics report.

You can generate a report for your computer by following these steps:

1. Open an elevated, administrator Command Prompt. One way to do this is to right-click Start and then select Command Prompt (Admin) on the shortcut menu.

2. Change to the documents folder in your user profile by entering the following at the prompt:

    cd %HomePath%\documents

3. Run Powercfg and generate the report by entering the following at the prompt:

    PowerCfg /Energy

4. Wait 1 to 2 minutes for the utility to perform the analysis and generate the report. Then display the report in the default browser by entering the following at the prompt:

    energy-report.html

Customizing Startup and Boot Configuration

Windows 10 provides the Startup And Recovery dialog box, the System Configuration utility, and the BCD Editor to help you modify the boot configuration and the startup process. The Startup And Recovery dialog box and the System Configuration utility are the easiest to use. Although a command-line professional may want to tune a computer with the BCD Editor, you can use the other tools to perform essentially the same tasks without all the fuss.

> **Pro Tip** Sometimes a device may fail to start due to issues with the boot options in firmware. On devices with firmware boot options that are configurable, you can access a Boot Options menu by pressing a designated function key, such as F8 or F12 during startup of the device. Some devices display a notice during startup regarding the key to press. However, increasingly, this menu is either hidden or completely inaccessible for all types of devices except for desktop PCs. On desktop PCs, the Boot Options menu and UEFI/BIOS firmware are where you go to disable Secure Boot and enable Legacy Boot, which is something you may need to do to enable loading additional operating systems.

Fine-Tuning Startup and Recovery Settings

One of the easiest ways to control the way your computer starts is to configure startup options by using the Startup And Recovery dialog box. The related options set the default operating system, how long to display the list of available operating systems, and how long to display recovery options when needed. You can optimize these settings to speed up the startup process by reducing wait times while also ensuring that you can access advanced options, which may be necessary for troubleshooting and recovery.

You access and configure startup options by completing the following steps:

1. In the Search box, type **SystemPropertiesAdvanced** in the Search box, and then press Enter to open the System Properties dialog box with the Advanced tab selected.

2. Under Startup And Recovery, click Settings to display the Startup And Recovery dialog box, shown in Figure 4-2.

3. If your computer has multiple operating systems, use the Default Operating System list to specify the operating system that you want to start by default.

4. Specify the display interval for the operating system list by selecting the Time To Display List Of Operating Systems check box and setting the desired interval in seconds. To speed up the startup process, you might use a value of 5 or 10 seconds.

5. Specify the display interval for the recovery options list by selecting the Time To Display Recovery Options When Needed check box and setting the desired interval in seconds. Again, to speed up the startup process, you might use a value of 5 or 10 seconds.

6. Under System Failure, select Write An Event To The System Log if you want to record events related to system failure. If you want your computer to automatically restart after a failure, select Automatically Restart.

7. Save your settings by clicking OK twice.

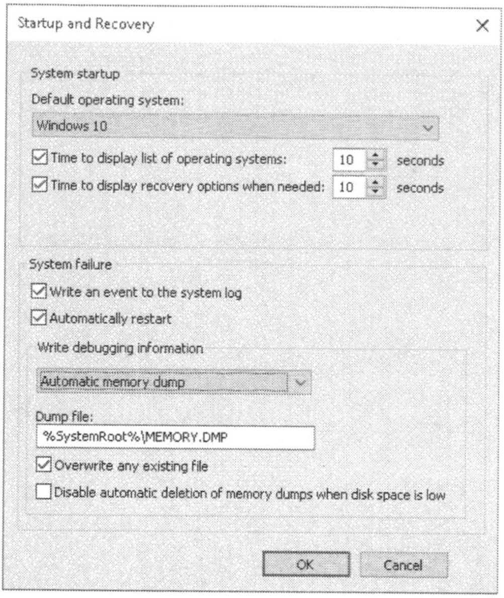

Figure 4-2 Configuring startup and recovery options

Changing Your Computer's Boot Configuration

As you've seen, the Startup And Recovery dialog box makes it easy to set basic startup options. To configure more advanced options and fine-tune the startup process, you can use the System Configuration utility (Msconfig.exe). Although you typically use this utility during troubleshooting, you also can use the utility to dig down deep into startup processes and change the way startup works.

The System Configuration utility is available by typing **msconfig.exe** in the Search box, and then pressing Enter. As shown in Figure 4-3, this utility has the following tabs:

- **General**   Allows you to configure normal startup, diagnostic startup, or selective startup

- **Boot**   Allows you to control the way to enable various Safe Boot modes and the way that individual startup-related processes work
- **Services**   Allows you to enable or disable system services
- **Startup**   Allows you to enable or disable startup processes
- **Tools**   Allows you to access various system management tools

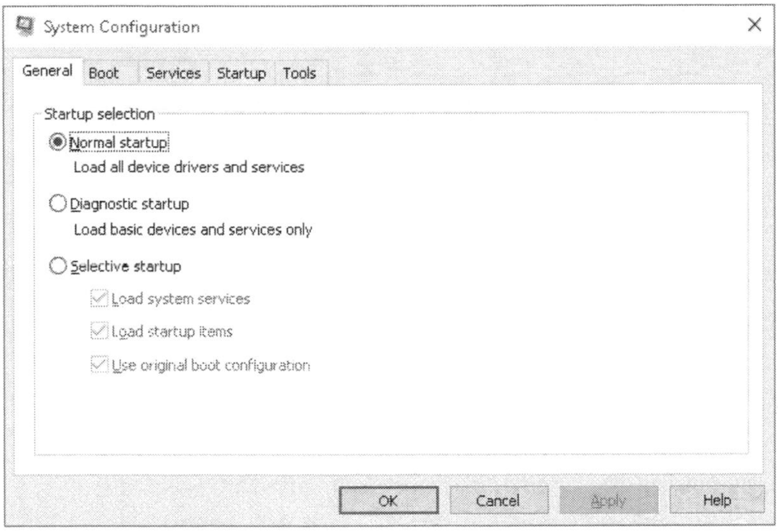

Figure 4-3 Fine-tuning startup with the System Configuration utility

You should know several important things about using the System Configuration utility:

- If you make changes on the Boot, Services, or Startup tabs, the Selective Startup option and related suboptions are automatically selected on the General tab.
- You should usually remove your selective or diagnostic options when you are finished troubleshooting your computer's problem. After you restart the computer and resolve any

problems, access the System Configuration utility again, restore the original settings, and then click OK.

- You must specifically elect to make changes permanent. Otherwise, your changes will be lost when you go back to normal startup.

Using the Selective and Diagnostic Startup Modes

Normal is the default startup mode. Normal startup ensures that Windows 10 loads all system configuration files and device drivers and runs all startup applications and enabled services. If your computer isn't performing properly or is generating errors at startup, you can use diagnostic or selective startup to try to determine the cause of the problem.

You use diagnostic startup to troubleshoot system problems. In diagnostic mode, your computer loads only basic device drivers and essential services. When you start the system in diagnostic mode, you can modify system settings to resolve configuration problems.

You use selective startup to identify problem areas in your computer's configuration. Selective startup is a modified boot configuration. Here, your computer only uses the system services and startup items you specify, which can help you identify settings that are causing system problems and correct them as necessary.

You can enable and use selective or diagnostic startup by completing these steps:

1. Type **msconfig** in the Search box, and then press Enter to display the System Configuration utility.

2. On the General tab, select either Diagnostic Startup or Selective Startup. If you choose Selective Startup, specify the items that you want your computer to use. Your choices are:

*   **Load System Services**   Sets the computer to load Windows services on startup. If you select this option, use the settings on the Services tab to specify which services are started.
*   **Load Startup Items**   Sets the computer to run applications designated for startup at boot time. If you select this option, you can enable and disable startup applications by using the options on the Startup tab.
*   **Use Original Boot Configuration**   Sets the computer to process the original boot configuration on startup instead of one you've created by modifying the boot settings with the System Configuration utility.

3. When you are ready to continue, click OK, and then reboot your computer. If you have problems rebooting your computer, restart the system in Safe Mode and repeat this procedure. Safe Mode appears automatically as an option after a failed boot.

Changing the Way Your Computer Boots

Windows 10 uses the Windows Boot Manager and a boot application to start the operating system. For troubleshooting, you can use the options on the System Configuration utility's Boot tab to control the boot partition, boot method, and boot options used by the operating system.

When your computer has multiple operating systems, you can specify that an operating system other than the current one should be used simply by clicking the related operating system entry. When working with operating system entries, you can select the following options:

- **Set As Default**   Sets the currently selected boot partition as the default partition. The default partition is selected automatically if you don't choose another option before the timeout interval.
- **Timeout**   Sets the amount of time the computer waits before using the default boot partition.
- **Delete**   Deletes an operating system entry. As the entry cannot be easily re-created, only delete an entry if absolutely necessary.

The Boot tab has other options as well, including:

- **Advanced Options**   Allows you to set boot options for number of processors, maximum memory, PCI locking, and debugging.
- **Safe Boot**   Sets the computer to start in Safe Mode, with additional flags for minimal, network, and alternate shell minimal boots. After you successfully boot your computer in Safe Mode, you can modify settings to resolve any configuration problems.
- **No GUI Boot**   Sets the computer to boot to the Windows prompt, which doesn't load the graphical components of the operating system. Booting to the prompt is useful when you are having problems with the video and graphical components of Windows 10.
- **Boot Log**   Turns on boot logging so that key startup events are written to an event log.
- **Base Video**   Forces the computer to use video graphics adapter (VGA) display settings. Use this mode when you are trying to resolve display settings, such as when the display mode is set to a size that the monitor cannot display.

- **OS Boot Information**   Starts the computer using verbose output so that you can view the details of startup activities prior to the loading of Windows graphical components.

All changes you make are stored as modified boot configuration data by the System Configuration utility. After you make changes and click OK, you can restart the computer to apply the changes temporarily. To go back to a normal startup after you've made and applied changes, you must start the utility, select Normal Startup on the General tab, and then click OK. You must then restart the computer so that the normal settings are used.

To make the standard or advanced boot options you've selected permanent, you must select the Make All Boot Settings Permanent check box on the Boot tab before clicking OK. In most cases, you won't want troubleshooting or debugging options to be permanent, so be sure to clear these options first.

Disabling Startup Applications and Services for Troubleshooting

Slow startup and errors experienced during startup can sometimes be related to applications and services run at startup. You manage startup apps using Task Manager and service startup using System Configuration.

When you believe that an application loaded at startup is causing problems with your computer, you can disable the program from starting and reboot your computer. If the problem is no longer present, you might have identified the problem and can remedy it by permanently disabling the automatic startup of the program. If the problem still occurs, you can try disabling other startup applications to see if this resolves the problem.

You can disable startup applications by following these steps:

1. Open Task Manager by right-clicking the Start button and select Task Manager on the shortcut menu. Alternatively, press the Windows logo key + X and then click Task Manager on the shortcut menu.

2. On the Startup tab, shown in Figure 4-4, all applications that run automatically at startup are listed by name, command path, and registry location.

3. Click any application that you do not want to load at startup to select it and then click Disable. Make sure you only disable programs that you've identified as potential problems, and do so only if you know how they are used by the operating system.

4. You should restart your computer to check the changes. Repeat this procedure as necessary to identify the program causing the system problems. If you can't identify an application as the cause of the problem, a Windows component, service, or device driver might be causing the problem you are experiencing. Some programs and housekeeping tasks are triggered by Scheduled Jobs, and the periodic triggering of these scheduled jobs might be the cause of the problem.

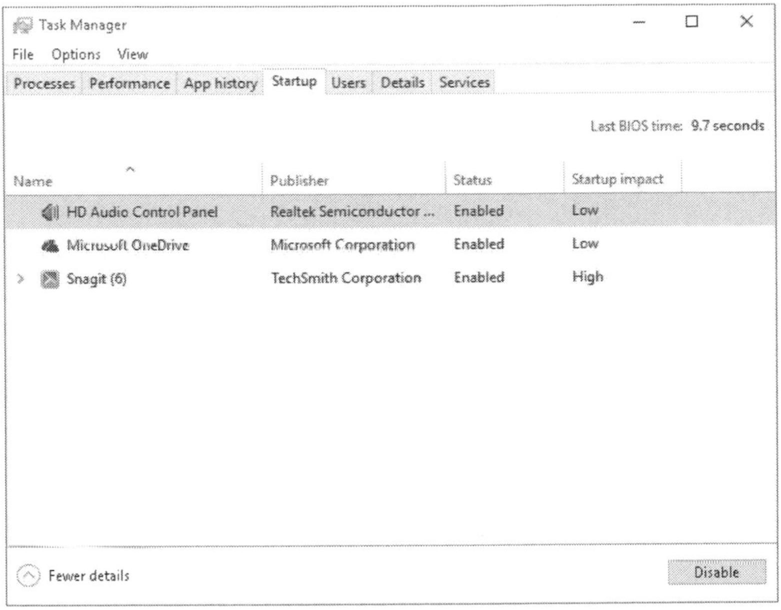

Figure 4-4 Viewing startup applications

If disabling a startup application resolves the problem, you may want to check with the application vendor to see if an updated executable is available. If so, install the update.

You can troubleshoot problems with system services in a similar way:

1. Open the System Configuration utility. The Services tab displays a list of all services installed on the computer, the origin of each service, and the state of each service, such as Running or Stopped.

2. Clear the check box next to any service that you do not want to run at startup. Make sure you only disable those services that you've identified as potential problems, and do so only if you know how they are used by the operating system.

3. Click OK. You should restart the computer to check the changes, so if you are prompted to restart the system, click Yes.

Otherwise, restart the computer manually. Repeat this procedure as necessary to identify the service causing the problem. If you can't identify a service as the cause of the problem, a Windows component, startup application, or device driver might be causing the problem you are experiencing. Some programs and housekeeping tasks are triggered by Scheduled Jobs, and the periodic triggering of these scheduled jobs might be the cause of the problem.

If disabling a service resolves the problem, you can then permanently disable the service using the Services utility or check with the service vendor to see if an updated executable is available for the service.

Customizing Boot Configuration with the BCD Editor

The BCD store contains information required by your computer to locate and load the operating system. There is a single entry for the Windows Boot Manager and one Windows Boot Loader entry for each instance of Windows installed on the computer.

Windows Boot Manager is itself a boot loader application. There are other boot loader applications as well, including:

* **Bootsector** The Windows Boot Sector Application
* **Fwbootmgr** The Firmware Boot Manager
* **Ntldr** The boot loader for legacy operating systems
* **Osloader** The boot loader for Windows operating systems
* **Resume** The Windows Resume Loader

You access and manage the BCD store by using the BCD Editor (Bcdedit.exe). The BCD Editor is a command-line utility that requires elevated, administrator privileges to perform management tasks. You can use the BCD Editor to view the entries in the BCD store by following these steps:

1. Press the Windows logo key+ X and then click Command Prompt (Admin) on the shortcut menu.

2. To view the entries in the BCD store, enter **bcdedit** at the command prompt.

3. To view the available commands, enter **bcdedit /?** at the command prompt.

> **Real World** The BCD Editor is an advanced command-line tool for IT professionals. If you make a mistake with the BCD Editor, your computer could end up in a nonbootable state, and you would need to initiate recovery. Because of this, only make changes when you are absolutely certain they will work.

Whenever you work with the BCD Editor, you work with the system BCD store, which contains the operating system boot entries and related boot settings. References in the BCD store can be specified by globally unique identifiers (GUIDs), such as {8c4305c4-243b-11e5-a00b-c54f98ee3b3b}, as well as by well-known identifiers, such as {bootloadersettings}.

A list of well-known identifiers and their usage follows. Both well-known identifiers and GUIDs are enclosed in curly braces. GUIDs have dashes as well.

{badmemory} Contains the global RAM defect list that can be inherited by any boot application entry.

{bootloadersettings} Contains the collection of global settings that should be inherited by all Windows Boot

Loader application entries.

{bootmgr}   Indicates the Windows Boot Manager entry.

{current}   Represents a virtual identifier that corresponds to the operating system boot entry for the operating system that is currently running.

{dbgsettings}   Contains the global debugger settings that can be inherited by any boot application entry.

{default}   Represents a virtual identifier that corresponds to the boot manager default application entry.

{emssettings}   Contains the global Emergency Management Services settings that can be inherited by any boot application entry.

{fwbootmgr}   Indicates the firmware boot manager entry. This entry is used on EFI systems.

{globalsettings}   Contains the collection of global settings that should be inherited by all boot application entries.

{hypervisorsettings}   Contains the hypervisor settings that can be inherited by any operating system loader entry.

{legacy}   Indicates the Windows Legacy OS Loader (Ntldr) that can be used to start Windows operating systems earlier than Windows Vista.

{memdiag}   Indicates the memory diagnostic application entry.

{ntldr}   Indicates the Windows Legacy OS Loader (Ntldr) that can be used to start operating systems earlier than Windows Vista.

{ramdiskoptions}   Contains the additional options required by the boot manager for RAM disk devices.

{resumeloadersettings}   Contains the collection of global

settings that should be inherited by all Windows resume-from-hibernation application entries.

The BCD Editor provides separate commands for creating, copying, and deleting entries in the BCD store. You can use the /create command to create identifier, application, and inherit entries in the BCD store. The syntax is:

```
bcdedit /create Identifier /d "Description"
```

where Identifier is a well-known identifier for the entry you want to create, such as:

```
bcdedit /create {ntldr} /d "Pre-Windows Vista
OS Loader"
```

You can create entries for specific boot loader applications as well, including:

- **Bootsector** Sets the boot sector for a real-mode application
- **OSLoader** Loads Windows Vista or later
- **Resume** Resumes the operating system from hibernation
- **Startup** Identifies a real-mode application

The syntax for creating entries for boot load applications is:

```
bcdedit /create /application AppType /d
"Description"
```

where AppType is one of the previously listed application types, such as:

```
bcdedit /create /application osloader /d
"Windows 10 Ent Ed"
```

You delete entries in the system store by using the /delete command and the following syntax:

```
bcdedit /delete Identifier
```

If you are trying to delete a well-known identifier, you must use the /f command to force deletion, such as:

```
bcdedit /delete {ntldr} /f
```

The /cleanup option is implied by default whenever you delete BCD entries. This option cleans up any other references to the entry being deleted to ensure that the data store doesn't have invalid references to the removed identifier. Entries are removed from the display order as well, and this could result in a different default operating system being set. To delete the entry and clean up all other references except the display order entry, you can use the /nocleanup command.

Other BCD editor commands you can use include:

- **/set** Used to set additional options and values for entries
- **/deletevalue** Used to delete additional options and values for entries
- **/displayorder** Used to change the display order of boot managers associated with a particular Windows Vista or later installation
- **/default** Used to change the default operating system entry

- **/timeout**   Used to change the timeout value associated with the default operating system
- **/bootsequence**   Used to boot to a particular operating system one time and then revert to the default boot order afterward

To learn more about subcommands and how they are used, type **bcedit**, type the subcommand name, type **/?** and then press Enter. For example, to learn how to use the /set subcommand, enter **bcdedit /set /?.**

Working with Automatic Recovery Mode

Your computer can start in safe or automatic recovery mode for a variety of reasons. Generally, safe mode is used when you select this option as part of troubleshooting and automatic recovery mode is used when Windows has detected a problem during a previous failed start. For example, after a sudden power loss, your computer may boot into automatic recovery mode.

Automatic recovery has several stages. During the initial stage, your device display a "Preparing Automatic Recovery" message while entering the preboot environment. During the next stage, your device will display a "Diagnosing Computer" message while loading the recovery menus and performing preliminary checks.

Next, your computer will display the Automatic Repair window, as shown in Figure 4-5. Here, if you simply click Restart, the computer will exit Automatic Recovery mode and attempt a normal start of the operating system.

Figure 4-5 Restart or continue to more options.

Real World   The window you see actually depends on how far Windows gets into the startup process. If the device boots but Windows fails to load, you'll see a Recovery window that states this. The Recovery window options are similar to those shown and perform the same actions. You can restart or continue to the Choose An Option window.

Generally, if you find yourself staring unexpectedly at the Automatic Repair window, you should always try a restart to see if the computer will start normally. If the restart fails, however, you'll then need to continue through the repair process by clicking Advanced Options.

As Figure 4-6 shows, the options at this point aren't really advanced. Instead, Windows is actually giving you two more chances to exit the repair and recovery process. If you click Continue, the computer will exit Automatic Recovery mode and attempt to continue loading the operating system. If you click Turn Off Your PC, the computer will exit Automatic Recovery mode and shutdown, allowing you to try to restart the computer normally later.

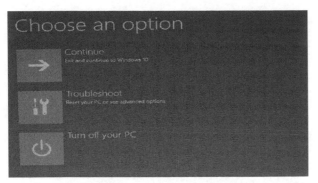

Figure 4-6 Exit the repair or continue.

The only option that lets you continue into the repair and recovery process is Troubleshoot. When you click Troubleshoot, you access the Troubleshoot window, shown in Figure 4-7. At this point, you've gone past your computer's sandboxed safety zone and entered dangerous territory.

Figure 4-7 Completely reset or continue.

Choose Reset This PC, and your computer will start the reset process which re-installs Windows and completely resets your device. All you need to do is follow the prompts. During the reset process, you'll be given the opportunity to specify whether to save files in your personal folders or remove them. All other data will be lost if it's stored on the same volume as the operating system. For example, if Windows is installed on the C drive, completing this process will destroy all other data on the C drive.

Choose Advanced Options to get to the actual Advanced Options window, shown in Figure 4-8.

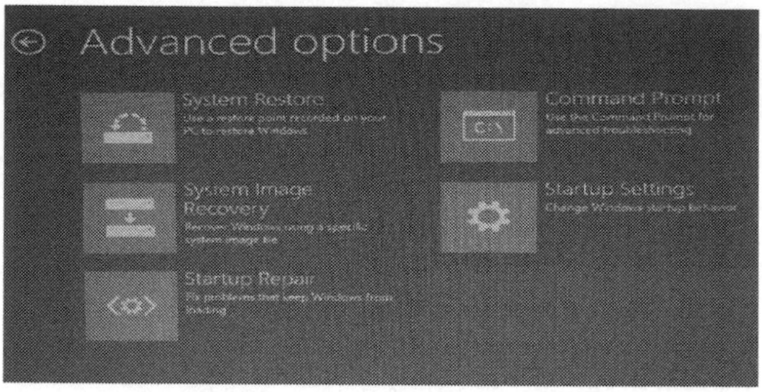

Figure 4-8 Completely reset your computer or continue.

How you use these options depends on the problem you are experiencing. My recommendation is the following:

1. On your first repair attempt, select Startup Repair to force Windows to enter repair mode. In this mode, Windows will try to detect issues that are causing startup problems, such as a missing boot file. Windows will then attempt to an automatic repair. If the repair is successful, your computer will boot normally.

2. If automatic repair fails, you can next try to repair the issue yourself by using the Startup Settings option as discussed in "Performing an Advanced or Safe Mode Boot" or by using the System Restore option.

For most people, the System Restore option may be the best choice. While you are working, your computer periodically creates restore points that save the system configuration. These restore points typically are created when you install programs or drivers but also when you make changes to the operating system that can affect the way the computer works. To try to use one of these restore points to restore your computer to a previous state, select System Restore and follow the prompts.

Performing an Advanced or Safe Mode Boot

Windows 10 needs access to specific system files to start properly. If the required files are missing or corrupt, your computer won't start and you'll need to use Startup Repair to try to resolve your computer's problem. Most of the time, repairing a damaged or missing file will fix such an issue; sometimes, you might need to continue troubleshooting to diagnose and resolve a deeper issue.

Usually, a computer fails to start because something has changed and your computer doesn't like the change. For example, you might have installed an update for a device driver that caused a system-wide conflict or failed partway through. Or a program you installed might have modified the system's configuration in such a way that prevents normal startup. Whatever the cause of the problem, if a Startup Repair doesn't fix things, you can try to resolve the problem using safe mode.

In safe mode, Windows 10 loads only basic files, services, and drivers, including those for the mouse, monitor, keyboard, mass storage, and base video. The monitor driver sets the basic settings and modes for the computer's monitor, and the base video driver sets the basic options for the computer's graphics card.

Because safe mode loads a limited set of configuration information, it can help you troubleshoot problems. When you have finished using safe mode, be sure to restart the computer using a normal startup. You will then be able to use the computer as you normally would.

Several Safe Mode options are available. The option you use depends on the type of problem you're experiencing. The main options are:

- **Safe Mode** Starts the computer with only basic files, services, and drivers during the initialization sequence. The drivers loaded include those for the mouse, monitor, keyboard, mass storage, and base video. No networking services or drivers are started.
- **Safe Mode With Networking** Starts the computer with basic files, services, and drivers, as well as services and drivers needed to start networking.
- **Safe Mode With Command Prompt** Starts the computer with basic files, services, and drivers, and then starts a command prompt instead of the Windows 10 graphical interface. No networking services or drivers are started. Start the Explorer shell from the command-line interface by pressing Ctrl+Shift+Esc to open Task Manager, clicking File, clicking New Task (Run) to open the Create New Task dialog box, typing explorer.exe, and then clicking OK.
- **Enable Boot Logging** Turns on boot logging to create a record of all startup events in the log files.
- **Enable Low Resolution Video** Turns on low-resolution display mode, which is useful if the system display is set to a mode that can't be used with the current monitor.

- **Disable Automatic Restart On System Failure**   Prevents Windows from restarting after a crash. If you don't set this option, Windows will restart automatically after a crash.
- **Disable Driver Signature Enforcement**   Starts the computer in Safe Mode without enforcing digital signature policy settings for device drivers. This can temporarily resolve a startup problem related to a device driver with an invalid or missing digital signature. After your computer is started, you can resolve the problem permanently by getting a new driver or changing the driver signature enforcement settings.
- **Disable Early Launch Anti-Malware Protection**   Starts the computer in Safe Mode without starting anti-malware software that runs as part of the startup bootstrap. This can temporarily resolve a startup problem related to invalid updates or changes to your anti-malware software. After your computer is started, you can resolve the problem permanently by updating, reinstalling or removing your anti-malware software.

You can use the System Configuration utility to start a computer in Safe Mode as discussed previously in this chapter under "Changing the Way Your Computer Boots." If your computer enters automatic recovery, you can start in Safe Mode by following these steps:

1. After your device loads the recovery environment, click Advanced Options.

2. At the Choose An Option prompt, click Troubleshoot. Next, at the Troubleshoot prompt, click Advanced Options.

3. The Advanced Options window provides several troubleshooting options, including the option to start a system restore or open a command prompt window. To continue, click Startup Settings.

4. As Figure 4-9 shows, the Startup Settings window gives you one last chance to go back while also telling you what's going to happen when you click Restart. (Yes, all these windows are designed to prevent you from accidentally making changes you'll regret.)

Figure 4-9 Last chance to go back before you restart in Safe Mode.

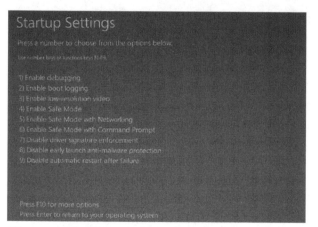

Figure 4-10 Choose the startup option for Safe Mode.

5. Click Restart. Next, you'll have the startup options shown in Figure 4-10. Use either the number keys or the function keys to select the mode you want to use.

If a problem reappears when you start in Safe Mode, you can eliminate the default settings and basic device drivers as possible causes. Begin your troubleshooting by looking at newly added devices or updated drivers. Use Safe Mode to remove the devices, reverse the updates, or install different versions of driver software. Restart your computer to test your changes.

If you are still having a problem starting the system normally and suspect that problems with hardware, software, or settings are to blame, go back to Safe Mode and try using System Restore to undo previous changes.

> **Real World**   Several of the devices I worked with in Safe Mode didn't function properly and I couldn't get to the Start menu or Search box. Luckily, I had pinned Command Prompt to the taskbar and was able to use an elevated prompt to get my work done, including starting Msconfig.exe so I could specify the Normal Startup option for when I restarted. On one device, however, even taskbar functionality was gone. To get to utilities, I pressed Ctrl+Shift+Esc to open Task Manager and then used the Run option on the File menu to run commands.

Resolving Restart or Shutdown Issues

Normally, you shut down or restart Windows 10 by clicking the Power button on the Start menu, and then clicking Restart or Shut Down as appropriate. Sometimes, however, Windows 10 won't resume, shut down, or restart normally, and you must try to resolve the problem.

Recovering from a Failed Resume

Windows 10 creates a snapshot of the current state of the computer whenever your computer enters sleep mode or hibernates. Windows Resume Loader handles sleep and hibernate operations. With sleep mode, this snapshot is created in memory and then read from memory by the resume loader when you wake the computer. With hibernate mode, this snapshot is written to disk and then read from disk by the resume loader when you wake the computer. These snapshots are what enable the Instant On and Fast Resume features.

Your computer may have a problem resuming for any of a variety of reasons that may include errors in the snapshot, physical errors in memory, and physical disk errors. Whatever the problem, Windows Resume Loader prompts you with a warning message similar to the following:

```
Windows Resume Loader
The last attempt to restart the system from
its previous location failed. Attempt to
restart again?

Continue with system restart
Delete restoration data and proceed to system
boot.

Enter=choose
```

The resume prompt gives you two options. You can try to continue with system restart, or you can delete restoration data and proceed to system boot. If you select Continue With System Restart, Windows

Resume Loader attempts to reload the system state again. If you select Delete Restoration Data And Proceed To System Boot, Windows Resume Loader deletes the saved state of the computer and restarts the computer. Although a full restart will typically resolve any problem, you'll lose any work that wasn't saved before the computer entered sleep or hibernate mode.

Forcing Your Computer to Shut Down

When there are unsaved files, locked processes, or both, your computer will not logoff and shut down immediately. Instead, you'll see a related prompt listing the files and processes that are causing the problem. With unsaved files, you'll usually want to save the open files and then exit the related program so that you can resume logging off and shutting down. With locked processes, you can wait for Windows to resolve the problem, either by getting a response from the program that allows Windows to close the program or by waiting until the timeout period has elapsed and letting Windows stop the program, which allows you to continue through the log off and shut down processes automatically.

That's the way Windows should work, but sometimes things go wrong. You can perform a hard shutdown by pressing and holding the device's power button or by unplugging the device. If your device has a removable battery, such as when you are working with a laptop, you can remove the battery to force the device to completely power down.

If you force the computer to shut down, the computer may enter Automatic Recovery mode when next started. See "Working with Automatic Recovery Mode" for pointers on how to exit this mode and continue with normal startup. After you start your computer, you may want to run Check Disk, as discussed in Chapter 9, to check for errors and problems that might have been caused by the hard shutdown.

Repairing a Computer to Enable Startup

Windows 10 includes the Startup Repair tool to automatically detect corrupted system files during startup and guide you through automated or manual recovery. The Startup Repair tool attempts to determine the cause of the startup failure by using startup logs and error reports, and then attempts to fix the problem automatically. If the Startup Repair tool is unable to resolve the problem, it restores your computer to the last known working state and provides diagnostics information and support options for further troubleshooting.

Every Windows 10 computer has a Window Recovery Environment (Windows RE) partition by default. This partition is created automatically when the operating system is installed. As a result, if your computer fails to shut down properly, the Automatic Recovery screen is shown the next time you start the computer. You can use the Automatic Recovery process to run the Startup Repair tool by following these steps:

1. After your device loads the recovery environment, click Advanced Options.

2. At the Choose An Option prompt, click Troubleshoot. Next, at the Troubleshoot prompt, click Advanced Options.

3. At the Advanced Options, click the Startup Repair option.

The Startup Repair tool checks for problems preventing your computer from starting. If problems are found, the tool tries to repair them to enable startup. The automated troubleshooting and repair process can take several minutes. During the first phase of the repair, you can click Cancel to exit.

If Startup Repair is successful, your computer will start. If Startup Repair is unable to find and correct problems, you'll see a note about this and will be able to send more information about the problem to Microsoft to help find solutions in the future. After selecting the option to send or not send information, you return to the Startup Repair dialog box.

To access advanced repair options, click the related link and follow the prompts to continue troubleshooting. Otherwise, click Finish. You may want to disconnect any external devices that you've recently connected to your computer and then try to start your computer again. Otherwise, ask your network administrator or your computer manufacturer for help.

Corrupted system files aren't the only types of problems that can prevent proper startup of the operating system. Many other types of problems can occur, but most of these problems occur because something on the system has changed. Often you can resolve startup issues using Safe Mode to recover or troubleshoot system problems. When you are finished using Safe Mode, be sure to restart the computer using a normal startup. You will then be able to use the computer as you normally would. See "Performing an Advanced or Safe Mode Boot," earlier in this chapter, for more information.

Chapter 5. Organizing, Searching, and Indexing

One of your computer's most important functions is to make it possible for you to create and store everything—from documents and pictures to songs, videos, and program data files. Windows 10 gives you many options for helping you organize, search for, and index these files. To get the most out of the available features, you need to master File Explorer and Windows Search.

Exploring Your Computer in New Ways

There are few components of the Windows operating system that you'll spend more time using than File Explorer. Every time you browse files and folders on your computer, you use File Explorer—whether you specifically open an Explorer window or you use the Open command in an application, such as Microsoft Word. Control Panel, the Computer window, the Network window, and even the Recycle Bin are different views for File Explorer.

As Figure 5-1 shows, File Explorer has an Address bar for quickly navigating disks and folders, a Search box for fast searches, and the following view panes:

- **Navigation**   Helps you quickly access favorites, homegroups, your computer, and your network. Drag any folder to Favorites to quickly create a shortcut to it; right-click and select Remove to delete a favorite.
- **Contents**   Provides the main working pane and shows the contents of your selected drive or folder. Use the View button

and View options to control whether item details, lists, or icons are shown.

- **Details** Shows information about a selected item. The details provided depend on the item selected and are different for drives, folders, documents, songs, videos, and shortcuts. Hide or show the Details pane by clicking Organize, clicking Layout, and then clicking Preview Pane.

- **Preview** Shows a preview of your selected document, picture, song, video, or other file type, as long as a preview control is available and configured for that file type. Use the Show/Hide Preview button to display or hide the Preview pane.

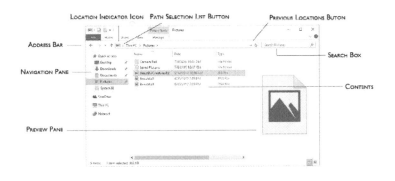

Figure 5-1 Exploring the drives, folders, and files on your computer.

So Long Libraries, Hello Quick Access

Microsoft continues to de-emphasize the idea of "library" folders. Libraries are predefined and provide a combined view of folders related to specific types of media, such as Documents, Music and Pictures. Generally, in Windows 10, the only time you work with libraries is when you click the Path Selection List button in File

Explorer and select Libraries. Then, as shown in Figure 5-2, File Explorer specifically states that each item listed is a library.

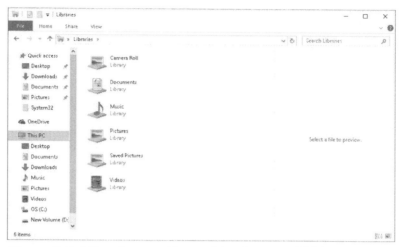

Figure 5-2 Libraries provide combined views of folders containing similar types of data.

When you are working with a library, such as the Documents library, you can right-click it and select Properties to get additional information about where that library's data comes from (see Figure 5-3). You can then use the options provided to add or remove folders from the library, and set default save locations.

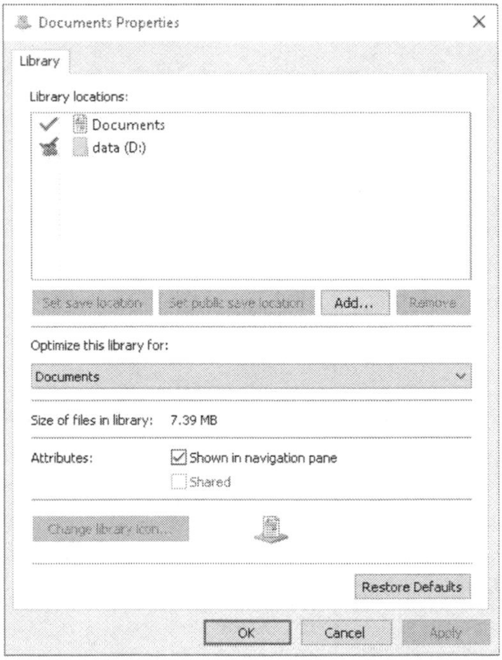

Figure 5-3 Use the Properties dialog box to manage the library.

Because library data can come from multiple folders, some users have
always found libraries a bit confusing. This is why Microsoft is de-
emphasizing the feature in favor of the This PC and Quick Access,
both of which are available in File Explorer.

When you select This PC as a location or This PC on the navigation
pane (see Figure 5-4), you have fast access to your personal folders,
including Documents, Music, Pictures and Videos.

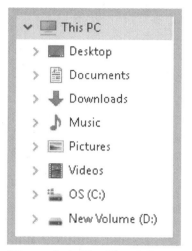

Figure 5-4 Use This PC to access drives and personal folders.

When Quick Access is expanded on the navigation pane (see Figure 5-5), you have fast access to any folder or file pinned to this panel. By default, Desktop, Downloads, Documents and Pictures are pinned to Quick Access.

Figure 5-5 Use Quick Access to access frequently used folders and files.

While working with File Explorer or any of its views, you can add a folder or file to Quick Access by right-clicking it and selecting Pin To Quick Access. To remove a pinned folder or file, right-click it on the Quick Access panel and then select Unpin From Quick Access.

When you are working with Quick Access, you may find that some folders and files don't have pins. Folders are added by Windows when you use them frequently and files are added when you've recently opened them. Because these items aren't actually pinned, they will be removed automatically when you use them less frequently.

To ensure a folder or file stays available, you can right-click it on the Quick Access panel and then select Pin To Quick Access. To remove an automatically added folder or file, right-click it on the Quick Access panel and then select Remove From Quick Access.

For privacy reasons, you may want to control whether folders and files are added to Quick Access. To do this, follow these steps:

1. In File Explorer, right-click the top of the Quick Access panel and select Options.

2. In the Folder Options dialog box, shown in Figure 5-6, you'll find options for controlling whether folders and files are added to Quick Access. Use the following techniques to manage Quick Access and then click OK:

- Clear the Show Frequently Used Folders checkbox if you no longer want frequently used folders to be added.
- Clear the Show Recently Used Files checkbox if you no longer want recently used files to be added.
- Click the Clear button to clear the history regarding frequently used folders and files.

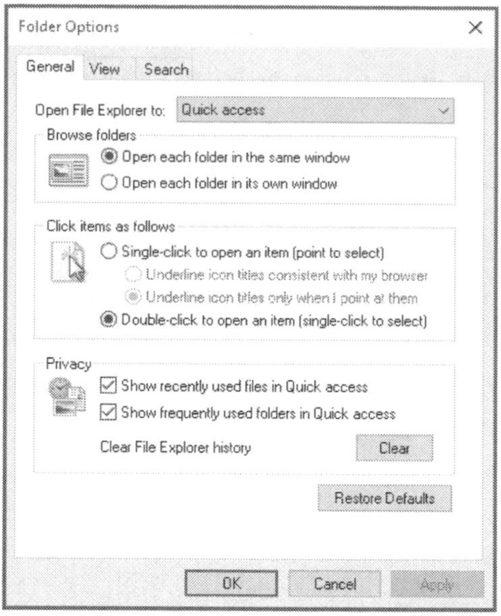

Figure 5-6 Manage Quick Access using Folder Options.

> **Tip**   By default, File Explorer opens with Quick Access selected in the main pane. If you'd rather have File Explorer open with This PC selected, select This PC on the Open File Explorer To list.

Address Bar Tips and Techniques

Every view of File Explorer, whether Control Panel, the Computer window, the Network window, or the basic Explorer view, has an Address bar that displays your current location as a series of links separated by clickable options buttons.

The address path includes a Location Indicator icon, a Path Selection list button, Location Path entries, and a Previous Locations button.

Location Path entries allow you to determine the current location. In the example shown in Figure 5-1, the location is:

This PC → Pictures

This PC provides access to your personal documents. Although the related folders are stored in your personal profile, you access them through the related libraries: Documents, Downloads, Music, Pictures, Videos, etc.

Consider the path shown in Figure 5-7:

This PC → New Volume (D:) → Family Photos

Figure 5-7 Viewing the Family Photos folder.

This tells you that the absolute path followed to get to the current location is D:\Family Photos on your computer.

When you are working with network paths in the Network window, you have quick access to network locations and shared resources. Click the Network entry in the path to display a list of remote computers and network resources, as shown in Figure 5-8. Double-click the name of a remote computer or network resource to list its shared resources, as shown in Figure 5-9.

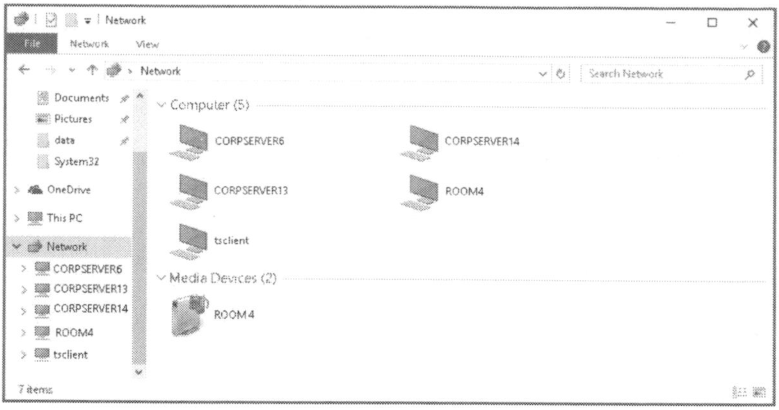

Figure 5-8 Using Network to access other computers.

Figure 5-9 Accessing shared resources on other computers.

You won't always see a full path, however. Many times, you'll see a relative or abbreviated path, such as when you follow a shortcut or browse to a path that cannot be fully listed. A relative or abbreviated path is indicated by the left-pointing chevron (<<), as shown in this example:

« History → Availability → New Materials

This tells you that the relative or abbreviated path of the current location is History\Availability\New Materials.

For ease of reference, I refer to Explorer's relative and absolute paths as navigation paths. When a navigation path is being displayed, you can always display the actual system path by clicking the Location Indictor icon or an empty area of the address path. For example, if I click the relative path listed previously, my computer shows the system path as E:\History\Availability\New Materials.

By default, the system path is selected, so you can copy it simply by pressing Ctrl+C. To display the navigation path again (instead of the system path), press Esc.

To the right of the Location Indicator icon is the Path Selection list button, which provides access to the available base locations. Selecting a base location allows you to quickly access key File Explorer views and perform related tasks.

The final control on the Address bar is the Previous Locations button, which provides a list of locations you've accessed recently. This location list can include folder locations, network drive locations, and web addresses. You can jump to a recently accessed location quickly by clicking the Previous Locations button and then clicking the desired location.

Keyboard Tips and Techniques for File Explorer

Putting File Explorer to work for you requires much more than simply learning to navigate the Address bar like a pro. Next, you need to learn about keyboard shortcuts that can make your everyday computing tasks easier. I'll go through the shortcuts you're likely to find the most helpful. The secret to your success is in being even more selective. Identify the techniques that will help you the most and commit those techniques to memory.

> **Note**   Generally, the keyboard shortcuts in this section work only when the main pane is the selected focus for File Explorer. This means you must be working in the main pane for the shortcut to work.

Most people who've worked with Windows for a while know that you right-click an item and select Properties to display the item's properties. There are two other ways to do the same thing:

* Hold the Alt key and then double-click the item.
* Select the item and then press Alt+Enter.

In Chapter 2, I discussed customizing the Start menu and pinning programs. Although you normally want only programs on the Start menu, you can folders and folder shortcuts to the Start menu as well. You do this by right-clicking the folder or folder shortcut, and then clicking Pin To Start menu. A hidden option displayed when you hold Shift before right-clicking a file is Copy As Path, which is used to copy the full path of the file to the clipboard.

With folders, holding Shift before right-clicking reveals three hidden options:

* **Copy As Path**   Copies the full path of the folder to the clipboard.
* **Open Command Windows Here**   Opens a command prompt with the initial path set to the folder location.

- **Open In New Process**   Opens the folder in a separate process. Otherwise, by default, all Explorer windows run in the same process.

File Explorer has several other shortcuts for working smarter with folders as well. When a folder is selected in the window:

- Press Alt and the Up Arrow key to jump to the parent folder of that folder.
- Press Enter to view the folder's contents. Then you can use press Alt and the Left Arrow key to go back.
- Press Ctrl+Shift+E to expand the folder tree so that the selected folder is shown in the Navigation pane.

File Explorer has Forward and Back buttons as well as a Recent Pages drop-down list. These buttons are easy enough to use, but you also can press Backspace to go back through the Recent Pages list. Within a folder, you can press a letter key or string of characters to quickly jump to the first file or folder starting with that letter or character string. For example, if you press C, File Explorer jumps to the first file or folder that starts with C. If you type **Chr**, File Explorer jumps to the first file or folder that starts with Chr.

> **Note**   Folder And Search Options can modify the way quick select works. Instead of jumping to the file or folder that starts with the letters you type, you also can configure File Explorer to enter the text in the Search box and begin a search of the current folder.

The Preview pane is handy, but it can take up a lot of workspace. You can quickly display or hide the Preview pane by pressing Alt+P. My preference is to not use the Preview pane at all. Instead of turning previews on and off, I hold Ctrl and use the mouse scroll button to cycle through the view settings. That way, I can quickly go from a detailed listing to a small, medium, or large icon listing.

If you're like me, you may prefer the Details pane instead of the Preview pane. The Details pane provides summary information, similar to what you see when you right-click a file or folder and select Properties. You can quickly display or hide the Preview pane by pressing Alt+Shift+P.

File Explorer provides a variety of ways to work with files and folders. You can press Ctrl+Shift+N to create a new folder. You can press F2 to rename a currently selected file or folder. While clicking a file or folder and pressing Del moves a file to the Recycle Bin, you can press Shift+Del to permanently remove a selected file or folder (bypassing the Recycle Bin).

Hold Ctrl and click to select multiple files and folders or deselect files and folders previously selected one by one. If you want to select a range of files or folders instead, click the first item to select it, hold Shift, and then click the final item. Now all items in the range, from the first item to final item, will be selected.

Other ways to select multiple files include:

* Using selection rectangles to select a group of files. Simply click an empty area near the first file and drag to draw a selection box around all the files you want to select.
* Using Ctrl and the spacebar to select individual items. While holding Ctrl, use the Up and Down Arrow keys to move

through a list of items and press the spacebar to select or deselect an item.

- Using Shift and the spacebar to select a range of items. Here, find the first item using the Up and Down Arrow keys. Next, hold Shift and use the arrow keys to expand your selection.

Customizing File Explorer

File Explorer settings control many aspects of the Windows operating system. Everything from whether hidden files are displayed to whether a single click opens an item and many dozens of other core options are configured by modifying settings in File Explorer.

Fine-Tuning Views & Details

File Explorer in Windows 10 is much smarter than File Explorer in early releases of Windows:

- When you select a picture, File Explorer adds Picture Tools to the toolbar.

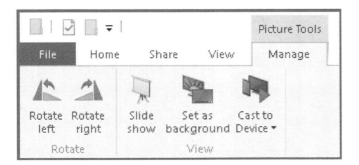

- When you select music, File Explorer adds Music Tools to the toolbar.

- When you select a program, File Explorer adds Application Tools to the toolbar.

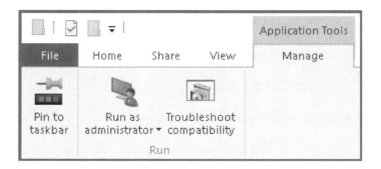

- When you select a video, File Explorer adds Video Tools to the toolbar.

Which tools are displayed depends on the type of file selected. File Explorer has many views that you can use to optimize the way files of various types are listed. Views include:

* Extra large, large, medium and small icons
* Tiles, list, content or details

When you are managing files, the most useful view is Details. The Details view lists columns of information about each file in a selected folder, such as Name, Type, Size and Date Created.

If you right-click in the column heading area, you'll see an option menu that allows you to easily add related columns of information.

If you right-click in the column heading area and then select More as an option, you'll be able to choose from a wide variety of details to add to the view of the selected folder.

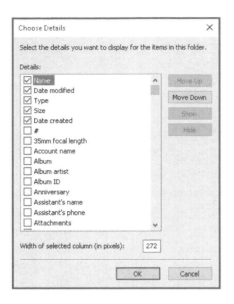

The details provided initially depend on the view template selected. If you frequently work with specific folders containing media, you may want to customize the template used so that additional details are displayed based on the folder and media type you are working with.

File Explorer has view templates for each basic media type as well as a template for General Items. The template assigned to a folder determines which details are shown when you are working with files.

The default view for most folders is General Items, which uses a template for folders containing mixed media. The Documents template is a basic template that doesn't have any media extensions. In contrast, the Music, Pictures, and Videos templates have media extensions that allow you to display tailored columns of information in details view. With the Pictures template, for example, you can display information about the dimensions, bit depth and more. With music, you can display information about the track number, title, contributing artists, album name, bit rate, length and more. Similar information is, of course, available on the Details pane in the related Properties dialog box. However, you can't see this information for multiple files in one place.

If you have write permissions on a folder, you can customize the folder's default view. You also can apply a favorite view to all folders of that type on the system. The folder view settings that you use are seen by all users who access the system, either locally or remotely.

You can configure custom views for folders by following these steps:

1. In File Explorer, right-click the folder you want to customize, and then select Properties.

2. Click the Customize tab, shown in Figure 5-11.

Figure 5-11 Optimizing default views for folders using templates

3. In the Optimize This Folder For list, choose the template you want to use, such as Pictures. To apply the view to subfolders of this folder, choose Also Apply This Template To All Subfolders.

4. Customize the folder preview, and then click OK to save your settings.

Instead of setting folder views one by one, you can apply a view, such as Details or Large Icons, to all the folders of a particular type or restore the default view to these folders. To apply a custom view to all the folders of a particular type, complete the following steps:

1. In File Explorer, right-click the folder you want to work with and then select Properties. In the Properties dialog box, ensure the folder type is set appropriately on the Customize tab and then click OK.

2. In File Explorer, use the options in the View list or on View menu to configure the folder view that you want to use, such as Large Icons or Details.

3. On the View toolbar in File Explorer, click Options, and then click Change Folder And Search Options.

4. In the Folder Options dialog box, select the View tab.

5. Do one of the following, and then click OK:

   ▪ To apply the current folder view to all folders of this type, click Apply To Folders.

   ▪ To restore all folders of this type to their default view, click Reset Folders.

You also may want all folders regardless of type to use the same default view. You can do this by following these steps:

1. In File Explorer, right-click the folder you want to work with, and then select Properties.

2. Select the Customize tab. Under Optimize This Folder For, choose General Items. Click OK.

3. In File Explorer, select the folder. Use the options in the View list or on the View menu to configure the folder view that you want to use, such as Large Icons.

4. On the View toolbar in File Explorer, click Options, and then click Change Folder And Search Options.

5. On the View tab, click Apply To Folders to apply the current folder view to all folders of this type. When prompted to confirm, click Yes.

6. Repeat this procedure four times, once each for the Documents, Pictures, Music, and Videos templates. In step 2, choose Documents, Pictures, Music, or Videos as appropriate.

Customizing Folder Options

You control the way File Explorer works by using settings in the Folder Options dialog box. Access this dialog box in File Explorer by clicking Options on the View toolbar, and then clicking Change Folder And Search Options. General tab and View tab options are shown in Figure 5-12.

Use the list that follows to help you understand how each option works, and then choose the configuration option that is best for the way you want File Explorer to work.

Open Each Folder In The Same Window   When selected, opens subfolders that you access in the same window. Otherwise, opens subfolders that you access in a new window.

Single-Click To Open An Item   When selected, selects an item when you point to it and opens the item when you click once. Otherwise, selects an item when you click it; opens the item when you double-click it.

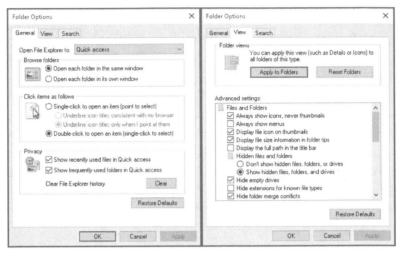

Figure 5-12 Optimizing File Explorer settings for the way you work

Always Show Icons, Never Thumbnails   When selected, does not create thumbnails. Instead, File Explorer shows the standard file and folder icons. Otherwise, shows large thumbnail images of the actual content for pictures and other types of files. When folders have many pictures, showing thumbnails can slow down the display because File Explorer has to create the thumbnail representation of each image.

Always Show Menus   When selected, always shows the menu bar, providing quick access to the menus. (You can also toggle this option by clicking Organize, pointing to Layout, and then selecting Menu Bar.) Otherwise, hides the menu bar; you must elect to display it by pressing the Alt key.

Display File Icon On Thumbnails   When selected, adds file icons to thumbnails it displays. Otherwise, displays thumbnails without file icons.

Display File Size Information In Folder Tips   When selected, displays a tooltip showing the creation date and time, the size of the folder, and a partial list of files when you move the mouse pointer over a folder name or folder icon. Otherwise, displays a tooltip showing the creation date and time when you move the mouse pointer over a folder name or folder icon.

Display The Full Path In The Title Bar   When selected and you press Alt+Tab to access the flip view, displays the actual file path instead of the folder name when you move the mouse pointer over a File Explorer window. Otherwise, when you press Alt+Tab to access the flip view, displays the folder name when you move the mouse pointer over a File Explorer window.

Hidden Files And Folders   When you select the related Show option, displays hidden files, folders, or drives. Otherwise, does not display hidden files, folders, or drives.

Hide Empty Drives   When selected, displays information about empty drives in the This PC window. Otherwise, does not display information about empty drives in the Computer window.

Hide Extensions For Known File Types   When selected, does not display file extensions for known file types. Otherwise, displays file extensions for known file types.

Hide Folder Merge Conflicts   When selected, merge conflicts aren't displayed for folders. Otherwise, displays merge conflicts.

Hide Protected Operating System Files   When selected, does not display operating system files. Otherwise, displays operating system files. Hidden operating system files are also referred to as super hidden files.

Launch Folder Windows In A Separate Process   When selected, runs in a separate process each time it is opened. Otherwise, Windows runs all instances of File Explorer in the same process.

Pro Tip   Although opening folder windows in a separate process requires more memory and generally slows down the process of opening new windows, it also means that each instance is independent of the others. Thus, if one instance crashes or hangs, it generally will not affect other instances of File Explorer. Also, if you often perform large file transfers using File Explorer, these transfers won't effect other File Explorer windows. Keep in mind that although using the same process saves memory and generally speeds up the process of opening new windows, it also means that all instances of File Explorer are dependent on each other. As a result, if one instance crashes, they all crash, and if one instance is in a pending or wait state, all instances could become locked.

Restore Previous Folder Windows At Logon   When selected, reopens folder windows you were using last time you logged on. Otherwise, folder windows aren't reopened.

Show Drive Letters   When selected, displays drive letters as part of the information on the Locations bar. Otherwise, does not display drive letters as part of the information on the Locations bar.

Show Encrypted Or Compressed NTFS Files In Color   When selected, lists encrypted files and compressed files using different colors. Normally, encrypted files are displayed with green text and compressed files are displayed with blue text. Otherwise, does not distinguish among encrypted, compressed, and normal files.

Show Pop-Up Description For Folder And Desktop Items
When selected, shows tooltips with additional information about a file or folder when you move the mouse over the file or folder. Otherwise, does not show tooltips with additional information about a file or folder when you move the mouse over the file or folder.

Show Preview Handlers In Preview Pane   When selected and the Preview pane is visible, displays previews of selected files and folders. Otherwise, when the Preview pane is visible, previews of selected files and folders aren't displayed.

Use Check Boxes To Select Items   When selected, displays check boxes that you can use to select files. Otherwise, allows you to select files, folders, and other items using only the standard selection techniques such as click, Shift+Click, and Ctrl+Click.

Use Sharing Wizard   When selected, uses the File Sharing wizard for configuring file sharing. Otherwise, uses the advanced file sharing options.

When Typing Into A List View   When you select Automatically Type... and are working with the list view, text you type is entered into the Search box. Otherwise, when you are working with the list view and press a letter key, the first file or folder with that letter is selected.

Searching and Indexing Your Computer

Your computer's drives probably have hundreds or even many thousands of documents, pictures, music, videos, and more, stored until you one day want to access them. The more digital stuff you have, the harder it is to find what you're looking for right now. This is where the Windows 10 search and indexing features come in.

> **Real World**   Your docs, pics, music and all your other files are a key reason to own a tablet, desktop or laptop PC. But just because you store your data doesn't mean that stored data will stay around forever. Ever heard of bit rot? Bit rot happens over a period of months and years when data on your drives remains stagnant. If you want to protect your data over time, you need to either move the data around or move the data to new drives, with the latter being preferable.

Windows Search Essentials

Whether you perform a search using the Search box on the toolbar or the Search box in File Explorer, the Windows Search service performs the search. The way Windows Search service looks for what you are trying to find depends on where you are searching and how your device is configured.

When you search using the Search box on the taskbar, the search service works as discussed in "Cortana & Search" in Chapter 1 and can include search results from Settings, Control Panel, personal files, apps and the web. In contrast, when you search using the Search box in File Explorer or any of its related views, such as Control Panel or This PC, the currently selected location sets the base location for the search. For example, if the base location is This PC > Documents, as shown in Figure 5-13, your search would include results from the Documents folder and the Work, Reports and School subfolders.

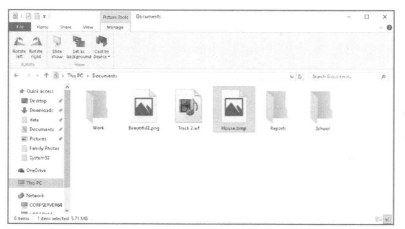

Figure 5-13 Working with File Explorer

Generally, you must click in the Search box prior to typing your search text. This means a basic search requires two steps:

1. In an Explorer window or related view, access the start location for your search.

2. Click in the Search box, and then enter the search text.

> **Note** The When Typing Into A List View option determines whether you have to click in the Search box before

entering search text. By default, you must click in the Search box, but if you enable Automatically Type Into The Search Box, any text you type into a list view is entered automatically in the Search box.

A general search involves Windows Search service matching the search text to words that appear in the title of any file or file folder, the properties of any indexed file or folder, and the contents of indexed documents in the currently selected folder and its subfolders. Results are returned to the Results Pane in File Explorer, and the Address bar is updated to reflect that you are viewing search results. Although the search results themselves are displayed in the previously selected view style, you may want to click View on the toolbar and then select Details. In the Details view, the results are listed by name, date modified, size, tags and folder path. If you click the Previous Locations button on the right side of the address path, you'll see the actual search text passed to the Windows Search service.

After the Windows Search service completes a search in the selected location, it automatically begins another search if you enter additional search text or if you change the search text. You can stop a search in progress at any time by clicking the Close button—the X on the right side of the Search box. You can repeat a search by clicking the Refresh button.

Understanding Localized Searches

By default, only a few specific locations on a computer are indexed, including personal profile folders, the Windows folder and the Start menu. The automatic indexing of selected files and folders is a key feature of Windows 10 that improves the search results and helps speed up the search process.

A localized search involves Windows Search service checking a specific location. When you perform a search in Control Panel, the search is localized to the names of related utilities and tasks. When you perform a search in the Network window, the search is localized to the names and ownership information for computers and devices listed therein.

Similarly, searches of Desktop and Recycle Bin are localized. For the desktop, Windows Search service matches against file names, file type information, and folder details related to items stored therein. For the Recycle Bin, Windows Search service matches against item names and original folder locations.

A Start menu search is much more broad than you might think. Windows Search service looks at the names of programs, the names of utilities, and tasks in Control Panel, and then looks at information related to indexed files in other locations.

Whenever you search in the This PC window, a drive folder, or any subfolder of a drive, you are performing a localized search as well. If the location you are searching is indexed, Windows Search service checks its index to try to find what you are looking for, and the search process is usually fairly quick. If the location you are searching isn't indexed, Windows Search service will try to find what you are looking for without the benefit of an index, and the search process can be fairly slow.

Fine-Tuning Windows Search

You can improve your search results by using the advanced search options and features built into Windows 10. These additional advanced features include search options for fine-tuning the search results and advanced filters that allow you to search in new ways, as well as options for managing which files and folders are indexed and saved searches that allow you to easily repeat custom searches.

Customizing Search Options

Search options control the way the Windows Search service searches your computer. The search service has several default behaviors. In indexed locations, the Windows Search service searches file names and contents. This means that it will look for matches to your search text in file names and folder names, file properties and folder properties, and the textual contents of files. Searches also extend to properties of zipped archives, which are compressed archival files, such as .ZIP, .CAB, .GZ, .TAR and .TGZ files. The contents of zipped archives aren't searched, however.

In nonindexed locations, the Windows Search service searches file and folder names only. This means it will look for matches to your search text only in file names and folder names. It will not look for matches to your search text in file and folder properties, or in the textual contents of files.

Windows Search service doesn't use natural language searches, but it does search subfolders of a selected location and allows partial matches. Disallowing natural language searches means you can't enter natural language questions as part of your search. Partial matching means that the service matches your search text to part of a word or phrase rather than to whole words only.

Figure 5-14 Searching your devices for files and folders

You can customize the search options by using the options on the Search Tools panel, shown in Figure 5-14. The Search Tools panel is displayed whenever you are performing a search, so if you haven't previously performed a search, the panel is hidden until you enter search text. Search options include:

* **Current Folder**   Limits the search to the current folder.
* **All Subfolders**   Expands the search to subfolders of the current folder (the default).
* **Date Modified**   Filters the search results according to one of the following preset dates: Today, Yesterday, This Week, Last Week, This Month, Last Month, This Year or Last Year. For example, if you are searching for a file you created the previous week, you'd select Last Week as your Date Modified filter.
* **Kind**   Filters the search results according to the general kind of file, such as all picture or all video files.

- **Size**   Filters the search results according to the approximate size of a file. Size filters have specific parameters, including Empty for files having zero bytes and Medium for 100 KB to 1 MB.

As you select search options, the related search parameters are added to the search text. For example, if you select the date modified as Yesterday and then specify the kind of file as Picture, the search is updated to include these parameters and the matching results are then displayed.

Although the default behaviors work well for most people, they are limiting, you can optimize the way search works by completing the following steps:

1. In File Explorer, click File on the menu bar, then click Options. Select the Search tab in the Folder Options dialog box.

2. Under How To Search, use the following option to configure how searches work:

- **Don't Use The Index When Searching In File Folders For System Files**   When selected, the Windows Search service ignores indexes when searching in file folders for system files. This forces the Windows Search service to examine the current state of system files, but it can be extremely slow. When not selected, the Windows Search service uses indexes to speed up the search process if indexes are available.

3. Under When Searching Non-indexed Locations, specify whether the Windows Search service includes system locations, compressed files, or both when searching nonindexed locations. If you often zip files and folders, you are

likely to improve your search results by including compressed files in searches.

4. Under When Searching Non-indexed Locations, specify whether the Windows Search service should always search file names and contents.

5. Click OK to save your search options.

> **Real World**   If you always want the service to search contents, you force the Windows Search service to ignore whether a folder is indexed when searching. This does not mean that indexes won't be used, however. When indexes are available, the Windows Search service will use them. When indexes aren't available, the Windows Search service will not be able to use indexes to speed up the search process, and this can result in slow searches.

Performing Advanced Searches with Filters

Sometimes you won't be able to use the standard search options to find what you are looking for. The date modified won't always fit neatly a present category; the file won't always be easily identifiable as a specific kind or relative size. In these cases, you can narrow your results by entering the search filters manually in the Search box.

Each search filter begins with a parameter name that begins with a keyword or keyword phrase followed by a colon. The parameter name is followed by a parameter value, such as a specific range of dates.

Search parameters you may want to use include:

- **Datecreated:**   Filters the search results according to the date on which files and folders were created. You can specify a range of dates. For example, you could enter Datecreated:09/02/2015..12/31/2015 to specify the date as being between 09/02/2015 and 12/31/2015. A set of predefined flags also can be used to set a general time period, such as Datecreated:Yesterday or Datecreated:Earlier This Week.

- **Datemodified:**   Filters the search results according to the date on which files and folders were last modified. You can specify a range of dates. For example, you could enter Datemodified:09/02/2015..12/31/2015 to specify the date as being between 09/02/2015 and 12/31/2015. A set of predefined flags also can be used to set a general time period, such as Datemodified:Yesterday or Datemodified:Earlier This Week.

- **Kind:**   Filters the search results according to the general kind of file, such as all picture or video files. A set of predefined flags can be used to set the general kind, but unlike other flags these must be separated from the filter identifier with an equal sign, such as Kind:=Calendar or Kind:=Video.

- **Type:**   Filters the search results according to the file type label or file extension. For example, you could use **type:"MP3 Format Sound"** or **type:mp3** to search for .mp3 audio files.

- **Owner:**   Filters the search results according to the owner of the file. For example, you could use **owner:tedg** or **owner:lisa** to search for files with these users set as the owner.

- **Size:**   Filters the search results according to the approximate size of a file. Size flags have specific parameters, including Empty for files having zero bytes and Medium for 100 KB to 1 MB. For example, you could specify that you are searching for a file between 100 KB and 1 MB by using the filter Size:Medium.

The available search filters are based on the names of indexable properties associated with files and folders. The basic syntax for a search filter is PropertyName: where PropertyName is the property name entered without spaces followed by a colon. For example, with music, you could search for a title of a song using Title: or the title of an album using Album:.

Because document files, picture files, video files, music files, and other types of files all have slightly different lists of indexable properties, they also have slightly different lists of search filters. A quick way to discover these is to follow these steps:

1. Open File Explorer. In the Navigation pane, your user name and then click Music.

2. In the main pane, you'll see songs listed by name, contributing artists, albums, track number, title, and type by default. Display a list of related headings by right-clicking an open area of the column headings.

3. Any of the headings shown can be used in your searches for music files. The related search filter is the heading name without spaces followed by a colon. You can learn about flags and options available with a filter by simply entering the filter in the Search box. For example, to search on bit rate, you could use the Bitrate: filter. If you enter bitrate: in the Search box, you'll see flags for voice and AM broadcasts, FM broadcasts, high-quality audio, and near-CD-quality audio.

4. To discover properties specific to documents, pictures, and videos, repeat this process, selecting Documents, Pictures, and Videos as appropriate instead of Music.

> **Note**   Although you can use any filter in any type of folder, the default folder view controls the column headings displayed by default as well as the headings that are listed when you right-click the column heading. As discussed earlier in the section "Fine-Tuning Folder Views & Details," File Explorer identifies folders as having mostly documents, mostly music, mostly pictures, or mostly videos, and then uses a template to set their default view.

You can use search filters with or without keywords. If you want to perform a filtered search with a keyword, click in the search window, type the keyword or phrase, and then enter the filter. If you want to begin a search without a keyword, click in the search window and then enter the filter. Just as you can use multiple keywords, you can use multiple filters in a single search. For example, you could search using the date modified, size, and kind filters. Searches that combine multiple filters and are difficult to re-create are the ones you'll likely want to save for later reuse.

Windows Search service allows you to perform logical AND searches as well as logical OR and logical NOT searches. AND (entered in all caps) acts as an operator to match exactly two or more keywords separated by AND operators. OR (entered in all caps) acts as an operator to match any of the keywords separated by OR operators. NOT (entered in all caps) acts as a selective operator to match one keyword but not another.

You use AND to perform complex searches that match multiple parameters. If file content searching is enabled, you could search for files containing the keyword Chicago and the keyword Miami using:

```
chicago AND miami
```

Here, only files containing both keywords are returned. Because the logical AND operation is implied whenever you enter multiple keywords in the Search box, you also could have simply entered:

```
chicago miami
```

You could limit the search to matching file names by using the Name: filter, such as:

name:better AND name:food

Here, only files whose name includes both better and food are returned. Logical OR operations can be handy as well. For example, you could search for either better or food or both better and food using:

```
Name:better OR Name:food
```

Here, files whose name includes either better or food are returned. To look for files who name includes better but not food, you could use the search parameters:

```
Name:better NOT Name:food
```

Searching by Kind or Type of File

When you are working with libraries and certain other folders, the Kind: and Type: filters are implied when you click in the Search box. These filters are also available when you are working with other folders, but you must enter the filter to use them. In either case, any file with a kind or type that matches your parameters is returned in the search results.

The kinds of files you can search for include:

- **Calendar**   Filters the search results so that only calendar items are included.
- **Communication**   Filters the search results so that only calendar, email, contact, and instant message items are included.
- **Contact**   Filters the search results so that only contact items are included.
- **Document**   Filters the search results so that only document files are included.
- **E-mail**   Filters the search results so that only email messages are included.
- **Feed**   Filters the search results so that only messages from RSS feeds are included.
- **Folder**   Filters the search results so that only folders are included.
- **Game**   Filters the search results so that only game data and other game files are included.
- **Instant Message**   Filters the search results so that only instant messages are included.
- **Journal**   Filters the search results so that only journal entries are included.
- **Link**   Filters the search results so that only links are included.
- **Movie**   Filters the search results so that only movie files are included.
- **Music**   Filters the search results so that only music files are included.

- **Note**   Filters the search results so that only note files are included.
- **Picture**   Filters the search results so that only pictures are included.
- **Playlist**   Filters the search results so that only to playlists for your music files.
- **Program**   Filters the search results so that program files are included.
- **Recorded TV**   Filters the search results so that recorded television programs are included.
- **Saved Search**   Filters the search results so that saved searches are included.
- **Task**   Filters the search results so that tasks are included.
- **Video**   Filters the search results so that video files are included.
- **Web History**   Filters the search results so that items from your web history are included.
- **Unknown**   Searches for any kind of file. You don't need to use this filter as it is implied when you don't provide a specific kind filter.

When performing kind or type searches, remember to enter your search keyword or keywords first and then either select the related option on the Search panel and choose a value, or enter Kind: or Type: followed by the appropriate parameter value. For example, if you know the file you are looking for is a video and the file name includes the keyword "vacation," you could search for it by following these steps:

1. In File Explorer, access the top-level folder from which you want to start searching.

2. Click in the Search box. Type **vacation kind:video**, and then press Enter.

The Type: filter allows you to search for a specific type of file by its file type label or file extension. For example, if you know the file you are looking for is a .wmv file and the file name includes the keyword "home," you could search for it by following these steps:

1. In File Explorer, access the top-level folder from which you want to start searching.
2. Click in the Search box. Type **home type:wmv**, and then press Enter.

Searching Using Date-Related Filters

Windows Search service tracks a variety of date-related properties, including:

- **Date Accessed**   Tracks the date a file was last accessed.
- **Date Archived**   Tracks the date a file was last archived.
- **Date Last Saved**   Tracks the date a file was last saved.
- **Date Created**   Tracks the date a file was created.
- **Date Modified**   Tracks the date a file was last modified.
- **Date Sent**   Tracks the date a message was sent.
- **Date Taken**   Tracks the date a picture was taken.

Generally, they all work in the same way. When you are working with a date filter, you can select a specific date, a general date, or a range of dates to search. Any file with a date that matches your parameters is returned in the search results.

You select specific dates by using the calendar provided, as shown in Figure 5-15. The calendar displays the current day and date by default.

Select a date or date range:

◄   July 2015   ►

Su	Mo	Tu	We	Th	Fr	Sa
			1	2	3	4
5	6	7	8	9	10	11
12	13	14	15	16	17	18
19	20	21	22	23	24	25
26	27	28	29	30	31	

Today
Yesterday
This week
Last week
This month
Last month
This year
Last year

Figure 5-15 Searching using date-related filters

The calendar has the several views:

- **Month** The month view is the default. While working with the month view, you can view other months in the calendar by using the right and left arrow buttons. Click and drag in the calendar to select a series of dates, such as the 5th through the 25th days of the month.
- **Year** The year view lists the months in a year. You can access the year view from the month view by clicking the month and year entry at the top of the calendar. While working with the year view, you can view other years in the calendar by using the right and left arrow buttons. Click and drag in the calendar to select a series of months, such as February through April.
- **Decade** The decade view lists the years in a 10-year period. You can access the decade view from the month view by clicking

twice at the top of the calendar. While working with the decade view, you can view other decades in the calendar by using the right and left arrow buttons. Click and drag in the calendar to select a series of years, such as 2010 to 2012.

- **Century** The century view lists the 10-year periods in a particular century. You can access the century view from the month view by clicking three times at the top of the calendar. While working with the century view, you can view other centuries in the calendar by using the right and left arrow buttons. Click and drag in the calendar to select a series of decades, such as 2000–2009 or 2010–2019.

The date-related filters accept abbreviated entries as well. Using an abbreviated entry, you can directly enter the date to search. The basic syntax varies by locality. For U.S. English, the syntax is:

```
Mm/Dd/Yyyy
```

or:

```
Mm/Dd/Yyyy .. Mm/Dd/Yyyy
```

where Mm is a one- or two-digit value for the month, Dd is a one- or two-digit value for the day of the month, and Yyyy is a four-digit value for the year. Knowing this, you could search for pictures taken between 1/1/2016 and 12/31/2016 by following these steps:

1. In File Explorer, access the top-level folder from which you want to start searching.

2. Click in the Search box. Optionally, type a keyword or phrase to search on.

3. Type **Datetaken: 1/1/2016 .. 12/31/2016**, and then press Enter to begin your search.

With date-related filters, you also can use the following predefined flags:

* **Yesterday**   Searches for files and folders created yesterday.
* **Earlier this week**   Searches for files and folders created earlier in the current week.
* **Last week**   Searches for files and folders created in the previous week.
* **Earlier this month**   Searches for files and folders created earlier in the current month.
* **Earlier this year**   Searches for files and folders created earlier in the current year.
* **A long time ago**   Searches for files and folders created prior to the current year.

You can search using the predefined flags by following these steps:

1. In File Explorer, access the top-level folder from which you want to start searching.
2. Click in the Search box. Optionally, type a keyword or phrase to search on.
3. Type the date-related filter you want to use, such as **Datetaken:**.
4. Type the preset label or click the preset button in the Search pane, and then press Enter to begin your search.

Windows Search service also allows you to use operators. Use the equal (=) operator to get an exact date match. For example, if you know a file was created on 12/15/2015, you can use the filter:

```
DateCreated:=12/15/2015
```

You also can use the less than, greater than, less than or equal to, greater than or equal to, or not equal to operators: <, >, <=, >=, <>. For example, you could look for files modified after 01/01/2014 by entering:

```
DateModified:>01/01/2014
```

As an alternative to the Mm/Dd/Yyyy .. Mm/Dd/Yyyy syntax, you could combine > and < searches using the AND operator. For example, you could look for files modified after 01/01/2014 but before 05/31/2014 by entering:

```
DateModified:>01/01/2014 AND
DateModified:<05/31/2014
```

Because the AND is always implied, you also could enter:

```
DateModified:>01/01/2014
DateModified:<05/31/2014
```

Or you could enter:

```
DateModified:(>01/01/2014 <05/31/2014)
```

This final syntax is closer to the one Windows Search service actually uses internally.

Searching Using Size-Related Filters

Windows Search service tracks a variety of size-related properties, including:

- **Dimensions:** Tracks the width and height of pictures.
- **Framewidth:** Tracks the width of frames in a video.
- **Frameheight:** Tracks the height of frames in a video.
- **Length:** Tracks the running time of songs and videos.
- **Size:** Tracks the size of the file as stored on the hard disk.

With the Dimensions: filter, you can search on the width and height of pictures. You can search using exact dimensions by using an equal sign and the dimensions in quotes, such as Dimensions:"1920 x 1020" or Dimensions:"2048 x 1536". The quotes and spaces are required to get a match. Implied in these examples is the equal (=) operator, so you also could enter Dimensions:="1920 x 1020" or Dimensions:="2048 x 1536". You also can use the less than, greater than, less than or equal to, greater than or equal to, or not equal to operators: <, >, <=, >=, <>.

The Framewidth: and Frameheight: filters can help search videos. For example, you could search for videos that are 320 x 240 by entering the search parameters:

```
framewidth:320 frameheight:240
```

Again, the equal (=) operator is implied, so you also could enter Framewidth:=320 Frameheight:=240. To search for videos with higher quality and larger frame sizes, you could use the search parameters:

```
framewidth:>320 frameheight:>240
```

Another handy size-related filter is Length:, which has the following flags:

- **Very Short**   For songs and videos less than a minute.
- **Short**   For songs and videos from 1 to 5 minutes in length.
- **Medium**   For songs and videos from 5 to 30 minutes in length.
- **Long**   For songs and videos from 30 to 60 minutes in length.
- **Very Long**   For songs and videos longer than 60 minutes.

Although you could enter numeric values for length, the search won't work as you expect. This is because the length is expressed internally in fractional seconds; you can see this by clicking the Location Indicator icon in the address path.

With the Size: filter, you can specify an approximate file size. Any file with an file size approximately matching your parameters is returned in the search results. The size options are:

- **Empty**   Allows you to search for empty files.
- **Tiny**   Allows you to search for files of 0 to 10 kilobytes.
- **Small**   Allows you to search for files of 10 to 100 kilobytes.
- **Medium**   Allows you to search for files of 100 kilobytes to 1 megabyte.
- **Large**   Allows you to search for files of 1 megabyte to 16 megabytes.
- **Huge**   Allows you to search for files of 16 megabytes to 128 megabytes.
- **Gigantic**   Allows you to search for files over 128 megabytes.

The size flags allow you to quickly find files that meet specific size criteria. For example, if you know the file you are looking for is medium in size and has the keyword "staff" or "monthly," you could search for it by following these steps:

1. In File Explorer, access the top-level folder from which you want to start searching.
2. Click in the Search box. Type **staff OR monthly size:medium**, and then press Enter.

The Size: filter accepts abbreviated entries as well. Using an abbreviated entry, you can directly enter the size parameters for the search. The basic syntax is:

```
size: SmallestSize .. LargestSize
```

where SmallestSize is the smallest file size that meets your parameters and LargestSize is the largest file size that meets your parameters. Use kb to specify a size in kilobytes, mb to specify a size in megabytes, and gb to specify a size in gigabytes. The kb, mb, and gb labels are required. If you don't use the appropriate label, Windows Search service won't return the expected results. Here's an example of how you could search for files between 50 KB and 2 MB:

1. In File Explorer, access the top-level folder from which you want to start searching.
2. Click in the Search box. Type **size:50kb .. 2mb**, and then press Enter.

You also can use the operators discussed previously, including <, >, <=, >=, and <>. For example, to search for files smaller than 900 KB in size, you would type **Size:<900kb** and press Enter to begin your search. To search for files greater than 900 KB in size, you would type **Size:>900kb** and press Enter to begin your search.

Saving Your Searches

You can save any search you perform in File Explorer. When you save a search, your search criteria are saved as a search folder so that you can rapidly perform an identical search in the future.

You can create a search folder by completing the following steps:

1. Perform a search in File Explorer, and then click Save Search on the Search panel.
2. In the Save As dialog box, accept the default name and location for the search folder or specify a new save location and name.
3. Click Save to create the search folder. Searches are saved with the .search-ms file extension.

By default, saved searches are stored in the Searches folder within your personal folders. You run a saved search at any time by double-clicking it in the Searches folder. Recent searches are also available on the Search pane in File Explorer when you click the Recent Searches option.

Saved Searches are represented by a blue icon with a magnifying glass and are listed with Saved Search as the type. When you open or double-click the saved search, the Windows Search service either retrieves the cached results of your previous search or performs a new search using the search criteria. The result is a list of matching files and folders that appear to be in the selected folder. The saved search does not actually contain any files or folders, however. A saved search's only content is the associated search string and result set.

You can work with saved search in the same way you work with files and folders. You can:

- Use Ctrl+X to cut and Ctrl+V to paste a saved search in a new location.
- Use Ctrl+C to copy and Ctrl+V to paste to create copies of saved searches.
- Press Delete to remove saved searches.

Although you cannot edit saved searches to update the search criteria, you can delete a saved search, configure the desired search criteria, and then save the new search using the old saved search name.

Indexing Your Computer

You tell the Windows Search service about locations that should be indexed by designating them as searched locations. After you've designated a folder as an indexed location, the Windows Search service is notified that it needs to update the related index whenever you modify the contents of the folder. You can manage the indexing of your computer's files and folders by adding or removing indexed locations, specifying file types to exclude, and rebuilding indexes as necessary.

> **Pro Tip** It's important to point out that encrypted files aren't indexed by default. This is designed to ensure that protected information isn't accidentally made available or

discoverable. Although a poor security practice, there is an advanced option for indexing encrypted files.

Customizing Indexed Locations

The Windows Search service indexes only a few locations by default. These locations are:

- **Offline files**   All offline file folders are indexed for fast searching.
- **Start menu**   All menu options are indexed for fast searching.
- **Users**   All personal folders of all users of the computer are indexed for fast searching.
- **Windows**   All system files are indexed for fast searching.

Tip   The quickest way to ensure that a folder is indexed is to add the folder to one of the folders in your personal profile, such as Documents or Pictures. Although application data folders are stored within user profiles, these folders are excluded from indexing by default. Because you don't want to index folders or files associated with application data, this is the desired setting in most instances.

The Indexing Options dialog box, shown in Figure 5-16, provides an overview of indexing on your computer, which includes the total number of items indexed and the current indexing state. The currently indexed locations are listed under Included Locations.

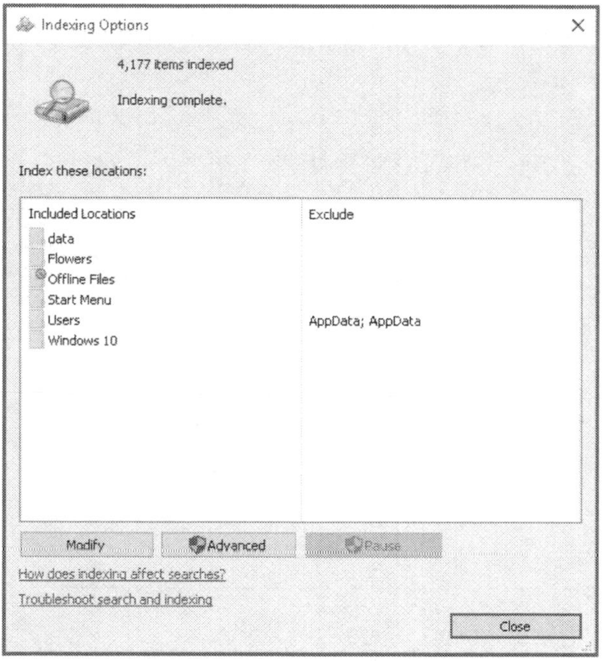

Figure 5-16 Setting indexing options

You can add or remove indexed locations by completing the
following steps:

1. In the Search box on the taskbar, type **Indexing Options**, and
    then press Enter. Or while working with the Search Tools in
    File Explorer, select Advanced Options and then select
    Change Indexed Locations.

2. Select a location and then click Modify. In the Indexed
    Locations dialog box, click Show All Locations to display
    hidden locations as well as standard locations.

3. Use the options provided to select locations to index, or clear
    check boxes for locations you no longer want to index. Click
    OK to save your changes.

The locations you can index include offline file folders, hard disk drives, and devices with removable storage. If a node can be expanded, you'll see an open triangle to the left of the location name. Click this to expand the location. For example, you could expand Local Disk (C:) to select a folder on the C: drive.

> **Note** Some system folders are excluded from indexing and are displayed dimmed to prevent them from being selected. If you enable indexing of the entire system drive, these system folders are excluded automatically. Keep in mind, however, that you usually don't want to index an entire drive. Instead, expand the drive location and select individual folders for indexing.

Including or Excluding Files by Type

Windows Search service can be configured to index file and folder names, file and folder properties, and file and folder contents. Windows Search service determines which types of files and folders to index according to the file extension.

The Windows Search service uses the information that it knows about file types and file extensions to help it index files more efficiently. Each file extension has a file filter associated with it, and this filter determines exactly whether and how files with a particular extension are indexed. For files included in the index, there are two general settings:

- **Index Properties Only** Ensures that only the properties of the file are indexed.

- **Index Properties And File Contents**   Ensures that the properties of the file are indexed and that the contents of the file can be indexed as well, if content indexing is enabled.

You can specify file types that the Windows Search service should include or exclude when indexing files by completing the following steps:

1. In the Search box on the taskbar, type **Indexing Options,** and then press Enter. Or while working with the Search Tools in File Explorer, select Advanced Options and then select Change Indexed Locations.

2. Click Advanced. On the Index Settings tab, select the Index Encrypted Files check box if you want the Windows Search service to index files that have been encrypted.

3. If you want to improve indexing of non-English characters, select the Treat Similar Words With Diacritics As Different Words check box. A diacritic is a mark above or below a letter that indicates a change in the way it is pronounced or stressed.

> **Note**   Selecting or clearing the options in Step 2 or 3 will cause the Windows Search service to completely rebuild the indexes on your computer.

4. On the File Types tab, each file extension and filter association is listed. If a file extension is selected, the Windows Search service includes files of this type when indexing. If a file extension is not selected, the Windows Search service excludes files of this type when indexing. Select or clear file extensions as appropriate.

> **Real World**   When you install new applications, those applications may register new filters with the Windows Search

service and configure related file extensions to use these filters. If a filter isn't available and you want to add support for a particular file extension, type the file extension in the text box provided and then click Add.

5. To change the way files with a particular extension are indexed, select the file extension and then click either Index Properties Only or Index Properties And File Contents. Only change the way indexing works when you are sure the indexing configuration you've chosen works. Although you can always stop indexing the contents of a particular file type, you'll rarely want to index the contents of a file type that isn't already being indexed.

6. Click OK to save your settings.

Resolving Indexing Problems

The Windows Search service must be running for you to perform searches. The service must also be running to index files. If you suspect there's a problem with searching or indexing, you should check the status of the Windows Search service. To do this, follow these steps:

1. In the Search box on the taskbar, type **View Local Services**, and then press Enter.

2. In the Services window, ensure the status of the Windows Search service is listed as Started. If the service isn't running, right-click Windows Search and then click Start. If the service is running and you suspect there's a problem with indexing, right-click and select Restart.

Other problems you may experience with searching and indexing have to do with corrupt indexes, improper index settings, and the index location running out of space. An indicator of a corrupt index is when your searches do not return the expected results or new documents are not being indexed properly. An indicator of improper index settings is when your searches fail or the Windows Search service generates bad file errors in the event logs. An indicator of the index location running out of space is when indexing of new documents fails and there are out-of-disk-space reports in the event logs for the Windows Search service.

The Windows Search service does a good job of automatically correcting some problems with indexes. For other types of problems, you'll find error reports in the form of Windows events in the system event logs. You can correct most problems with searching and indexing by completing the following steps:

1. In the Search box on the taskbar, type **Indexing Options**, and then press Enter. Or while working with the Search Tools in File Explorer, select Advanced Options and then select Change Indexed Locations.

2. Click Advanced. If you suspect your computer's indexes are corrupt, click Rebuild. Windows 10 rebuilds the indexes on your computer by stopping the Windows Search service, clearing out indexes, and then starting the Windows Search service. Indexes also are rebuilt automatically whenever you restart your computer.

3. By default, the Windows Search service creates indexes in the %ProgramData%\Microsoft folder. If the related drive is low on space or if you want to try to balance the workload by using other hard disk drives, you may want to change the index location. To do this, click Select New under Index Location. In the Browse For Folder dialog box, select the disk drive and folder in which the index should be stored, and then click OK.

The next time you restart your computer or the Windows Search service, indexes will be created in the new location.

4. Click OK. In the Indexing Options dialog box, you can track the status of reindexing files by watching the number of indexed items increase. The indexing status indicates whether indexing is complete or in progress.

Chapter 6. Managing Your Apps

Windows 10 runs two different types of software: desktop programs and desktop apps. For general discussion in this book, I refer to programs and apps interchangeably. However, in this chapter, I must now distinguish between the two:

* Desktop programs are software that you install and configure using media or Windows Installer.
* Desktop apps are software that you download and install from the Windows store.

I will discuss apps first to give a context and then focus on programs.

Working with Desktop Apps

Generally, you purchase apps in the Windows store and install apps over the Internet. However, apps can also be developed in-house or by third-party developers and deployed using policy settings. You manage apps using techniques similar to desktop programs. However, apps have many distinct characteristics.

Zeroing in on Apps

Desktop apps are automatically added to Start when you install them and will have a tile. A tile makes it easy to work with the app. Right-click the tile to display management options. Management options depend on the type of tile. Live tiles can update their contents, and these updates can be turned on or off by right-clicking and selecting Turn Live Tile On or Turn Live Tile Off as appropriate. As discussed in Chapter 2 under "Making the Start Menu Work for You," tiles can be displayed in several sizes, and you can make a tile smaller or larger as needed. If you no longer want a tile to be displayed on Start, you can right-click the tile and choose the Unpin From Start option.

If you unpin an app, it's still accessible by clicking the All Apps button. All Apps is the Windows 10 equivalent to the Programs menu in early release of Windows. In contrast, desktop programs may not be added to Start or Apps automatically. For more information, see the "Making Programs Available" section later in this chapter.

Windows 10 apps with live tiles start updating immediately after installation. Unlike programs where you typically have only one foreground program, multiple apps can share the screen and remain in the foreground. Apps can open other apps and share the screen with them; one app also can use multiple monitors.

Getting, Installing and Running Apps

Out of the box, computers running Windows 10 can install only trusted app packages that come from the Windows Store. You can access the Windows Store, shown in Figure 6-1, using the Store options on Start and the toolbar. If you are logged on to your device with a connected account, you'll be logged into the store automatically and can begin browsing for apps. While you can download any free app without having to provide payment information, the first time you purchase a paid app, you'll need to provide complete details for a credit, debit or other card.

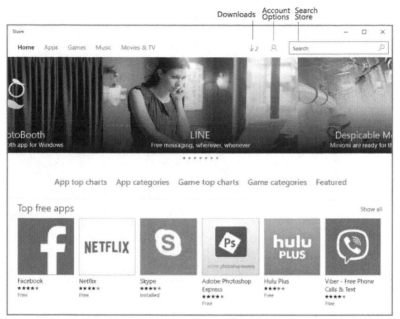

Figure 6-1 Visiting the Windows Store

Connecting Your Account to the Store

Sometimes you'll be working with a local account or domain account that isn't connected to a Microsoft account. For example, you may prefer not having Microsoft track information about your every online activity and therefore opt not to use a connected account. Don't worry, you can still get apps from the Windows Store.

If you need to login and have an Outlook.com, Hotmail, Live.com, MSN or other valid account in the Microsoft network, follow these steps to get connected to the store:

1. Click Account Options on the toolbar and then click Sign In.
2. When prompted to choose an account, click Microsoft Account.

3. Enter the email address and password for your Microsoft account and then click Sign In.

4. When prompted for your current Windows password, as shown in Figure 6-2, do one of the following:

▪ Provide your password and click Next to connect your current account to the Microsoft account and thereafter, you'll need to log in to your Windows device using the Microsoft account and password.

▪ Specify that you don't want switch to a Microsoft account for login by clicking the Sign In To Just This App Instead link. This option ensures your Microsoft account is used only for signing in to the Store.

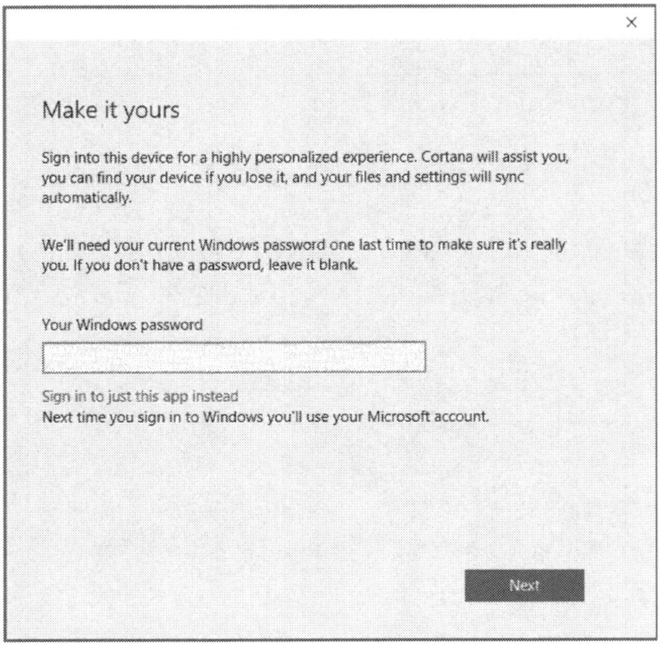

Figure 6-2 Connecting your account

If you need to login and don't have an Outlook.com, Hotmail, Live.com, MSN or other valid account in the Microsoft network, follow these steps to get connected to the store:

1. Click Account Options on the toolbar and then click Sign In.

2. When prompted to choose an account, click the Create One link.

3. Enter your first and last name in the text boxes provided.

4. Next, you are prompted for an email address to use for accessing Microsoft networks. This email address can be your work or home email address, but should be one that only you have access to as it will be the address used for recovering your account and verifying your identity if needed.

> **Tip** If you don't want to connect an existing email address into the Microsoft network, you can click the Get A New Email Address link and then enter a unique identifier for a new outlook.com email address.

5. Whether you entered your email address or created a new one, you must next enter a password. This password is for accessing the Microsoft network and should not be the same one you use for login or email access.

6. Use the selection lists provided to specify your country of origin and birthdate and then click Next.

7. Protect your account by entering a phone number that can be used to validate your account. Or click the Add An Alternate Email Instead link and then enter an alternate email address. When you are ready to continue, click Next twice.

8. When prompted for your current Windows password, as shown previously in Figure 6-2, do one of the following:

- Provide your password and click Next to connect your current account to the Microsoft account and thereafter, you'll need to log in to your Windows device using the Microsoft account and password.
- Specify that you don't want switch to a Microsoft account for login by clicking the Sign In To Just This App Instead link. This option ensures your Microsoft account is used only for signing in to the Store.

Finding and Installing Your Apps

Once you are signed in to the Store, you can get and install apps. Browse the store to find apps. Get and install an app, simply by clicking it's purchase button. With free apps, you simply click the Free button. The first time you purchase a paid app, however, you'll need to enter payment information.

Apps that are in the process of being downloaded and installed are shown on the Downloads And Installs page, which is accessed by clicking the Downloads option on the toolbar. If there's a problem downloading and installing an app, you'll see an error, as shown in Figure 6-3. Get more information about the error by clicking the See Details link. Try to download and install the app again by clicking the Retry option.

Figure 6-3 Checking the downloads and installs queue.

If you've made previous purchases on other devices, you'll find those purchases in your media library. Click Account Options on the toolbar and then click My Library. Apps that you've purchased but aren't yet installed have a download icon, as shown in Figure 6-4.

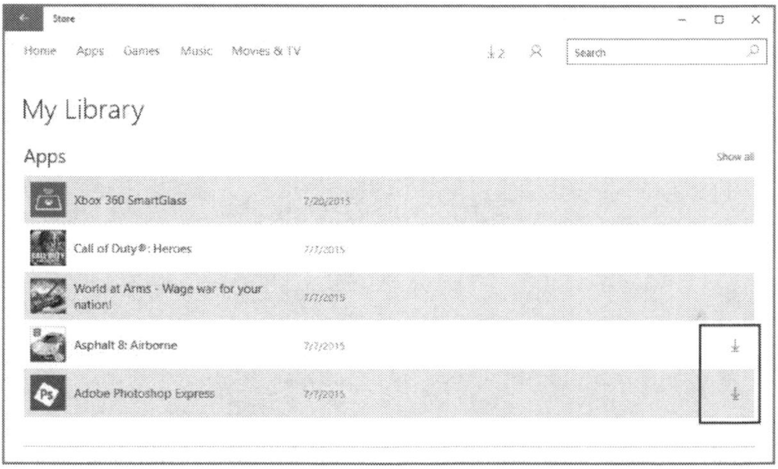

Figure 6-4 Getting downloads from your library.

By default, apps are updated automatically so you don't have to worry about checking for updates and installing them. While this is usually a good thing, you may not want apps to be updated automatically if you frequently use more costly mobile data instead of wi-fi. If so, you can specify that you don't want apps to be updated automatically by following these steps:

1. Click Account Options and then select Settings.
2. On the Settings page, set Update Apps Automatically to Off by clicking it.
3. If you turn off automatic updates, you'll then need to manually check for updates periodically, by clicking the Downloads option and then clicking the Check For Updates button.

While you are working with Settings, you may also want to specify that the Windows Store app only updates its live tile when you are connected to wi-fi. To do this, set the Only Update The Tile... option to Off.

Real World   When Update Apps Automatically is set to On, Windows 10 checks for updates to all installed apps daily. The daily check occurs every 20 hours. Thus, if the update check starts at 4:00 PM today, it'll start at 12:00 PM tomorrow and 8:00 AM the day after. If this time is missed, Windows 10 performs the check and any subsequent updates as soon as possible after the scheduled start is missed. Although the check and updates occur regardless of whether the computer is running on AC power or battery, Windows 10 won't check for updates when you are using mobile data and will instead wait until you have a wi-fi connection.

Installing Desktop Programs

You install desktop apps via the Windows Store, as discussed in the previous section. You install programs using a downloaded installer or installation media. Part of the installation process involves checking the credentials and prompting for consent if the user doesn't have appropriate privileges. As part of installing a program, you might also need to specify whether you want to make the program only available to you or to all users of the computer.

With older programs, Windows might not be able to properly determine the permissions required for installation. Solve this problem by canceling the installation and then re-running the setup program with elevated privileges. To do this, locate the executable file for the installer. Right-click this file, and then click Run As Administrator.

With a downloaded installer, you typically need to double-click the file you downloaded to begin the setup process. Next, you may be prompted to confirm that you want to make changes to your computer, as shown in Figure 6-5. If so, click Yes and begin the setup process. Follow the prompts to complete the installation.

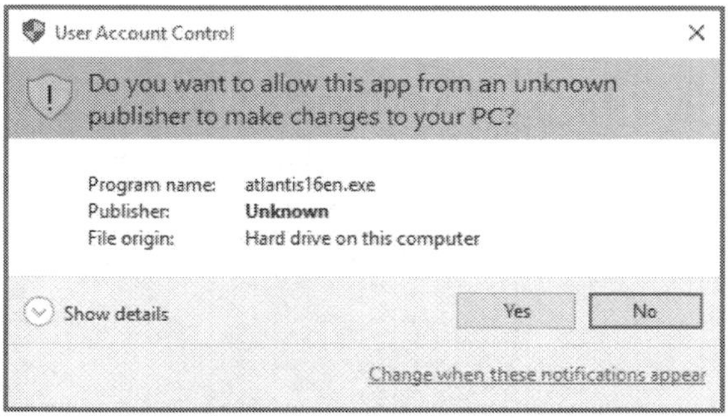

Figure 6-5 Confirm the changes to your computer.

Not all downloaded programs use direct installation. With some downloaded programs, you'll be prompted for a folder location where the setup files can be extracted and stored. Afterward, you'll then need to initiate setup by running the setup program for the application. Typically, this program is named Setup.exe.

To install an application using installation media, you insert the disc in the DVD drive. Windows should then check for an autorun file, such as Autorun.inf. If present, the autorun file specifies the action that the operating system should take and might also define other installation parameters. Autorun in turn invokes a setup program, such as Setup.exe.

If the autorun process doesn't start for some reason, access the installation media in File Explorer, as shown in Figure 6-6 and then double-click the setup program. Next, you may be prompted to confirm that you want to make changes to your computer. If so, click Yes to continue and begin the setup process. Follow the prompts to complete the installation.

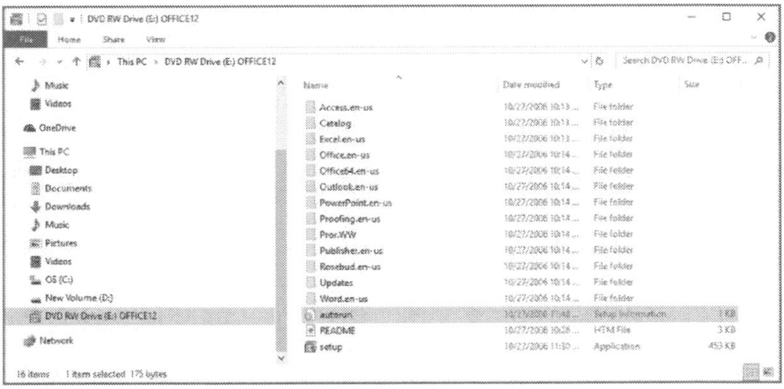

Figure 6-6 Start setup manually if needed.

Compliant versus Legacy Applications

The way that applications are installed and run, where applications write data, and what permissions applications have is controlled by User Account Control (UAC). Applications used with Windows 10 are divided into two general categories. Either they are UAC-complaint or considered to be legacy applications.

Compliant applications use UAC to reduce the attack surface of the operating system. This prevents unauthorized applications from installing or running without the user's consent and restricts the default privileges granted to applications. Both of which make it harder for malicious software to take over a computer.

Applications that run on Windows 10 derive their security context from the current user's access token. By default, UAC turns all users into standard users even if they are administrators. Before an administrator user can use administrator privileges, she must consent to the elevation. During the elevation process, a new access token is created containing the user's privileges, and this new access token is used to start the elevated application.

Whether applications need to run with standard or administrator privileges depends on the actions the application performs. Administrator user applications differ from standard user applications because they require elevated privileges to run and perform core tasks. Once started in elevated mode, an application with a user's administrator access token can perform tasks that require elevated privileges and can also write to system locations of the registry and the file system.

In contrast, standard user applications don't require elevated privileges to run or to perform core tasks. Once started in standard user mode, an application with a user's standard access token must request elevated privileges to perform administration tasks. For all other tasks, the application runs using standard user privileges and can only write data to nonsystem locations of the registry and the file system.

Applications not written for UAC compliance run with a user's standard access token by default and must use a special compatibility mode. This compatibility mode allow the non-compliant application to use virtualized views of file and registry locations. When the non-compliant application attempts to write to a system location, Windows 10 gives the application a private copy of the file or registry value. Any changes are then written to this private copy, and this private copy is then stored in your profile data. If the application attempts to read or write to this system location again, Windows 10 gives the application the private copy from your profile to work with. For more information about UAC and related prompts, see "Fine-Tuning Control Prompts" in Chapter 3.

Setting Run Levels for Applications

Generally, only applications running with an administrator user access token run in elevated mode. Sometimes, however, you'll want an application running with a standard user access token to be in elevated mode. For example, you might want to open the Command Prompt window in elevated mode so that you can perform administration tasks.

There are two basic ways to set the run level for applications. You can run an application once as an administrator or you can always run an application as an administrator. To run an application once as an administrator, right-click the application's menu item on Start, and then click Run As Administrator. Or if an application shortcut is pinned to the taskbar, you must right-click the pinned item, right-click the item again in the jump list, and then click Run As Administrator.

UAC controls whether you can elevate applications in this way:

- If you are using an administrator user account and prompting for consent is enabled, you are prompted for consent before the application is elevated and run in administrator mode.
- If you are using a standard user account and prompting is enabled, you are prompted for consent before the application is elevated and run in administrator mode.
- If you are using a standard user account and prompting is disabled, the application will fail to run.

You also can mark an application so that it always runs with administrator privileges, which is useful for resolving compatibility issues with legacy applications that require administrator privileges. This approach also is useful for UAC-compliant applications that normally run in standard mode but that you use to perform administration tasks.

To mark a program to always run as an administrator, follow these steps:

1. Locate the program shortcut by right-clicking the program on Start and selecting Open File Location. This opens File Explorer with the .exe file for the program selected.

2. Right-click the program's .exe file, select Send To and then select Desktop (Create Shortcut).

3. On the desktop, right-click the shortcut and then select Properties.

4. In the Properties dialog box, on the Compatibility tab, select Run This Program As An Administrator and then click Apply.

The program will now always run with the access token for an administrator user. Keep in mind that if you are using a standard account and prompting is disabled, the program will fail to run. If note that if the option is dimmed (unavailable), the application is blocked from always running at an elevated level, the application does not require administrator credentials to run, or you are not logged on as an administrator.

Application Setup and Compatibility

Most applications have a setup program that uses InstallShield, or Windows Installer. When you start the setup program, the installer helps you through the installation process and should also make it easier to uninstall the program if necessary. With older applications, the setup program might use an outdated version of one of these installers, which might mean the uninstall process won't completely uninstall the program.

Regardless of whether a program has a current installer, you should consider the possibility that you will need to recover your computer if something goes wrong with the installation. To help ensure that you can recover your computer, make sure System Restore is enabled for the drive on which you are installing the program by typing System Restore in the Search box and pressing Enter to open the System Properties dialog box to the System Protection tab, as shown in Figure 6-7. With System Restore enabled, Windows automatically creates checkpoint before installing the program. Then if a problem occurs, you can use this checkpoint to recover your computer.

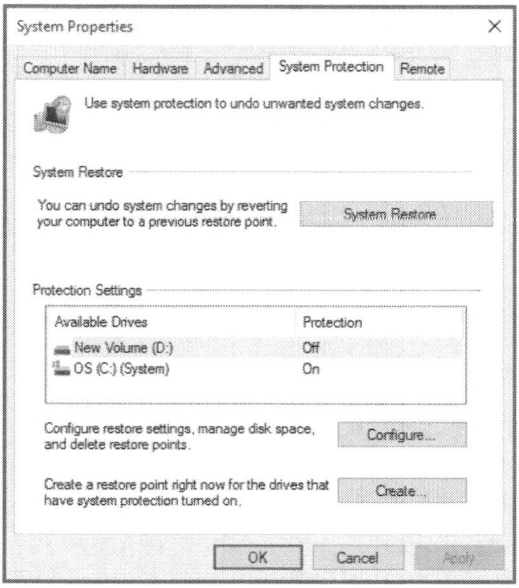

Figure 6-7 Confirm that System Restore is enabled.

Although the installers for most current programs automatically trigger the creation of a restore point before making any changes to a computer, the installers for older programs might not. You can manually create a restore point, by selecting the system drive on the Protection Settings panel and then clicking Create. Then, if you run into problems, you can try to uninstall the program or use System

Restore to recover the computer to the state it was in prior to installing the program.

Generally, Windows 10 checks for potential compatibility problems before you install applications. If it detects a problem, you might see a Program Compatibility Assistant dialog box after you start a program's installer. Often, this dialog box contains information about the known compatibility issues with the program and a possible solution. With some legacy applications, the Program Compatibility Assistant might display a message that the program is blocked due to compatibility issues. Programs get blocked because they cause a known stability issue with Windows, and you can't create an immediate work around to the problem. Your options will be limited. Generally, you'll either be able to check for solutions online or cancel the installation. If you check for solutions online, the typical solution requires you to purchase a current version of the program.

If the installation continues but fails for any reason before it is fully complete (or fails to properly notify the operating system regarding completion), you will also see the Program Compatibility Assistant dialog box. In this case, if the program installed correctly, click This Program Installed Correctly. If the program didn't install correctly, click Reinstall Using Recommended Settings to allow the Program Compatibility Assistant to apply compatibility fixes, and then try again to run the installer.

When you start programs, Windows 10 uses the Program Compatibility Assistant to automatically make changes for known compatibility issues as well. If the Program Compatibility Assistant detects a known compatibility issue when you run an application, it notifies you about the problem and provides possible solutions. You can then either accept the solutions or you can manually configure compatibility as discussed in "Resolving Compatibility Issues" later in this chapter.

Making Programs Available

After installation, most desktop programs should have related tiles on the Start menu and related options on the Apps list. This occurs because a program's shortcuts are placed in the appropriate subfolder of the Start Menu\Programs folder for all users so that any user who logs on has access to that program. Some programs prompt you during installation to choose whether you want to install the program for all users or only for the currently logged-on user. Other programs simply install themselves only for the current user.

If setup installs a program so that it is available only to the currently logged-on user and you want other users to have access to the program, you need to do one of the following:

* Log on to the computer with each user account that should have access to the program, and then rerun Setup to make the program available to these users. Then you also need to run Setup again when a new user account is added to the computer and that user needs access to the program.
* For programs that don't require per-user settings to be added to the registry before running, you can in some cases make the program available to all users on a computer by adding the appropriate shortcuts to the Start Menu\Programs folder for all users. Simply copy or move the program shortcuts from the

currently logged-on user's profile to the Start Menu\Programs folder for all users.

To make a program available to all users on a computer, you can copy or move a program's shortcuts by completing the following steps:

1. In File Explorer, make sure you can view hidden files and protected system files. Click File and then click Change Folder And Search Options. On the View tab, select Show Hidden Files, Folders, And Drives and clear the Hide Protected Operating System Files checkbox.

2. Access the currently logged-on user's Programs folder. This is a hidden folder under %UserProfile%\AppData\ Roaming\Microsoft\Windows\Start Menu.

3. In the Programs folder, right-click the folder for the program group or the shortcut you want to work with, and then click Copy or Cut on the shortcut menu.

4. Next, navigate to the Start Menu\Programs folder for all users. This hidden folder is under %SystemDrive%\ ProgramData\Microsoft\Windows\.

5. In the Programs folder, right-click an open space, and then click Paste. The program group or shortcut should now be available to all users of the computer.

Resolving Compatibility Issues

To get older programs to run, you might sometimes need to adjust compatibility options. Some programs won't install or run on Windows 10 even if they work on earlier releases of Windows. As discussed previously, if you try to install a program that has known compatibility problems, Windows 10 displays a warning prompt telling you about the compatibility issue. Generally, you shouldn't continue installing or running a program with known compatibility problems, unless there are known fixes that can be applied. That said, if a program will not install or run properly, you may be able to get the program to run by adjusting its compatibility settings.

You can manage compatibility settings using the Program Compatibility Wizard, or you can edit the program's compatibility settings directly by using the program's Properties dialog box. Both techniques work the same way. Keep in mind programs that are part of Windows 10 cannot be run in Compatibility mode—they don't need to be and for these programs the Compatibility options are not available.

To have Windows 10 try to automatically detect compatibility issues using the Program Compatibility Troubleshooter Wizard locate the program shortcut by right-clicking the program on Start and selecting Open File Location. This opens File Explorer with the .exe file for the program selected. Next, right-click the program shortcut, and then click Troubleshoot Compatibility to start the Program Compatibility Troubleshooter Wizard.

The wizard tries to automatically detect compatibility issues. If issues are detected, the wizard applies fixes and allows you to run the program with the recommended fixes. To do this, click Try Recommended Settings and then click Test The Program. After running the program, click Next, and then do one of the following:

* Click Yes, Save These Settings For This Program if the compatibility settings resolved the problem and you want to keep the settings.

- Click No, Try Again Using Different Settings if the compatibility settings didn't resolve the problem and you want to repeat this process from the beginning.
- Click No, Report The Problem To Microsoft And Check Online For A Solution if the compatibility settings didn't resolve the problem and you'd like to check for an online solution.
- Click Cancel if you want to discard the compatibility settings and exit the wizard.

If a program you have already installed won't run correctly, you might want to edit the compatibility settings directly rather than by using the wizard. You can do this by following these steps.

1. Locate the program shortcut by right-clicking the program on Start and selecting Open File Location. This opens File Explorer with the .exe file for the program selected. Next, right-click the program shortcut, and then click Properties.

2. In the Properties dialog box, click the Compatibility tab. Any option you select is applied to the currently logged-on user for the program shortcut. To apply the setting to all users on the computer and regardless of which shortcut is used to start the program, click Change Setting For All Users to open the Compatibility For All Users tab, and then select the compatibility settings that you want to use for all users who log on to the computer.

3. Select the Run This Program In Compatibility Mode For check box, and then use the selection menu to choose the operating system for which the program was designed, such as Windows 7.

4. For very old legacy programs, use the display options in the Settings panel to restrict the video display settings for the

program. Options include Reduced Color Mode with either 8-bit (256) color or 16-bit (65536) color, Run In 640 × 480 Screen Resolution, and Disable Display Scaling Of High DPI Settings.

5.   Click OK. Double-click the shortcut to run the program and test the compatibility settings. If you still have problems running the program, modify the compatibility settings and use different options. For example, if you thought the program was created for Windows 7 but it was really created for Windows Vista, change the compatibility mode.

Managing Desktop Programs and Features

Windows 10 provides many ways to work with desktop programs and windows components. You can:

- Add or remove Windows Features
- Designate default programs
- Configure AutoPlay options
- Manage file extensions and associations
- Modify, repair and remove programs
- Troubleshooting running programs

These options are discussed in the sections that follow.

Adding and Removing Windows Features

Operating system components are considered Windows features that can be turned on or off by following these steps:

1. Type Windows Features in the Search box and then press Enter. This opens the Windows Features dialog box. (Alternatively, in Control Panel click Programs. Then under Programs And Features, click Turn Windows Features On Or Off.)

2. As shown in Figure 6-8, select the check boxes for features to turn them on, or clear the check boxes for features to turn them off.

3. When you click OK, Windows 10 reconfigures components to reflect any changes you made.

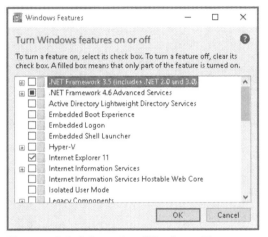

Figure 6-8 Managing Windows Features.

Designating Default Programs

Default programs determine which programs are used with which types of files and how Windows handles files on media or devices. You configure default programs based on the types of files those programs support, either globally for all users of a computer or only for the current user. As individual user defaults override global defaults, you could select Groove Music as the global default for all types of files it supports, and then all users of the computer would use

Groove Music to play the sound, audio, and video files it supports. But if John who also uses your computer wanted to use Apple iTunes instead as the default player for sound and audio files, you could configure iTunes to be his default player for the types of media files iTunes supports.

You can configure global default programs for you and everyone else who uses your computer by following these steps:

1. Type Default Programs in the Search box and then press Enter. This opens the Default Programs page in Control Panel, which can also be opened by clicking Programs and then clicking Default Programs when working with Control Panel.

2. Select Set Program Access And Computer Defaults. You'll see the dialog box shown in Figure 6-9.

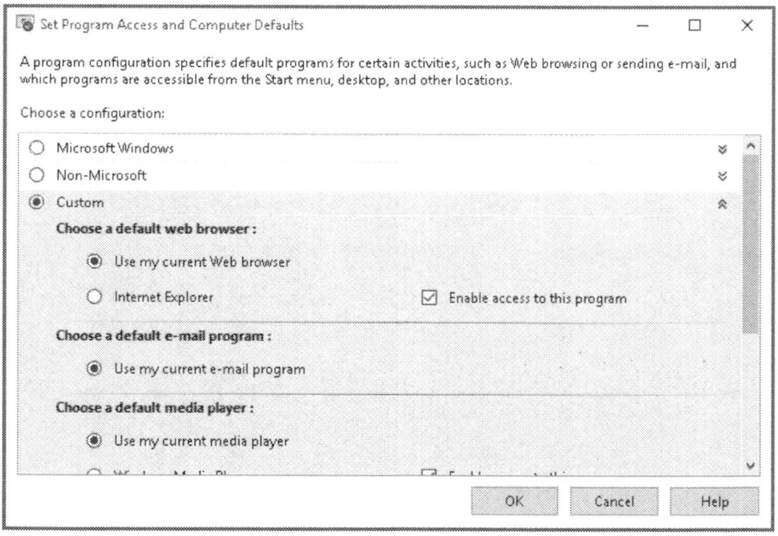

Figure 6-9 Choosing default programs for all users

3. Choose a configuration from one of the following options:

- **Microsoft Windows**   Choose this option to set the currently installed Windows programs as the default programs for browsing the web, sending email, playing media files, etcetera

- **Non-Microsoft**   Choose this option to set non-Microsoft programs (when available) as the default programs for browsing the web, sending email, playing media files, etcetera

- **Custom**   Choose this option if you want to specify the default programs for browsing the web, sending email, playing media files, etcetera

4. Select OK to save the settings.

To override global defaults, you can set default programs for yourself or other users of your computer. You can configure default programs for you or anyone else by following these steps:

1. Log on as the user you want to configure. Type Default Programs in the Search box and then press Enter. Or click Programs and then click Default Programs when working with Control Panel.

2. Next, select Set Your Default Programs.

3. Select a program you want to work with in the Programs list.

4. If you want the program to be the default for all the file types and protocols it supports, select Set This Program As Default.

5. If you want the program to be the default for specific file types and protocols, select Choose Defaults For This Program. Select the file extensions for which the program should be the default, and then select Save.

6. Repeat Steps 3-5 as appropriate. Select OK to save the settings.

Configuring AutoPlay Options

In Windows 10, AutoPlay options determine how Windows handles files on media and devices. You can configure separate AutoPlay options for each type of media and device your computer can handle by following these steps:

1. Type Default Programs in the Search box and then press Enter. Or click Programs and then click Default Programs when working with Control Panel.

2. Click Change AutoPlay Settings. This displays the AutoPlay page in Control Panel.

3. As shown in Figure 6-10, use the media selection list to set the default AutoPlay option for each media type. Although the actions available depend on the type of media and whether your computer has a program for playing the media type, the general actions you can choose include:

- Import
- Play
- Install Or Run
- Take No Action
- Open Folder To View Files
- Ask Me Every Time

4. Click Save to save your settings.

> **Note** For removable drives (USB memory sticks, etc.), you can specify an overall default or a default for each media type. To specify an overall default, clear the Choose What To Do check box and then select a preferred default. To specify individual defaults, select the Choose What To Do check box and then select a default action for each media type.

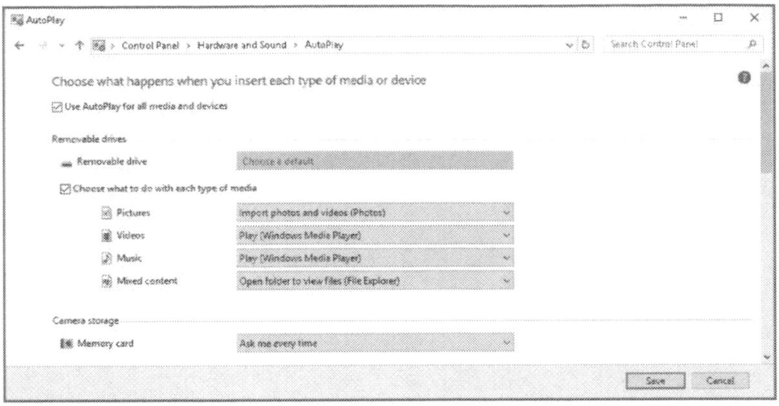

Figure 6-10 Setting AutoPlay options for media and devices.

Working with the Command Path

Windows uses the command path to locate executables. Using the PATH command, you can view the current command path for executables simply by entering **path** on a line by itself when working with the Command Prompt. In Windows PowerShell, you enter **$env:path** on a line by itself to get the same information. In the output from either technique, observe that Windows uses a semicolon (;) to separate individual paths, marking where one file path ends and another begins, such as:

```
PATH=C:\WINDOWS\system32;C:\WINDOWS;C:\WINDOWS\System32\
Wbem;C:\WINDOWS\System32\WindowsPowerShell\v1.0\
```

Paths are searched in order, with the last path in the PATH user variable is the last one searched. Because these paths determine where Windows looks for executables and scripts, it's important to ensure the paths are correct for the way you use Windows.

During logon, system and user environment variables are used to set the command path. The path defined in the PATH system variable sets the base path. The path defined in the PATH user variable adds to the base path. Knowing this, you can add to the command path by following these steps:

1. Type **SystemPropertiesAdvanced** in the Search box, and then press Enter to open the System Properties dialog box with the Advanced tab selected.

2. Click Environment Variables. Under User Variables, click New (or Edit if you previously created a user path). This opens the User Variable dialog box.

3. Enter Path as the variable name and then type the paths to include in the PATH variable. Be sure to use a semicolon (;) to separate individual paths, as shown in Figure 6-11.

4. Click OK three times to close all open dialog boxes.

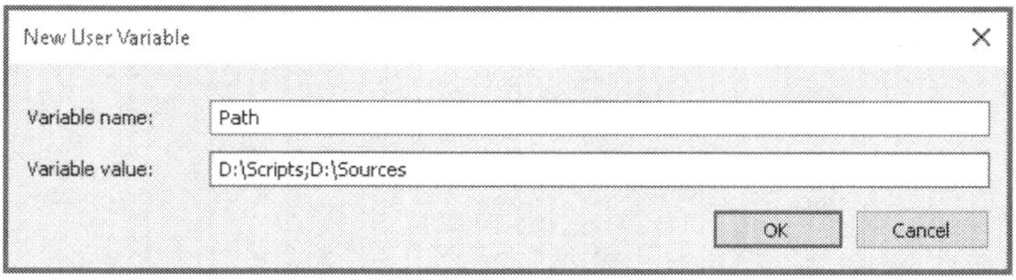

Figure 6-11 Adding to the command path.

> **Note**   Although the user path is added to the command path immediately, the path is not updated in any open command prompt or PowerShell windows. Close and re-open those windows to update their working environment.

If you make a mistake or no longer want to add a user path to the command path, delete the additional paths by following these steps:

1. Type **SystemPropertiesAdvanced** in the Search box, and then press Enter to open the System Properties dialog box with the Advanced tab selected.

2. Click Environment Variables. Under User Variables, click Path and then click Delete.

3. Click OK twice to close all open dialog boxes.

Working with File Extensions and Associations

Windows uses file extensions and file associations to determine which applications to open for which types of files. File extensions allow you to execute a command by using just the command name. File associations allow you to double-click a file and open the file automatically in a related application.

Two types of file extensions are used:

- File extensions for executables
- File extensions for applications

Executable files are defined with the %PATHEXT% environment variable and can be set using the Environment Variables dialog box. To view the current settings for this variable, enter **set pathext** at the command line or enter **$env:pathext** at a PowerShell prompt. The default setting is:

```
PATHEXT=.COM;.EXE;.BAT;.CMD;.VBS;.VBE;.JS;
.JSE;.WSF;.WSH;.MSC.
```

With this setting, the command line knows any files ending with this extension are executable. The order of file extensions in the %PATHEXT% variable sets the search order used by Windows on a per-directory basis. Thus, if a particular directory in the command path has multiple executables that match the command name provided, a .com file would be executed before an .exe file, and so on.

File extensions for applications are referred to as file associations. File associations are what enable you to pass arguments to executables and to open documents, worksheets, or other application files by double-clicking their file icons.

Each known extension on your computer has a file association that you can view at a command prompt by entering **assoc** followed by the extension, such as **assoc .doc** or **assoc .docx**. For example, if you enter assoc .docx at the command prompt and you've installed Word, the output is similar to the following:

```
.docx=Word.Document.15
```

Each file association in turn specifies the file type for the file extension. This can be viewed at a command prompt by entering **ftype** followed by the file association, such as **ftype Word.Document.12**. The output tells you what program is run for this type of file:

```
Word.Document.15="C:\Program Files\Microsoft
Office\Office15\WINWORD.EXE" /n /dde
```

Here, the output shows Winword.exe is used to open .docx files.

Extensions for executables also have a corresponding file association and file type. For some executables, the file type is the extension text without the period followed by the keyword file, such as cmdfile, exefile, or batfile, and the file association specifies that the first parameter passed is the command name and that other parameters should be passed on to the application. For example, if you enter **assoc .exe** to see the file associations for .exe executables, you'll see the file type is exefile. If you then enter **ftype exefile**, you'll see the file association is set to the following:

```
exefile="%1" %*
```

This means that when you run an .exe file Windows uses first value as the command to run and anything else as a parameter to pass to the executable.

You can associate a file type (or protocol) with a specific application by following these steps:

1. Type Default Programs in the Search box and then press Enter. Or click Programs and then click Default Programs when working with Control Panel.

2. Click Associate A File Type Or Protocol With A Program.

3. On the Set Associations page, current file associations are listed by file extension and the current default for that extension. To change the file association for an extension, click the file extension, and then click Change Program.

4. Use the How Do You Want To Open dialog box, shown in Figure 6-12, to specify the default program to use. Programs registered in the operating system as supporting files with the selected extension are listed automatically. Simply click a recommended program to set it as the default for the selected extension. Or click More Apps to view other programs that might also support the selected extension.

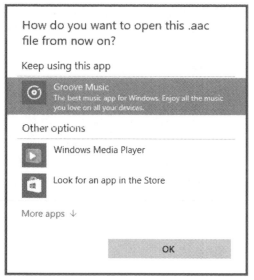

Figure 6-12 Associating file extensions with other programs.

Managing, Repairing, and Uninstalling Desktop Programs

Windows 10 considers any program you've installed on a computer or made available for a network installation to be an installed program. You use the setup program that comes with the program to install programs, and the Programs And Features page in Control Panel to manage programs.

The basic steps for working with programs follow:

1. Type Programs And Features in the Search box and then press Enter. Or click Programs and then click Programs And Features when working with Control Panel.

2. As shown in Figure 6-13, you should see a list of installed programs. In the Name list, right-click the program you want

to work with. The options available depend on the program you are working with and include:

- **Uninstall**   Choose this option to uninstall the program
- **Uninstall/Change**   Choose this option to uninstall or modify a program
- **Change**   Choose this option to modify the program's configuration
- **Repair**   Choose this option to repair the program's installation

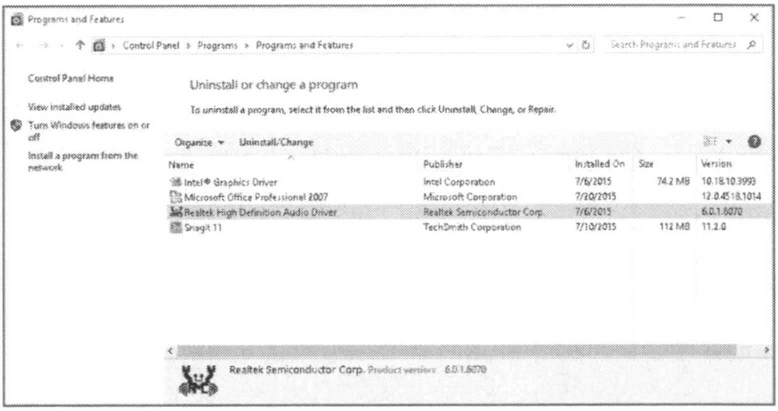

Figure 6-13 Managing installed programs in Control Panel.

The management options available depend on the installer program used during setup of the application and the version of the installer. Most software applications use InstallShield or Windows Installer, but not necessarily the most recent version. If the uninstall process fails, you often can resolve any problem simply by rerunning the uninstaller for the program.

When you are uninstalling programs, keep the following in mind:

- Windows warns you if you try to uninstall a program while other users are logged on. Using the Switch Accounts option, other users can be logged in but not active. Before uninstalling programs that others might be using you should have those users log off. If you don't do this, you might cause other users to lose data or experience other problems.
- Windows only allows you to remove programs that were installed with a Windows-compatible setup program. Legacy programs might have a separate uninstall utility that doesn't use InstallShield or Windows Installer. Some legacy programs work by copying their data files to a program folder and these you uninstall simply by deleting the related folder.
- Many uninstall programs leave behind data either inadvertently or by design. Because of this, you'll often find folders for these applications within the Program Files folder. Although you could delete these folders, they might contain important data files or custom user settings that could be used again if you reinstall the program.

Managing Currently Running Apps, Programs and Processes

In Windows 10, you can view and work with your computer's currently running apps, programs and processes by using Task Manager. Open Task Manager by pressing Ctrl+Shift+Esc or by right-clicking the lower-left corner of the screen and then clicking Task Manager on the shortcut menu.

By default, Task Manager displays a summary list of all running apps and programs, as shown in Figure 6-14. When you click an apps or program in the list, you can manage it. To exit an app or program (which might be necessary when it is not responding), click it in the Task list, and then click End Task. To display other management options, right-click the app or program in the Task list.

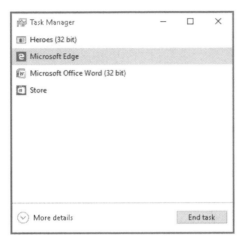

Figure 6-14 Using the summary view in task manager to view running apps and programs.

When working with the summary view, you can click More Details to open the full Task Manager. You'll then see detailed information about running programs, apps and processes, as shown in Figure 6-15. The Processes tab lists each item running on the computer under three general headings:

- **Apps**   Shows desktop apps and programs that you've started.
- **Background Processes**   Shows processes being run in the background by Windows.
- **Windows Processes**   Shows all other processes running on the computer.

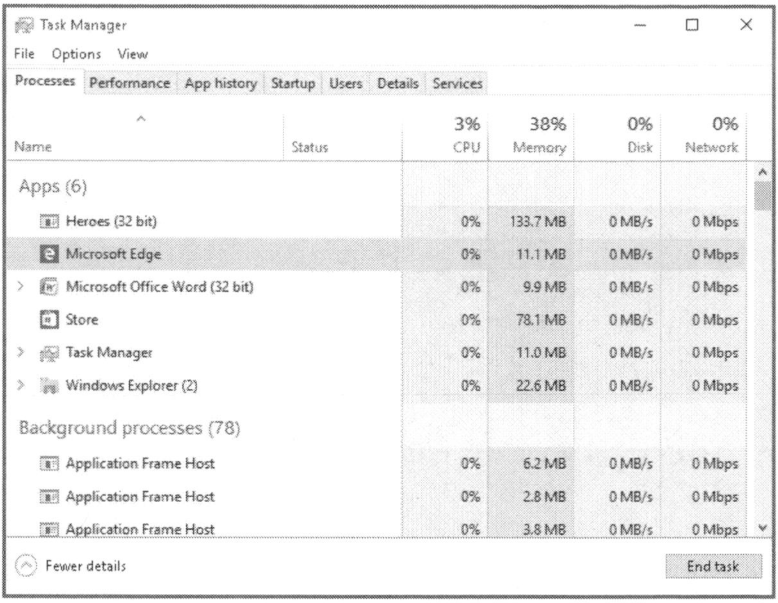

Figure 6-15 Getting an expanded view of running apps, programs and processes.

Apps, programs and processes are listed by name, status, CPU usage, memory usage, disk usage, and network usage. A blank status indicates a normal state. As with the summary view, you can exit an application or stop a running process by clicking the item in the Task list, and then clicking End Task.

Some items with related windows or processes can be expanded. Double-click an item to see details for the related windows or processes. Display more management options by right-clicking an item in the Task list. The options include:

- **Open File Location**   Opens the folder containing the executable file for the application or process in File Explorer

- **Create Dump File** Creates a memory dump file for the selected process
- **Go To Details** Opens the Details tab with the process selected
- **Properties** Opens the Properties dialog box for the executable file.

Although programs you are running are listed under the Apps heading, programs being run by any other users (such as when you switch context) are listed as Background Processes. Select the Users tab to view information about resources being used by other users.

Chapter 7. Tracking System Performance and Health

Your computer's performance levels are directly related to its health. Whether you have a desktop, laptop, or tablet PC, your computer was designed to be paused (by putting it in sleep mode) and resumed. All that pausing and resuming can have unintended consequences on the overall performance of your computer, especially after days or weeks of pause and resume. So the first thing I ask anyone experiencing a problem with a Windows device is this: When was the last time you shut down and then restarted device?

Beyond a simple restart, there are several things you need to know to understand issues that can affect your computer's performance. You need to understand what CPU, memory and disk resources the computer has—which are the best indicators of potential performance. You need to determine what is currently happening on your computer in terms of running applications, processes, and services—Task Manager makes this easy. And you need to know what problems (if any) your computer is experiencing—the best way to track problems is to examine the event logs.

Getting to Know Your Computer's Hardware

Your computer's performance capabilities are relative to its hardware configuration. It's relative because your computer's actual performance depends on many factors, including whether you've followed the tips and techniques discussed in this book to squeeze every last bit of power out of your computer while making the most of the included features and options.

To understand your computer's performance capabilities, you need information about your computer's processor, physical memory (RAM), graphics card, and primary hard disk. Get this information using the System Information utility shown in Figure 7-1.

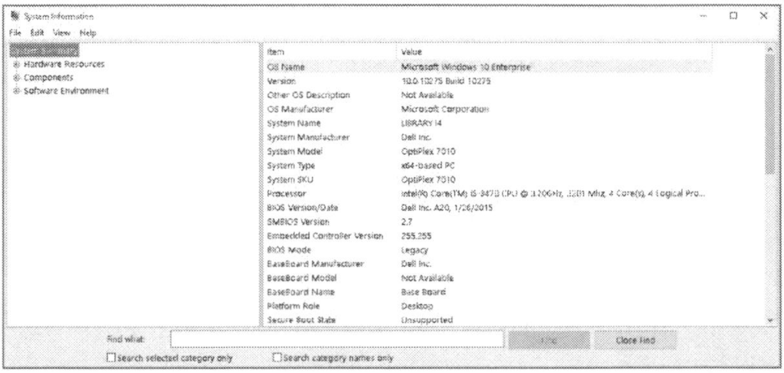

Figure 7-1 Checking your computer's hardware, architecture and resources.

After you start System Information by typing **msinfo32** in the Search box and pressing Enter, you can use the System Summary to answer most of your questions about your computer's hardware, architecture and memory, including:

* Operating system edition, such as Enterprise edition
* System type, such as x64-based PC
* Processor, such as Intel Core I5
* BIOS version
* Physical memory and virtual memory
* Hyper-V capabilities

> **Note**   The processor details also provide an easy way to verify the processor speed and the number of processor cores.

To determine what graphics card your computer has and its capabilities, expand Components by double-clicking its entry and then select Display. You'll then see the name of the graphics card and the size of the RAM on the graphics card. Graphics memory is different from standard memory. The current screen resolution and color bit depth are also listed.

You can learn more about the storage capabilities of your computer by expanding Storage under Components and then selecting Drives. You'll then see information about all fixed and removable drives available, including whether they are compressed, the file system type, the total size and the amount of available free space.

If you want to learn more about the networking capabilities of your computer, expand Network under Components and then select Adapter. You'll then see information about all network adapters available, including the adapter type and the current TCP/IP settings.

> **Note**   While you are viewing the detailed information, click File and then select Print to print any of this information for future reference.

Clearly, your computer's system type, processor, and RAM have a big impact on overall performance. If your computer has an older or single-core processor, you may be able to boost performance dramatically by upgrading the processor. However, performing a processor upgrade isn't the easiest thing to do. Many things can go wrong, and your older computer probably won't be able to use the latest processors anyway. At best, you might be able to upgrade to a similar class CPU that is only marginally faster; so instead of trying to upgrade the processor, I recommend determining whether you can add more RAM to your computer. If your computer has less than 8 GB of RAM, you may be able to improve performance by installing more memory. Remember, the memory must operate at a speed compatible with your computer's motherboard and system bus, and you can't mix and match different types of memory. Often, you'll have the best chances for success if you remove your existing memory and replace it with the new memory.

Your computer's primary hard disk also has a big impact on overall performance. The primary hard disk is the one most used by the operating system and programs. If you have an older computer and its primary drive is slow, you may see a significant reduction in boot and wake from sleep times by upgrading the primary hard disk to a newer model that is faster and supports caching. However, moving your primary disk isn't very easy; these two tricks will save you a lot of time and heartache:

* Try moving your computer's paging file to a faster, newer disk, as discussed in "Fine-Tuning Virtual Memory" in Chapter 9.
* Try using Windows ReadyBoost to shift some of your computer's system cache reads and writes to faster flash memory. See "Enhancing Performance with ReadyBoost" in Chapter 9.

If your computer's primary drive has relatively good performance, you can maintain relatively good disk performance by:

* Running a full check disk on your primary hard drive periodically. Be sure to perform error repair and bad sector recovery as well.
* Defragmenting your primary hard drive periodically. While you can defragment other drives, fragmentation of the primary hard drive is what most affects performance.
* Cleaning up your primary hard drive at least once every other month and always ensuring that your primary drive has at least 15 percent of its disk space free.

> **Note**   DiskCleanup and other disk utilities are discussed in Chapter 9.

Graphics memory can also affect relative performance levels. Look at:

* **Shared system memory**   A reflection of physical memory (RAM) that is shared between the graphics card and the CPU. Shared memory used by the graphics card leaves less physical memory available for applications and the operating system.
* **Dedicated graphics memory**   A reflection of the actual memory on its graphics card or cards. If your computer has little dedicated graphics memory, installing a new graphics card with 2 GB or more of dedicated RAM would substantially increase relative performance levels.
* **Total available graphics memory**   A combination of shared memory and dedicated memory. If your computer has 2 GB of dedicated graphics memory and 4 GB of shared graphics memory, it has 6 GB of total available memory for graphics.

Following this, if your computer has 12 GB of RAM, and 4 GB of that currently is being used by the graphics card to perform graphics rendering for a graphic-intensive application or program, only 8 GB is available for other uses. In this case, you'd have a better experience if you added RAM, upgraded to a graphics card with a higher amount of dedicated memory.

You can squeeze extra performance out of your computer by using the techniques I've discussed here, as well as other techniques I've discussed previously. For example, if your computer doesn't have a high-end graphics card, you may be able to improve overall performance by turning off graphics-intensive features of the operating system, as discussed in "Optimizing Interface Performance" in Chapter 2.

Checking Current Performance Levels

"Managing Currently Running Apps, Programs and Processes" in Chapter 6 discussed basic techniques for working with Task Manager. Now let's take a closer look. You can start Task Manager by pressing Ctrl+Shift+Esc or by right-clicking the lower-left corner of the screen and then clicking Task Manager on the shortcut menu. The Processes tab shows the status of currently running programs. You can switch to a program and make it active by selecting the application and then clicking Switch To, and you can start a new program by following these steps:

1. Click Run New Task on the File menu. This opens the Create New Task dialog box, shown in Figure 7-2.
2. Enter a command to run the application and then click OK. For example, you can run the System Information utility by entering **msinfo32**.

> **Note** Run the application with elevated privileges by selecting the Create This Task With Administrative Privileges.

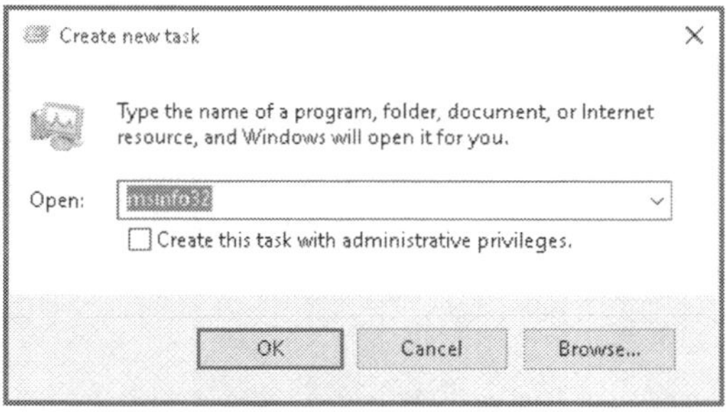

Figure 7-2 Using Task Manager to run a program.

When you start an application or run a command, Windows 10 starts one or more processes to handle the related program. Processes that you start are called interactive processes. If an application is active and selected, the interactive process has control over the keyboard and mouse until you switch control by terminating the program or selecting a different application. When an application's process has control, it's said to be running in the foreground.

Tracking Applications and Processes

Processes can also run in the background. For processes you started, this means that programs that aren't currently active can continue to operate; however, they generally aren't given the same priority as active processes. Windows also has background processes that run independently of your user session. These processes are related to startup applications, scheduled tasks, housekeeping activities, and so on.

The Details tab in Task Manager, shown in Figure 7-3, provides detailed information about running processes, including those from the operating system, local services, the interactive user logged on to the local console (you), and all other users. If your computer isn't responding well, you can use this information to determine which processes are over-consuming system resources. The default columns are:

* **Name**   Shows the name of the process or related executable
* **PID**   Shows the ID number of the process
* **Status**   Shows the status of the process, such as Running
* **User Name**   Shows the name of the user or system service running the process
* **CPU**   Shows the percentage of CPU utilization for the process
* **Memory** (Private Working Set)   Shows the amount of memory the process is currently using
* **Description**   Provides details or proper name of the process

Name	PID	Status	User name	CPU	Memory (p...	Description
ApplicationFrameHo...	6996	Running	libco	00	3,036 K	Application Frame H...
ApplicationFrameHo...	1164	Running	edt	00	6,416 K	Application Frame H...
ApplicationFrameHo...	388	Running	tedg	00	2,880 K	Application Frame H...
ApplicationFrameHo...	2936	Running	tedg	00	5,568 K	Application Frame H...
audiodg.exe	6784	Running	LOCAL SE...	00	2,344 K	Windows Audio Devi...
browser_broker.exe	7924	Running	tedg	00	1,608 K	Browser_Broker
csrss.exe	492	Running	SYSTEM	00	620 K	Client Server Runtime...
csrss.exe	2220	Running	SYSTEM	00	588 K	Client Server Runtime...
csrss.exe	5756	Running	SYSTEM	00	604 K	Client Server Runtime...
csrss.exe	11292	Running	SYSTEM	00	600 K	Client Server Runtime...
csrss.exe	204	Running	SYSTEM	00	956 K	Client Server Runtime...
csrss.exe	11384	Running	SYSTEM	00	476 K	Client Server Runtime...
dasHost.exe	1344	Running	LOCAL SE...	00	4,092 K	Device Association Fr...
dwm.exe	1756	Running	DWM-3	00	6,240 K	Desktop Window Ma...
dwm.exe	368	Running	DWM-4	00	11,164 K	Desktop Window Ma...

Figure 7-3 Tracking resource usage by processes

To get even more information, you can add columns to the Processes tab. Right click one of the default columns and choose Select Columns. Use the dialog box provided to select the columns to add. For troubleshooting performance and related issues, you might want to add these columns:

* **Base Priority** Indicates the priority of the process, relative to other running processes. When there is resource contention between a higher-priority process and a lower-priority process, the higher-priority process will be given more resources relative to the lower-priority process. The priorities from lowest to highest are: Low, Below Normal, Normal, Above Normal, High, and RealTime. Most processes have a Normal priority by default.

* **CPU Time** Shows the total CPU cycle time used by a process since it was started. If you want to see the processes that are using the most CPU time, display this column and then click the column header to sort process entries by CPU time.

* **Handles** Shows the current number of file handles maintained by the process. Use the handle count to gauge how dependent the process is on the file system. Each file handle requires system memory to be maintained.

* **I/O Reads, I/O Writes** Shows the total number of disk input/output (I/O) reads or writes since the process was started. Together, the number of I/O reads and writes tells you how much disk I/O activity is related to the process.

* **Page Faults** Shows the number of page faults actively occurring because of the process. A page fault occurs when a process requests a page in memory and Windows can't find the page at the requested location. If the requested page is elsewhere in memory, the fault is called a soft page fault. If the requested

page must be retrieved from disk, the fault is called a hard page fault. While hard faults can cause significant delays, most processors can handle a large number of soft faults.

- **Paged Pool, NP Pool**   Shows paged pool memory usage. Paged pool is an area of system memory for objects that can be written to disk when they aren't used.

- **NP Pool**   Shows nonpaged pool memory usage. Paged pool is Nonpaged pool is an area of system memory for objects that can't be written to disk. Processes that require a large amount of nonpaged pool memory can affect performance, especially when they are vying for resources with other processes.

- **Peak Working Set**   Shows the highest amount of memory used by the process. The difference between current memory usage and peak memory usage is important to note; some applications use a lot of memory when performing certain tasks, which can degrade performance when they are vying for resources with other processes.

- **Threads**   Shows the current number of threads that the process is using. Most modern applications are multithreaded. Multithreading allows concurrent execution of process requests. Some applications can dynamically control the number of concurrently executing threads to improve application performance, but too many threads can actually reduce performance because the operating system has to switch thread contexts too frequently.

Pay particular attention to the System Idle Process. This process tracks the amount of system resources that aren't being used. Thus, a 99 in the CPU column of the System Idle Process means that 99 percent of system resources currently aren't being used. Also remember that a single application can start multiple processes. To be sure you are tracking or managing the right process for an application, right-click the application on the Processes tab and select Go To Details.

To stop an application, you'll usually want to target the main application process as well as dependent processes, either by right-clicking the application on the Details tab and then clicking End Task or by right-clicking the main application process on the Processes tab and then clicking End Task. You can also right-click the main process or a dependent process on the Details tab, and then select End Process Tree.

Tracking Performance and Resource Usage

All running processes, whether operating actively or in the background, affect the performance of your computer. At times, your computer may seem less responsive than usual and you may want to try to determine why. The Performance tab in Task Manager provides a quick way to check system resource usage and relative performance levels.

Usage graphs are provided to help you understand how CPU, memory, disk and Ethernet resources are being used. Summary graphs for each resource are provided in the left pane. The Update Speed setting, on the View menu, determines how often graphs are updated.

When you select a resource in the left pane, more detailed information is provided in the main pane. The detailed usage graph for CPU shows either the overall utilization or the utilization of individual processor cores. Switch between the views by right-clicking the CPU graph in the main pane, pointing to Change Graph To and then selecting either Overall Utilization or Logical Processors as appropriate.

Figure 7-4 shows the resource usage for a computer with four CPU cores under normal usage conditions. This computer's CPU cores are operating normally and are not heavily taxed. The few peaks shown are not remarkable; they probably occurred when applications were opened or new tasks were started. The memory usage levels are also normal and not remarkable, as are disk usage levels. Of interest, however, is the relatively high Ethernet usage, which is indicative of large transfers in progress or possibly video streaming.

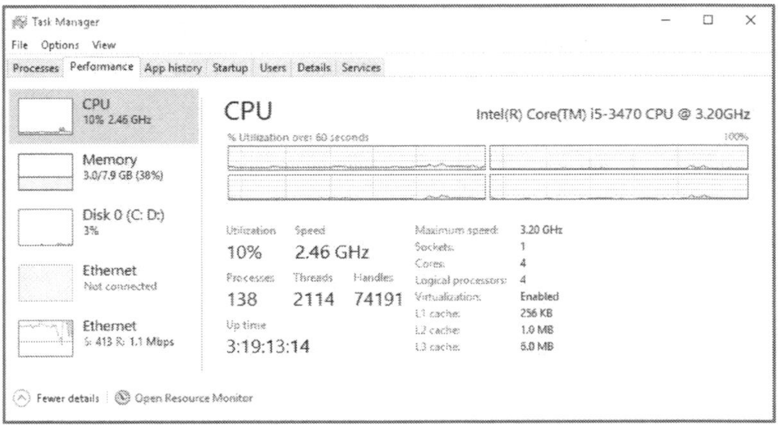

Figure 7-4 Tracking resource usage under average usage conditions

Contrast this to the resource usage for the same computer shown in Figure 7-5. In this case, the computer is experiencing higher resource usage with disk utilization at 100% and Ethernet usage peaking frequently to 100%. The continuing peaks and high usage levels of disk and Ethernet usage in this instance are remarkable, especially if they represent normal usage conditions. However, this computer doesn't have a performance problem related to its memory or CPUs. Rather, it is simply performing disk- and Ethernet-intensive operations, and those operations are ongoing.

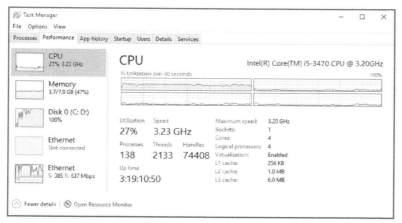

Figure 7-5 Tracking resource usage under high usage conditions

Note You can view a close-up of the CPU graphs by double-clicking in the Performance tab. Double-clicking again returns you to normal viewing mode.

However, if CPU usage were consistently and continually high on all CPUs, you would want to examine running applications and their processes to get a better understanding of what is happening on the computer. You might, for example, be running processor-intensive applications, or you simply might need to consider upgrading your computer's CPUs to perform the kinds of tasks you want to perform.

Memory is often a source of performance problems. The Performance tab's Memory graph shows the amount of physical memory currently being used by the computer, graphed to reflect the percentage of total memory. The Memory Usage History graph shows physical memory usage plotted over time. If your computer is consistently low on available memory, you might want to consider tuning or adding memory.

The computer shown in the examples doesn't have a memory issue. In the second example, the computer is using 3.7 GB of memory and still has 4.2 GB of available memory. But if memory usage were considerably and consistently higher, you would want to examine running processes and take a closer look at what was happening on the computer. For example, applications running in the background, such as a virus checker, software updaters or backup software, might be using memory resources, or you simply might need to consider upgrading your computer's memory to perform the kinds of tasks you want to perform.

Under the CPU Utilization graph are statistics related to the total number of handles, threads, and processes, as well as total up time of the computer since it was last started. In the example, the computer is quite active, with 74,408 open handles, 2133 active threads, and 138 running processes. Of particular note are the details regarding the CPU. If you ever have a question about the CPU configured, this is where you look. The details tell you:

- The maximum processor speed, which is 3.20 GHz in this instance.
- The Sockets value tells you the number of physical processors. This computer has 1.
- The Cores value tells you how many processor cores the computer has. This computer has 4.

- The Logical Processors value tells you how many logical processors the computer has (which isn't necessarily the same as the number of cores). This computer has 4.
- The Virtualization value specifies whether virtualization is enabled, which it is on this computer.
- The L1, L2, and L3 values specify the size of each memory cache, which are integrated into the processor.

> **Pro Tip** You can show kernel usage by clicking Show Kernel Times on the View menu. Tracking kernel CPU usage can help you better understand how the operating system is using the CPU. Usage by the kernel is plotted in a different color and reflects total usage.

Select Memory in the left pane to view statistics related to memory usage. As shown in Figure 7-6, usage statistics include:

- **In Use**   Displays the amount of memory currently being used.
- **Committed**   Displays physical memory in use for which space has been reserved in the paging file, followed by the commit limit, which is determined by the size of the paging file.
- **Cached**   Displays the amount of memory marked as "in use" for system caching. This essentially is the amount of memory currently reserved for when a process needs it.
- **Available**   Displays the amount of RAM available for use by processes.
- **Paged Pool**   Shows the amount of non-critical kernel memory that is paged to virtual memory.
- **Non-paged Pool**   Shows the amount of critical kernel memory that is resident in physical memory.

> **Note** Critical portions of kernel memory used by the operating system must operate in physical RAM and can't be paged to virtual memory. The rest of kernel memory can be paged to virtual memory.

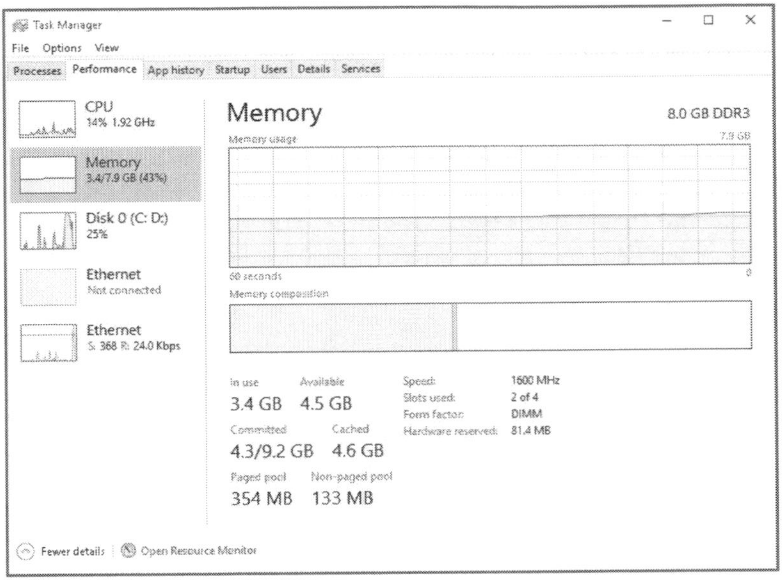

Figure 7-6 Tracking processor and memory usage under high usage conditions

Of particular note is the Committed value. Here the committed value is shown in gigabytes (GB), but it could also be shown in MB.

The Commit value shows the virtual memory currently in use followed by the total amount of virtual memory available. This is important because virtual memory is memory stored on disk in one or more paging files. If the current page file usage, reflected by current virtual memory usage, is consistently close to the maximum value, you might want to add physical memory, increase the amount of virtual memory, or both.

The Memory panel can also answer your questions about the exact type of memory your computer has and whether you can add more memory. In the example, the computer has 8.0 GB of DDR3 memory configured. That memory operates at a speed of 1600 MHz. As only 2 of 4 available memory slots are used, you could add memory using the 2 remaining slots. You would add memory using two 1600 MHz DDR3 DIMMs.

Event Logging and Viewing

Windows 10 stores warnings, errors, and other information generated for tracking purposes in the event logs. There are two general types of event logs. Windows logs are a type of log file that the operating system uses to record general system events related to applications, security, setup, and system components. Applications and services logs are a type of log file that specific applications and services use to record application-specific or service-specific events.

Digging into the Event Logs

Event logs use a proprietary format that is readable only in the Event Viewer utility, which can be accessed by typing **Event Viewer** in the Search box, and pressing Enter. As long as you have administrator privileges on your computer, you can access the event logs and use them to track system health and system security issues.

The Windows logs that you should track closely are:

* **Application**   Records events logged by applications, such as an error that results in a system fault

- **Security**   Records events configured for auditing, including user logon and logoff
- **Setup**   Records events logged by the operating system during setup, as well as whenever the installed state of components change, such as when you apply a patch or service pack to the operating system
- **System**   Records events logged by the operating system, its services, and its components—especially state changes and failures to load or start

If you are experiencing a problem with a specific application or service, you can check for a related applications and services log. For example, you can use the Windows PowerShell log to help you resolve issues related to Windows PowerShell, or you can use the Microsoft\Windows\Audio\Operational log to examine issues related to the Windows Audio service.

In Event Viewer, you can work with your computer's event logs in the following ways:

- To view all errors and warnings for all logs, expand Custom Views and then select Administrative Events. The main page displays a list of all warning and error events for the server.
- To view events in a specific log, expand the Windows Logs node, the Applications And Services Logs node, or both. Select the log you want to view, such as Application.

While you are working with a particular event log, use the information in the Source column to determine which component logged a particular event. In the example shown in Figure 7-7, the computer's DNS client is the source of the event.

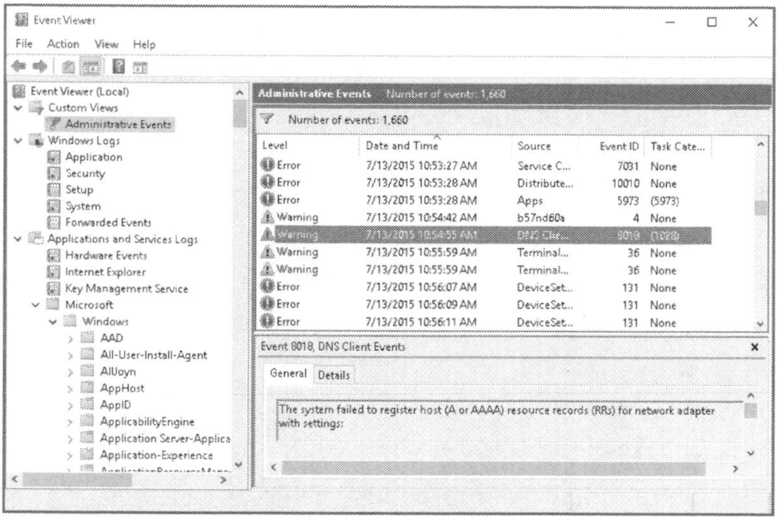

Figure 7-7 Examining events in the Event Viewer

The logged details for an event provide a quick overview of when, where, and how an event occurred. The event level tells you the seriousness of the event. An informational event is usually related to a successful action. A warning event tells you about a less serious (and often only temporarily) problem that occurred, such as an error detected on a disk device during paging. An error event tells you about a more serious but noncritical problem that occurred, such as a write failure to a disk device. A critical event tells you about a serious problem for which there is no recovery.

Resolving Performance Issues with the Logs

You'll frequently see warnings and errors, and you don't need to try to determine the cause and resolution for each and every one. However, if your computer is experiencing performance issues or other problems, you should look for warnings and errors that could possibly be related to the problem, because they can help you find a resolution to the problem. Be sure to review the detailed event information as part of your troubleshooting. Click the Event Log Online Help link if you think you need more information.

If you spend just a few minutes in the event logs, you'll see just how much information your computer tracks. Wading through all that information to find what you're looking for isn't always easy, so you may need to filter the event logs to focus in on the specific information you need.

Earlier I mentioned that when you select the Administrative Events node, you see a list of all errors and warnings for all logs. That selective view of the event logs is created using a filter, and you can create your own filters to help sort through the logs by following these steps:

1. Start Event Viewer by typing **Event Viewer** in the Search box, and then pressing Enter.

2. In the left pane, right-click the Custom Views node, and then click Create Custom View.

3. Use the Logged drop-down list to select a timeframe for logging events, such as the Last 24 Hours, Last 7 Days, or Last 30 Days.

4. Use the Event Level check boxes to specify the level of events to include. Usually, you'll want to look for Critical, Warning, and Error events. Select Verbose to get additional details.

5. Create a custom view for either a specific set of logs or a specific set of event sources by doing one of the following:

■ Use the Event Logs drop-down list to select event logs to include. Select multiple event logs by selecting their check boxes. If you select specific event logs, all other event logs are excluded.

- Use the Event Sources drop-down list to select event sources to include. Select multiple event sources by selecting their check boxes. If you select specific event sources, all other event sources are excluded.

6. Optionally, use the User box to specify users that should be included.

Real World Many events are logged with the user listed as N/A, for not applicable. Events directly related to your logon and interactions with active applications may be logged with your user name, but not always. Other events may be logged with the user as System (the local system account used for running system processes and handling system-level tasks), Local Service (the local service account, which has fewer privileges than system), or Network Service (the local network service account, which has fewer privileges than system but also has access to network resources).

---

7. Click OK. Type a name and description for the custom view, and then specify where to save the custom view. By default, custom views are saved under the Custom Views node. You can create a new node by clicking New Folder, entering a name for the folder, and then clicking OK.

8. Click OK to close the Save Filter To Custom View dialog box. You should now see a filtered list of events.

Chapter 8. Analyzing and Logging Performance

Windows 10 provides many tools to help you track performance. The previous chapter discussed ways you could track current and relative performance and provided techniques for determining resource usage using Task Manager and uncovering problems using the Event Logs. Although these tools are excellent, you might need to dig deeper to diagnose complex problems and optimize performance.

Additional tools for resolving performance issues include:

- **Action Center**   Allows you to check for problems that are affecting performance and try to find solutions using automated processes.
- **Reliability Monitor**   Allows you to analyze reliability issues that are affecting performance and determine their causes.
- **Resource Monitor**   Allows you to track resource usage on the computer. The information provided is similar to Task Manager but more detailed.
- **Performance Monitor**   Allows you to log performance data, watch resource usage over time, and determine areas that can be optimized.

Resolving Failures and Reliability Issues

Windows 10 includes an automated diagnostics framework for detecting and diagnosing many common problems with applications, hardware devices, and Windows itself. Restart Manager and Action

Center are the core components of this framework that you'll interact with.

Windows 10 uses Restart Manager to shut down and restart applications automatically. If Windows diagnostics detects that an application has stopped responding, Restart Manager attempts to stop the application's primary process and then restart the application. Problem reports related to nonresponsive applications are logged in the Action Center, as are problem reports for other types of failures.

Checking for Problems That Are Affecting Performance

After you install a device, Windows 10 attempts to detect the hardware and install the device automatically. If Windows 10 detects the device but cannot install the device automatically, you may find a related solution in Action Center. Typically, Action Center opens automatically, allowing you to begin troubleshooting immediately.

Similarly, if Windows diagnostics detects a problem with a hardware device or Windows component, Windows 10 displays a notification telling you there is a problem. If you click this notification, Windows 10 displays more information, including possible fixes that can help you resolve the problem.

On the far-right side of the taskbar, you'll find the notification area, which also has a notification icon for Action Center. If you move your mouse pointer over the Action Center icon, a tooltip provides information about current notifications. Clicking this icon opens the Action Center notification panel (see Figure 8-1).

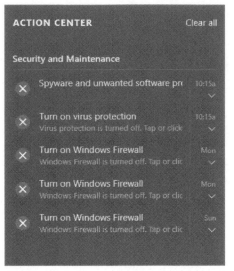

Figure 8-1 Examining notifications in Action Center

In Action Center, you'll see notifications under one or two general categories, with the most common category being Security And Maintenance. Each notification has an Expand/Collapse button and a Close button. Click Expand to get more details, if available. Click Close to clear the notification.

Action Center notification settings control whether you are notified about problems. To stop being notified about problems with a particular app, right-click a related notification in Action Center and then select Turn Off Notifications For This App.

Although Action Center provides insights into possible issues, you really need to open Control Panel and access the Security And Maintenance page, shown in Figure 8-2, to learn more about detected issues. Open this page by typing **Security And Maintenance** in the Search box and pressing Enter.

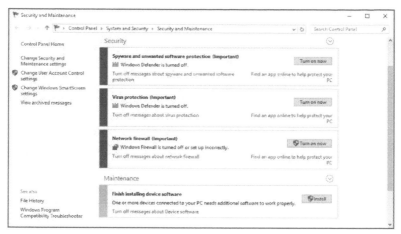

Figure 8-2 Getting information about detected issues with solutions

While working with the Security And Maintenance page in Control Panel, you can click the Security or Maintenance heading to expand the section and view more detailed information. Expand the Security area to get more information about the status and configuration of your computer's core security components. Known problems are color-coded. Red-coded issues are warnings about important problems that need your attention. Orange-coded issues are cautions about problems that you might want to review.

Notification settings control whether you are notified about problems. To view and manage these settings, click Change Security And Maintenance Settings in the left pane. Then turn notifications for messages on or off by selecting or clearing check boxes.

While automated reported and detection works fairly well, some problems can be missed by the diagnostics framework. If you suspect that your computer has problems that hasn't been identified, you can initiate automatic problem detection simply by opening Security And

Maintenance, expanding the Maintenance panel, and then clicking Check For Solutions. When this process is complete, your computer is updated to include all newly discovered problems, and solutions are provided if known.

If automated diagnostics detects problems for which there are no solutions available, you'll see the Problem Reporting dialog box and be able to send a problem report. Click Cancel if you don't want to send a report.

If automated diagnostics detects problems for which solutions are available, you can resolve the problems immediately. Each known problem will have a solution button. Click the View Problem Response button to display a page providing more information about the problem. Note the following:

* When a configuration issue is causing a problem, you'll find a description of the problem and a step-by-step guide for modifying the configuration to resolve the problem.
* When a driver or software issue is causing a problem, you'll find a link to download and install the latest driver or software update.

Analyzing Reliability Issues That Are Affecting Performance

Windows 10 tracks the relative reliability of your computer in Reliability Monitor. You can use the related reports to determine how stable your computer is and what components, applications, or devices have caused problems. When you are working with the Security And Maintenance page in Control Panel, you can access reliability reports by expanding the Maintenance panel, scrolling down, and then clicking View Reliability History.

Reliability Monitor tracks changes to the computer and compares them to changes in system stability. This gives you a graphical representation of the relationship between changes in the configuration and changes in stability. By recording software installation, software removal, application failures, hardware failures, and Windows failures, and key events regarding the configuration of your computer, Reliability Monitors gives you a timeline of changes large and small and information about their effect on reliability. You can use this information to pinpoint changes that are causing stability problems. For example, if you see a sudden drop in stability, you can click a data point and then expand the related data set to find the specific event that caused the problem.

Reliability Monitor displays stability data by days or weeks. The default view is days. To view history by weeks, click the Weeks option for View By.

Your computer's stability is graphed with values ranging from 1, meaning extremely poor reliability, to 10, meaning extremely high reliability. A graph for a computer experiencing reliability problems will be similar to the one shown in Figure 8-3.

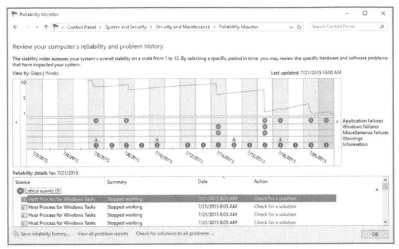

Figure 8-3 Checking your computer's reliability

> **Note**   The graph has left and right scroll buttons. By
> scrolling left, you can see reliability data for earlier dates. You
> can scroll right to go to later dates.

In this example, the reliability of the computer has been severely
impacted by a series of failures. Failures and other reliability events
are summarized on the graph relative to the selected time period,
either by day or by week. Failures are divided into three categories:

- **Application Failures**   Tracks failures caused by running
  applications. An application that stopped working or stopped
  responding is tracked as an application failure.
- **Windows Failures**   Tracks failures caused by Windows
  components and system hardware. A hardware error that
  occurred is tracked as a Windows failure, as are errors related to
  component configuration.

- **Miscellaneous Failures** Tracks other types of failures that occur, such as failures caused by an unexpected shutdown of the operating system.

Reliability Monitor tags failures that have affected stability as critical. Events tagged as warnings indicate a potential to affect stability. For example, failed Windows Updates are marked as warnings because most updates need to be applied to ensure reliability and stability.

You'll also see that successful Windows updates, successful application installations, and many other system activities are logged using informational events. Although these activities don't represent failures, they do have an effect on the overall stability of your computer.

Clicking a column in the graph displays details for the events that occurred on that day or during a selected week. Events are listed by source, summary, and date. Under Action, you'll see several possible actions, depending on the type of event.

If Windows detected a critical problem and resolved it automatically, a View Problem Response link allows you to display information about how Windows resolved the problem. If the critical problem is unresolved, a Check For A Solution link lets you report the problem and check for a solution. For warnings and informational events, a View Technical Details link provides detailed technical information about the event.

The bottom panel of Reliability Monitor provides three additional options. You can:

- Click Save Reliability History and use the dialog box provided to select a save location and file name for a Reliability Monitor report. The report will contain complete details about the computer's stability, formatted using XML. You can view the report at any time in Internet Explorer by double-clicking the file. If you attach a report to an email message, you can send the report to someone who can help you with troubleshooting.

- Click View All Problem Reports to open the Problem Reports window and access a history of all identified problems and their status. Most problems have a status of Report Sent, Not Reported, More Data Required, or No Solution Available. To clear the history, click Clear All Problem Reports.

- Click Check For Solutions To All Problems to start automated diagnostics. When diagnostic testing is complete, Action Center shows any newly discovered problems and also provides solutions if known.

When you view all problem reports, the Problem Reports page in Control Panel, shown in Figure 8-4, lists problems that you can report by source, summary, date, and status. The status shows whether the problem has or has not been sent. The status also shows when Microsoft needs more information from the general user community to resolve a problem, as well as when there is no solution available for a particular problem.

> **Real World** Although it may seem rather odd that Windows lists problems as having no solution available, remember how diagnostics works. Diagnostics looks for specific types of Windows, application, and hardware failures. Some problems can be solved with updates and patches.

Others, such as compatibility issues, may simply be a result of the way in which an application was written. Also remember that if a solution is available for a problem, the solution is shown in Action Center.

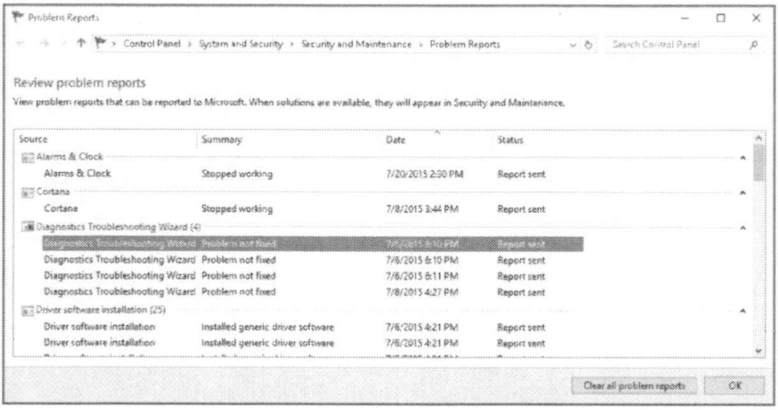

Figure 8-4 Checking all problems that have been detected

Regardless of the problem status, you can do something in Problem Reports that you can't always do in Reliability Monitor: You can right-click a problem and choose Check For Solution to re-check for a solution to a problem. You also can right-click a problem and choose View Solution to get more information about a problem that's been resolved or View Technical Details to get technical details about a problem.

Tip It's important to point out that only problems with solutions are shown on the Security And Maintenance page. If you want to see a complete list of all problems your computer has encountered with apps, devices, driver installation and more, you need to review the All Problem Reports page in Control Panel. Although Reliability Monitor provides a link to open this page, you also can open this page by typing **All Problem Reports** in the Search box and pressing Enter.

Diagnosing and Resolving Problems with Troubleshooters

Windows 10 tracks failed installation, unresponsive conditions, and other problems. Should an installation fail or an application become unresponsive, the built-in diagnostics creates notifications and problem reports and either provides a ready solution or allows you to check for a solution. Many other automated responses to problems are handled with troubleshooters.

The standard troubleshooters include:

- **Hardware And Devices troubleshooter**   Detects and resolves problems preventing the computer from properly using a device.
- **Homegroup troubleshooter**   Detects and resolves problems preventing the computer from sharing files in a homegroup.
- **Incoming Connections troubleshooter**   Detects and resolves problems preventing the computer from being connected to.
- **Internet Connections troubleshooter**   Detects and resolves problems preventing the computer from connecting to the Internet or an intranet.
- **Network Adapter troubleshooter**   Detects and resolves problems related to Ethernet, wireless, and other network adapters.
- **Playing Audio troubleshooter**   Detects and resolves problems preventing the computer from playing sound.
- **Power troubleshooter**   Detects and resolves problems that affect power management, sleep, hibernation, or resume.

- **Printer troubleshooter**   Detects and resolves problems preventing the computer from using a printer.
- **Program Compatibility troubleshooter**   Detects and resolves problems preventing a program from running on the computer.
- **Recording Audio troubleshooter**   Detects and resolves problems preventing the computer from recording sound.
- **System Maintenance troubleshooter**   Performs routine maintenance if you don't.

If Windows PowerShell is installed, related services are running, and troubleshooting is enabled, the troubleshooters can automatically detect and diagnose many common problems. If you suspect a problem that hasn't been detected, you can start a troubleshooter manually by following these steps:

1. If you are working with the Security And Maintenance page in Control Panel, scroll down, and then click the Troubleshooting link. Alternatively, type **Troubleshooting** in the Search box and press Enter.

2. As shown in Figure 8-5, links on the Troubleshooting page provide access to troubleshooters according to tasks you might want to perform. For example, you could click Run Programs Made For Previous Versions Of Windows to start the Program Compatibility troubleshooter.

3. If you don't see an appropriate task, click View All in the left pane to display a list of all available troubleshooters by name, and then click the troubleshooter you want to start.

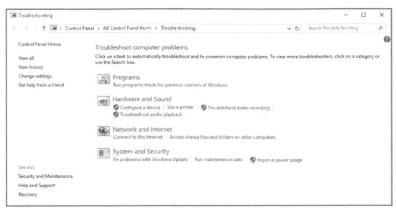

Figure 8-5 Resolving problems with the troubleshooters

When you are working with the Troubleshooting page, note the View All, View History, and Change Settings options in the left pane. Selecting View All shows all available troubleshooters, listed alphabetically by name, description, location, category, and publisher. When a troubleshooter is listed as Local, the troubleshooter is available on your computer. When a troubleshooter is listed as Online, the troubleshooter is available online and will be downloaded and run each time you use it.

While you are working with the Troubleshooting page, don't overlook the View History option. The troubleshooting history shows you the troubleshooters run under your user account and when they were run. Click Include Troubleshooters That Were Run As An Administrator to view troubleshooters run with administrator privileges. More importantly, if you click an entry in the history, you can view and print a detailed troubleshooting report. The report shows the issues found and the fixes Windows tried, which can be as helpful as the troubleshooters themselves.

The Change Settings option on the Troubleshooting page is also useful, because it allows you to manage how troubleshooters are used. By default, Windows checks for routine maintenance issues and alerts you when a troubleshooter can help fix a problem. Windows also allows you and other users to browse for available troubleshooters online and begins troubleshooting immediately when you start a troubleshooter.

Problems with hardware devices can be particularly difficult to resolve. If you suspect that a device isn't working properly, you can use Device Manager to verify whether the device is working properly. Start Device Manager by typing **Device Manager** in the Search box, and then pressing Enter; then examine the status of your computer's devices.

A device that is malfunctioning will have an error or warning icon. To view information about the error, right-click the device and then select Properties. For malfunctioning devices, the device properties will show an error status code and a suggested resolution for the code.

You can resolve many hardware device problems by reinstalling or updating the device driver. In Device Manager, right-click the device you want to work with, and then select Properties. On the Driver tab, click the Update Driver button and follow the prompts to reinstall or update the driver as appropriate.

You can also uninstall a driver and let Windows 10 reinstall the current version of the driver files from the driver store. In Device Manager, right-click the device, and then select Uninstall on the Driver tab. Click OK to confirm. If reinstalling the device driver doesn't work, check to make sure the device is properly inserted and connected. You may need to disconnect and reconnect the device (while ensuring that the computer is powered down and unplugged as appropriate and necessary).

If you are still unable to get the device to work properly, check the device manufacturer's website for alternative versions of the device driver. You may find that an older version of a device driver is more stable than the latest version.

Examining Resource Usage in Detail

Resource Monitor should be one of your tools of choice for performance tuning. You use Resource Monitor to track resource usage on the computer. The information provided is similar to Task Manager but more detailed.

You can open Resource Monitor by typing **Resource Monitor** in the Search box, and then pressing Enter. As Figure 8-6 shows, Resource Monitor provides resources usage statistics for four categories:

- **CPU** Shows the current CPU utilization and the maximum CPU frequency (as related to processor idling). If you expand the CPU entry (by clicking the options button), you'll see a list of currently running executables by name, process ID (PID), description, status, number of threads used, current CPU utilization, and average CPU utilization.
- **Disk** Shows the number of kilobytes per second being read from or written to disk and the highest percentage of usage. If you expand the Disk entry (by clicking the options button), you'll see a list of currently running executables that are performing or have performed I/O operations by name, process

ID (PID), file being read or written, average number of bytes being read per second, average number of bytes being written per second, total number of bytes being read and written per second, I/O priority, and the associated disk response time.

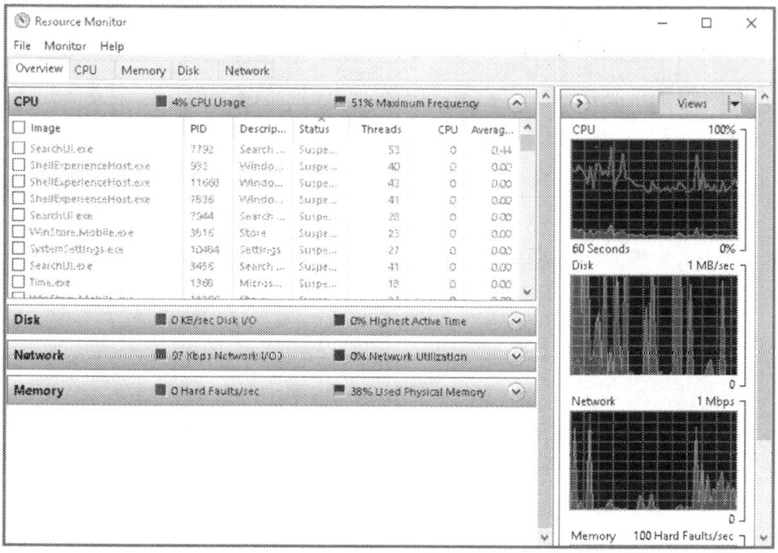

Figure 8-6 Tracking resource usage details

- **Network**   Shows the current network bandwidth utilization in kilobytes and the percentage of total bandwidth utilization. If you expand the Network entry (by clicking the options button), you'll see a list of currently running executables that are transferring or have transferred data on the network by name, process ID (PID), computer or IP address being contacted, average number of bytes being sent per second, average number of bytes received per second, and total bytes sent or received per second.

- **Memory**   Shows the current memory utilization and the number of hard faults occurring per second. If you expand the Memory entry (by clicking the options button), you'll see a list of currently running executables by name, process ID (PID), hard faults per second, commit memory in KB, working set memory in KB, shareable memory in KB, and private (nonshareable) memory in KB.

The Overview tab displays a general overview of all resource data for each of the four areas tracked. Expand the panels to see more details, or select the individual tabs to take a closer look at specific usage.

One of the most useful features of Resource Monitor is the usage filter. On the Overview tab, you can filter by any combination of processes running on the computer simply by selecting the related check boxes on the CPU panel. In the example shown in Figure 8-7, the data is filtered to focus on resource usage related to a specific application: Winword.exe. I've also added resource usage data for System processes.

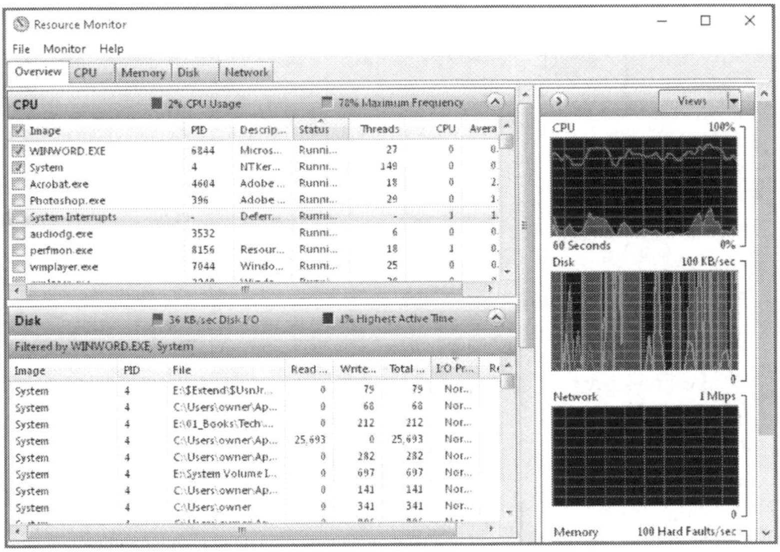

Figure 8-7 Getting more detailed information

After you've filtered the usage activity, the graphs highlight resource usage specific to the processes you've selected. As disk usage, network usage, and memory usage data are similarly filtered, you can see exactly what the selected processes are doing on your computer.

You can apply filters on the CPU, Memory, Disk, and Network tabs as well. The filters are global and affect what you see on all other tabs. Because of this, don't forget to remove filters you've applied if you want to examine other processes or view overall usage data again. To do this, simply clear the process check boxes that apply the filters.

Recording and Analyzing Performance Data

You need to record performance data and analyze it to know what's really happening on your computer. Logging performance data isn't something you should do haphazardly. You should have a clear plan before you begin, and that plan should define specifically why you want to log performance data. For example, you might think that an application you are using has a memory leak that is causing your computer to perform poorly, and you could prove this by logging memory usage data while working with the application.

Logging Performance Data

Although Resource Monitor and Task Manager tell you what's happening on your computer, they don't delve deep enough to help you resolve every performance problem you'll encounter—this is where Performance Monitor is useful.

Performance Monitor, shown in Figure 8-8, graphs usage statistics for sets of performance parameters that you've selected for display. Open this utility by typing **Performance Monitor** in the Search box, and then pressing Enter.

Performance parameters that you track are referred to as counters. When you install certain applications on your computer, Performance Monitor might be updated with a set of counters for tracking related performance. Similarly, performance counters may be added when you install certain services and add-ons for Windows.

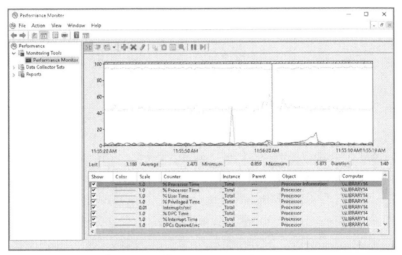

Figure 8-8 Analyzing performance metrics

Performance Monitor has several key features. A legend, displayed at the bottom of the details pane, shows the color and line style used for each counter. A value bar, displayed between the graph and the legend, shows values related to the counter you've selected in the graph or in the legend. A toolbar, displayed above the graph, provides the basic functions and options for working with Performance Monitor. Each toolbar button has a keyboard shortcut as well.

The toolbar buttons and their shortcut keys are as follows:

- **View Current Activity** CTRL+T; switches the view so that current activity being logged is displayed.
- **View Log Data** CTRL+L; switches the view so that data from a performance log can be replayed.
- **Change Graph Type** CTRL+G; switches the view to toggle between bar graph, report list, and graph format.
- **Add** CTRL+N; displays the Add Counters dialog box, which lets you add counters to track.
- **Delete** DELETE key; removes the currently selected counter so that it is no longer tracked.
- **Highlight** CTRL+H; highlights the currently selected counter with a white line so that it is more easy to see. To turn the Highlight function off, select the counter and press CTRL+H again.
- **Copy Properties** CTRL+C; creates a copy of the counter list, along with the individual configuration of each counter, and puts it on the Windows Clipboard as an Extensible Markup Language (XML) file.
- **Paste Counter List** CTRL+V; pastes a copied counter list into Performance Monitor so that it is used as the current counter set. If you saved a counter list to a file, you simply open the file, copy the contents of the file to the Clipboard, and then press CTRL+V in Performance Monitor to use that counter list.
- **Properties** CTRL+Q; displays the Properties dialog box for a select item.
- **Freeze Display** CTRL+F; freezes the display so that Performance Monitor no longer updates the performance information. Press CTRL+F again to resume sampling.

- **Update Data** CTRL+U; updates the display by one sampling interval. When you freeze the display, Performance Monitor still gathers performance information; it just doesn't update the display using the new information. To update the display while it is frozen, use this option.

The graphing update interval is configurable, but it is set to 1 second by default. Because you'll often need to track many counters to identify a performance problem, you'll find that recording the performance data in a log and then analyzing the log data is typically the best approach. Performance Monitor also allows you to configure alerts that send messages when certain events occur.

To work effectively with Performance Monitor, you need to understand the difference between performance counters and performance objects. Performance counters represent the measurable properties of performance objects. A performance object can be a physical part of the operating system, such as the memory, the processor, or the paging file; a logical component, such as a logical disk or print queue; or a software element, such as a process or a thread.

Performance object instances represent single occurrences of performance objects. If a particular object has multiple instances, such as when a computer has multiple processors, you can use an object instance to track a specific occurrence of that object. You could also elect to track all instances of an object, such as when you want to monitor all processors on your computer.

The most common performance objects you'll want to monitor include:

- **Cache**   Represents the file system cache, which is an area of physical memory that indicates application I/O activity.
- **LogicalDisk**   Represents the logical volumes on your computer.
- **Memory**   Represents memory performance for system cache (including pooled, paged memory and pooled, nonpaged memory), physical memory, and virtual memory.
- **Network Interface**   Represents the network adapters configured on your computer.
- **Objects**   Represents the number of events, processes, sections, semaphores, and threads on your computer.
- **Paging File**   Represents page file current and peak usage.
- **PhysicalDisk**   Represents hard disk read/write activity as well as data transfers, hard faults, and soft faults.
- **Print Queue**   Represents print jobs, spooling, and print queue activity.
- **Process**   Represents all processes running on your computer.
- **Processor**   Represents processor idle time, idle states, usage, deferred procedure calls, and interrupts.
- **System**   Represents system-level counters, including processes, threads, context switching of threads, file system control operations, system calls, and system uptime.
- **Thread**   Represents all running threads and allows you to examine usage statistics for individual threads by process ID.

Each of these performance objects has a set of counters that can be tracked.

Choosing Counters to Monitor

Performance Monitor displays information only for counters that you're tracking. You'll find counters related to just about every logical and physical aspect of your computer. The easiest way to learn about these counters is to read the explanations available when you select a counter. To do this, start Performance Monitor, click Add on the toolbar, expand an object in the Available Counters list, and then select the Show Description check box. Now when you scroll through the list of counters for the selected object you'll see a detailed description of what the counter represents and how it can be used.

When you are configuring monitoring for a particular object, pay particular attention to the instances of that object that will be tracked. You can configure tracking for all instances of an object or for specific instances. For example, when you track the Physical Disk object, you have a choice of tracking all physical disk instances or specific physical disk instances. If you think a particular disk is going bad or experiencing other problems, you could monitor just that disk instance.

The two special instance types you should know are:

- **_Total**   Tracks all instances of a counter in total, rather than separately. Use _Total to track the overall performance of all instances of a related counter. For example, if your computer has four processor cores, you could track their processor usage in total rather than separately for each processor core.
- **<All Instances>**   Tracks all instances of a counter separately, rather than in total. Use <All Instances> to track all instances of a related counter separately. For example, if your computer has

four processor cores, you could track processor usage individually for all processor instances.

Performance Monitor allows you to view performance data as graphed current data, line data, histogram data, and report data. By clicking View Current Activity on the toolbar or pressing Ctrl+T, you can be sure you are viewing a graph of current activity. You can switch between the view types by clicking Change Graph Type or pressing Ctrl+G.

In the Histogram Bar view, Performance Monitor represents the performance data by using a bar graph with the last sampling value for each counter graphed. The sizes of the bars within the graph are adjusted automatically based on the number of performance counters being tracked and can be adjusted to accommodate hundreds of counters, which is useful because it allows you to track multiple counters more easily than other views.

In the Report view, Performance Monitor represents the performance data in a report list format. In this view, objects and their counters are listed in alphabetical order and performance data is displayed numerically rather than graphed. If you are trying to determine specific performance values for many different counters, this is the best view to use because the actual values are always shown.

You can select counters to monitor by following these steps:

1. Click Add on the toolbar or press Ctrl+N to display the Add Counters dialog box (see Figure 8-9). Note that only administrators of the local computer and members of the local Performance Log users group can monitor performance data.

2. In the Available Counters section, performance objects are listed alphabetically. Click an object entry to select all related counters, or expand an object entry and then select individual counters by clicking them.

3. When you select an object or any of its counters, you see the related instances. Choose _Total to track all instances of a counter in total or <All Instances> to track all instances of a counter separately.

4. After you've selected an object or a group of counters for an object as well as the object instances, click Add to add the counters to the graph.

5. Repeat steps 2–3 to add other performance parameters. Click OK when you have finished and are ready to start graphing performance.

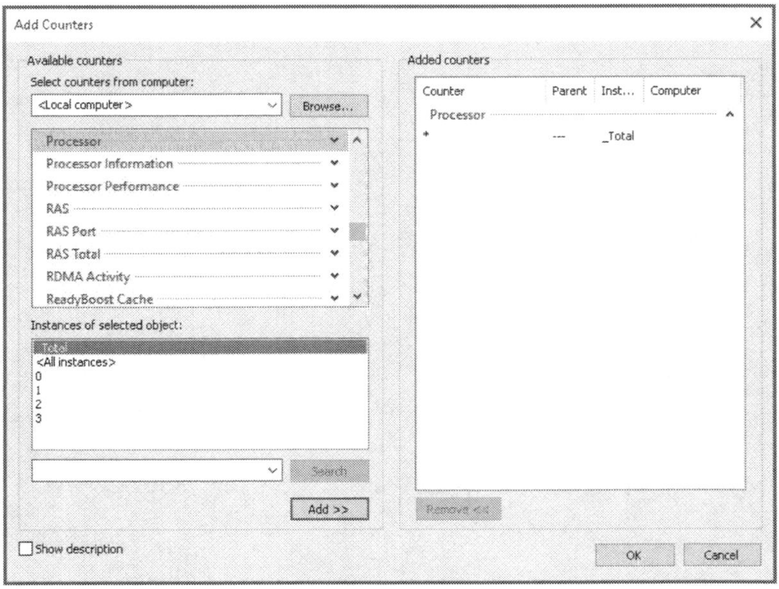

Figure 8-9 Adding counters to track

> **Tip** Don't try to graph too many counters or counter instances at once. You'll make the display too difficult to read, and you'll use system resources.

Identifying Performance Bottlenecks

The way your computer performs depends primarily on its memory configuration, its processors, its hard disks, and its networking components, each of which can act as a bottleneck that keeps your computer from performing at its best.

Your computer's memory is often the source of the biggest performance issues, and you should always rule out memory problems before examining other areas of the system. Because computers use both physical and virtual memory, look specifically at physical memory, caching, and virtual memory. Virtual memory is paged to disk and represented by the paging file. Look specifically at:

* Memory\Available Bytes
* Memory\Committed Bytes
* Memory\Commit Limit

If your computer has very little available memory, you might need to add memory. Generally, you want the available memory under normal usage conditions to be no less than 5 percent of the total physical memory on the computer. If your computer has a high ratio of committed bytes to total physical memory on the system, you might need to add memory as well. Generally, you want the committed bytes value to be no more than 75 percent of the total physical memory.

You should also look at memory page faults. To do this, track:

- Memory\Page Faults/sec
- Memory\Pages Input/sec
- Memory\Page Reads/sec

A page fault occurs when a process requests a page in memory and the operating system can't find it at the requested location. If the requested page is elsewhere in memory, the fault is called a soft page fault. If the requested page must be retrieved from disk, the fault is called a hard page fault. Most processors can handle large numbers of soft faults, but hard faults can cause performance problems.

Page Faults/sec is the overall rate at which the processor handles all types of page faults. Pages Input/sec is the total number of pages read from disk to resolve hard page faults. Page Reads/sec is the total disk reads needed to resolve hard page faults. Pages Input/sec will be greater than or equal to Page Reads/sec and can give you a good idea of your hard page fault rate. A high number of hard page faults could indicate that you need to increase the amount of memory or reduce the cache size on the computer.

For deeper problems, take a look at the page pool and the nonpaged pool by using Memory\Pool Paged Bytes and Memory\Pool Nonpaged Bytes. The paged pool is an area of system memory for objects that can be written to disk when they aren't used. The nonpaged pool is an area of system memory for objects that can't be written to disk.

If the size of the paged pool is large relative to the total amount of physical memory, you might need to add memory to your computer.

If the size of the nonpaged pool is large relative to the total amount of virtual memory allocated, you might want to increase the virtual memory size.

Focus on your computer's processor after you have eliminated memory as a potential bottleneck source. If the computer's processors are the performance bottleneck, adding memory or faster drives won't resolve your performance problem. Instead, you might need to upgrade the processors to faster clock speeds or add processors. Look specifically at:

* System\Processor Queue Length
* Processor\% Processor Time

System\Processor Queue Length tracks the number of threads waiting to be executed. These threads are queued in an area shared by all processors. Generally, you want very few queued threads per processor. Otherwise, you may need to upgrade or add processors.

Processor\% Processor Time tracks the percentage of time a processor is executing a nonidle thread. If the % Processor Time values are high and the network interface and disk I/O throughput rates are relatively low, you may need to upgrade or add processors.

Your computer's hard disks and networking components may be causes of bottlenecks as well. Accessing memory is much faster than reading from disk or retrieving data over a network. If your computer has to do a lot of reads and writes, whether to disk or over the network, its overall performance can be degraded. To reduce the amount of disk activity, you want the computer to manage memory very efficiently and page to disk only when necessary. See "Fine-Tuning Virtual Memory" in Chapter 9 for details.

If you've fine-tuned virtual memory and are still having problems, you may want to track counters related to disk I/O activity. Specifically, you should monitor:

- PhysicalDisk\% Disk Time
- PhysicalDisk\Disk Writes/sec,
- PhysicalDisk\Disk Reads/sec
- PhysicalDisk\CurrentDisk Queue Length

PhysicalDisk\% Disk Time gives you a good picture of overall drive performance. Be sure to monitor % Disk Time for all hard disk drives on the computer, and use this counter in conjunction with Processor\% Processor Time and Network Interface Connection\Bytes Total/sec. If the % Disk Time value is high and the processor and network connection values aren't high, your computer's disk drives might be the source of a performance bottleneck.

The number of reads and writes per second reveals how much disk I/O activity there is. The disk queue length indicates the number of read or write requests that are waiting to be processed. Generally, you want very few waiting requests.

Although memory, processors, and hard disks have the biggest actual impact on performance, your perception about the speed and performance of your computer may be tied directly to its networking components. If your computer is still using a dial-up modem to connect to the Internet, your connection will be slow and transferring data will be painfully slow. Wireless connections can also seem very slow, especially if your network hasn't been upgraded to the latest and greatest high-speed wireless technologies.

Network latency can affect your experience. A long delay, or high degree of latency, between when a request is made and the time it's received can make your computer seem very slow. You can't do much about latency. It's a function of the type of connection and the route the request takes to your computer. On the other hand, the total capacity of your computer to handle requests and the amount of bandwidth available are factors you can control.

The capacity of your network card can be a limiting factor. Older computers may use 10/100 network cards instead of newer 100/1000 network cards. Someone might have configured a 100/1000 card for 100 Mbps, or the card might be configured for half duplex instead of full duplex. If you suspect a capacity problem with a network card, you should always check its configuration.

You can determine the throughput and current activity on your computer's network cards by using the following counters:

- Network Interface\Bytes Received/sec
- Network Interface\Bytes Sent/sec
- Network Interface\Bytes Total/sec
- Network Interface\Current Bandwidth

Compare these values in conjunction with PhysicalDisk\% Disk Time and Processor\% Processor Time. If the disk time and processor time values are low but the network values are very high, you might have a capacity problem. Solve the problem by optimizing the network card settings or by adding a network card. Remember that the hubs and routers on your network can also limit the networking speed. If your network card is 1 Gbps and you want to operate at this speed, your network hubs and routers must support 1 Gbps.

Chapter 9. Optimizing Performance Tips and Techniques

No discussion on optimizing Windows 10 is complete without a few final tips and techniques for boosting overall performance—and that's exactly what you'll find in this chapter. As you set out to use these tips and techniques, remember that your computer's performance is in your control. You'll need to fine-tune settings occasionally to keep things running smoothly. You'll need to perform maintenance as necessary. And you'll need to operate your computer while keeping in mind its relative performance ratings.

Optimizing Power Management Settings for Performance

Regardless of what type of device you have, don't overlook the impact of power settings on your computer's performance. Power management settings are designed to save energy, but there is a direct tradeoff between power savings and performance. I covered the basic options for turning off the screen and entering sleep mode in "Configuring When the Screen Turns Off" in Chapter 3. Now let's look at how can use power plans and optimize advanced power settings for the way you work.

Selecting and Using Power Plans

You use the Power Options page in Control Panel to manage your computer's power plans. Power plans are collections of power management settings that control power usage and consumption. A computer can have multiple power plans, but only one can be active at any particular time.

> **Note** You need administrative privileges to manage power plans and other advanced power options. Because of this, you may find the related settings are dimmed and cannot be set unless you click the Change Settings That Are Currently Unavailable link.

Open the Power Options page by typing **Power Options** in the Search box, and then pressing Enter. Specify the power plan to use by click it in the Preferred Plans list. As shown in Figure 9-1, most computers have two or three default power plans:

- **Balanced** Balances energy usage and system performance. The processor speeds up when more resources are used and slows down when less are needed.
- **High Performance** Optimizes the computer for performance while increasing energy usage. The plan ensures that you always have enough power for using graphics-intensive programs or playing multimedia games.
- **Power Saver** Reduces power consumption while decreasing performance. The plan slows down the processor to conserve power.

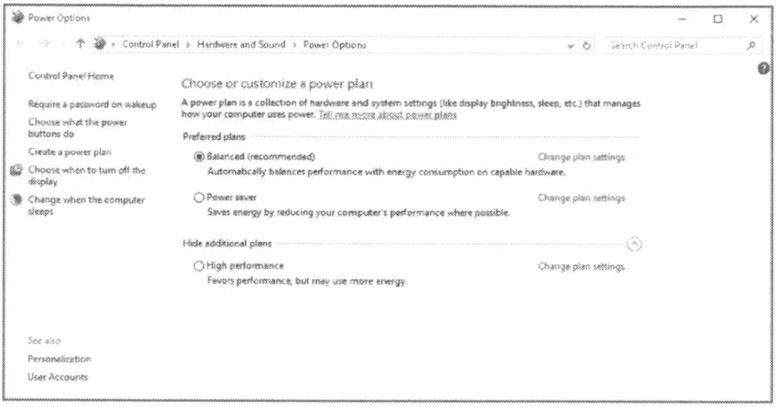

Figure 9-1 Configuring power plans

Power plans have basic and advanced settings. Basic settings control when a computer turns off its display and when it enters sleep mode. And if you are using a device with a battery, you'll have separate plugged in and on battery options. Advanced settings determine precisely whether and when power management components are shut down and how those components are configured for performance. And you'll like wise have different advanced options for when the computer is plugged in and on battery.

The available advanced settings depend on the type of computer you are using and include:

- **Battery\Reserve Battery Level**   Determines the percentage of battery remaining that initiates reserve power mode. Typical default is 7 percent, meaning enter reserve power mode when battery power reaches 7 percent remaining. A reserve level of 5 to 18 percent is often best.
- **Desktop Background Settings\Slide Show**   Determines whether the slide show feature for the desktop background is

available or paused. Default is Available. Set to Paused to disable background slide shows on the desktop.

- **Display\Turn Off Display After**   Determines whether and when a computer's display is turned off to conserve power. Choosing Never disables this feature. Specific value in minutes sets inactive duration before the display is turned off.

- **Hard Disk\Turn Off Hard Disk After**   Determines whether and when a computer's hard disk is turned off to conserve power. Choosing Never (0) disables turning off the hard disk. Specific value in minutes sets inactive duration before hard disk is turned off.

- **Multimedia Settings\When Playing Video**   Determines the power optimization mode used when playing video. Use Optimize Video Quality for best quality playback. Use Balanced for a balanced approach to adjusting playback quality to save power. Use Optimize Power Savings for active approach to adjusting playback quality to save power.

- **Multimedia Settings\When Sharing Media**   Determines what the computer does when a device or another computer plays media from the computer. Use Allow The Computer To Enter Away Mode to ensure computer will not enter sleep mode when sharing media. Use Allow The Computer To Sleep to allow the computer to enter sleep mode when inactive. Use Prevent Idling To Sleep to allow the computer to enter sleep mode only if set by user.

- **PCI Express\Link State Power Management**   Determines the power saving mode to use with Peripheral Component Interconnect (PCI) Express devices connected to the computer. Set this option to Off, Moderate Power Savings, or Maximum Power Savings.

- **Power Buttons And Lid\Power Button Action**   Specifies the action to take when someone pushes and holds the computer's power button. Set this option to Do Nothing, Sleep, Hibernate, or Shutdown.

- **Power Buttons And Lid\Sleep Button Action**   Sets the default action for the sleep button. Use this setting to override the computer's default action. Set this option to Do Nothing, Sleep, or Hibernate (as permitted).

- **Processor Power Management\Maximum Processor State**   Sets a maximum or peak performance state for the computer's processor. Lower to save power at a direct cost to responsiveness and computational speed. At 50 percent or below can cause a significant reduction in performance and responsiveness.

- **Processor Power Management\Minimum Processor State**   Sets a minimum performance state for the computer's processor. Lower to save power at a direct cost to responsiveness and computational speed. 5 percent reduces responsiveness while offering substantial power savings. 50 percent helps to balance responsiveness and while moderately saving power. 100 percent maximize responsiveness but doesn't saving power.

- **Processor Power Management\System Cooling Policy**   Determines whether the operating system increases the fan speed before slowing the processor. Passive limitedly enables, and the processor may run hot. Active fully enables to help cool the processor.

- **PlanName\Require A Password On Wakeup**   Determines whether a password is required when a computer wakes from sleep. Set to Yes or No. With domain computers, controlled through Group Policy.

- **Sleep\Allow Hybrid Sleep**   Specifies whether the computer uses hybrid sleep mode rather than the sleep mode used in earlier versions of Windows. Set to On or Off. Hybrid sleep mode puts the computer in a low-power state until the user resumes using the computer. If the battery runs low, the computer hibernates.

- **Sleep\Allow Wake Timers** Determines whether timed events should be allowed to wake the computer from a sleep state. Use Disable to prevent. Use Enable to allow.
- **Sleep\Hibernate After** Determines whether and when a computer hibernates to conserve power. Not normally used unless battery power runs low. Use Never to disable. Specific value in minutes sets inactive duration before the computer hibernates.
- **Sleep\Sleep After** Determines whether and when a computer enters a sleep state to conserve power. Use Never to disable. Specific value in minutes sets inactive duration before the computer sleeps.
- **USB Settings\USB Selective Suspend Setting** Determines whether the USB selective suspend feature is available. Use Disabled to turn off selective suspend. Use Enabled to allow selective suspend.
- **Wireless Adapter Settings\Power Saving Mode** Specifies the power saving mode to use with any wireless adapters connected to the computer. Set to Maximum Performance, Low Power Saving, Medium Power Saving, or Maximum Power Saving.

Real World Differences in the advanced settings are what set the default power plans apart. As an example, the High Performance plan ensures performance by allowing the computer's processor to always run at 100 percent power consumption, whereas the Power Saver and the Balanced

---

plans reduce energy consumption by configuring the processor to use a minimum power consumption rate of 5 percent and a maximum rate of 100 percent.

You can manage power plans from the command line by using the Power Configuration (Powercfg.exe) utility. Type **powercfg -l** at the command prompt to list the power plans configured on a computer by name and globally unique identifier (GUID). When you know the GUID for a power plan, you can work with it in a variety of ways:

- Enter **powercfg –q** followed by a GUID to view the settings of the related plan.
- Enter **powercfg –d** followed by a GUID to delete the related plan.
- Enter **powercfg –s** followed by a GUID to set the related plan as the active plan.

If you want to see a complete list of all available parameters, enter **powercfg /?** at the command prompt.

Creating and Optimizing Power Plans

In addition to the preferred power plans included with Windows 10, you can create power plans and optimize existing power plans as needed.

You can create a power plan by following these steps:

1. On the Power Options page, click Create A Power Plan in the left pane, and then select the default power plan that is closest to the type of plan you want to create.

2. In the Plan Name field, type a descriptive name for the plan; then click Next.

3. Use the Turn Off The Display drop-down list to specify whether or when the computer's display automatically turns off. Choose Never to disable this feature. Note that if you are using a device with a battery, you'll have separate plugged in and on battery options.

4. Use the Put The Computer To Sleep drop-down list to specify whether or when the computer automatically enters sleep mode. Choose Never to disable this feature. Note that if you are using a device with a battery, you'll have separate plugged in and on battery options.

5. Click Create to create the plan. On the Power Options page, the plan you created is selected by default.

6. Click Change Plan Settings for your new plan, and then click Change Advanced Power Settings.

7. Configure the advanced power options as appropriate, and then click OK to save your power plan.

You can optimize an existing power plan by following these steps:

1. On the Power Options page, select the power plan you want to configure, and then click Change Plan Settings.

2. Use the Turn Off Display drop-down list to specify whether or when the computer's display automatically turns off. Choose Never to disable this feature. Note that if you are using a device with a battery, you'll have separate plugged in and on battery options.

3. Use the Put The Computer To Sleep drop-down list to specify whether or when the computer automatically enters sleep mode. Choose Never to disable this feature. Note that if you are using a device with a battery, you'll have separate plugged in and on battery options.

4. To configure advanced options, click Change Advanced Power Settings, and then use the Power Options dialog box to configure your desired settings. Click OK to save any changes you've made.

5. Click Save Changes to update the power plan.

Resolving Power Problems That Are Affecting Performance

When it comes to power plans and power management, an aspect that's often overlooked is compatibility. To enter and exit sleep states, your computer must support a Standby sleep state. Similarly, to use hybrid sleep and hibernate, your computer must support the Hibernate and Hybrid Sleep states. One of Windows 10's top features—Fast Startup—is also a sleep state that must be supported.

To determine the sleep states supported by entering **powercfg -a** at the command prompt. As Figure 9-2 shows, this option lists the available sleep states on the computer and the reasons why a particular sleep state is not supported. If your computer does not support hybrid sleep or fast startup, you should ensure that the related settings are not enabled in firmware.

Figure 9-2 Determining the supported sleep states

Every running application and every installed device must support power management for your computer to manage power and sleep states effectively. If an application is causing pause and resume problems, you can check with the developer for an update or newer version that fixes the problem. You can verify that the installed devices support power management appropriately by typing **powercfg -energy** at an elevated, administrator command prompt. As shown in the following example, Powercfg provides details about each review step and also lets you know if problems were found.

```
powercfg -energy

Enabling tracing for 60 seconds...
Observing system behavior...
Analyzing trace data...
Analysis complete.

Energy efficiency problems were found.

14 Errors
11 Warnings
28 Informational

See C:\Users\owner\Documents\energy-
report.html for more details.
```

When the Power Configuration utility finishes tracing and analyzing your computer, review the energy report generated by the utility in a web browser. As Figure 9-3 shows, the analysis results are what you want to focus on.

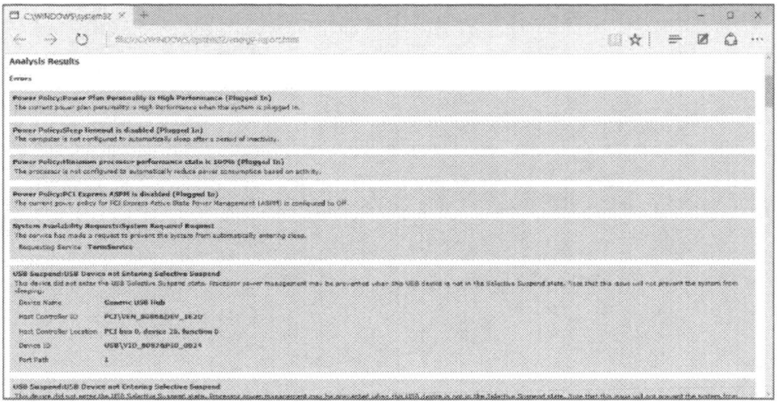

Figure 9-3 Reviewing the analysis results

Read the errors, warnings, and informational messages. If possible, take appropriate action to resolve errors. If a device has a power management issue, you may be able to resolve the problem by installing an updated driver or by changing the device's configuration options.

However, there are many caveats. Active devices, such as an audio device playing music, could prevent your computer from entering sleep mode during the analysis. This is normal, and success or failure is determined by the type of device and the power management settings.

The same device can generate a series of errors. For example, on my computer, a USB audio device prevented the system from automatically entering sleep mode during the analysis, and several other USB related errors were related to this device.

Other common errors you'll see relate to the display or a particular device that may have had pending update requests during the testing. If there were pending requests for the display or any other device, these requests would prevent the computer from automatically powering off the display or the device, and also would prevent the computer from automatically entering a low-power sleep state.

You can get more information about pending requests made by device drivers by typing **powercfg –requests** at the command prompt. In the following example, a USB audio device has pending requests.

```
powercfg -requests

DISPLAY:
None.

SYSTEM:
[DRIVER] USB Audio Device
(USB\VID_05A7&PID_1020&MI_00\6&2eafe1b7&0&000
0)
An audio stream is currently in use.

AWAYMODE:
None.
```

In this example, note the device identifier: USB\VID_05A7&PID_1020. Each error in the power report is associated with a specific device as well. To know for sure whether a device has a sleep and resume problem, you need to examine the detailed power support information available when you type **powercfg -devicequery all_devices_verbose** at a command prompt.

Because the information is so detailed, you'll want to redirect the command output to a text file, as shown in this example.

```
powercfg -devicequery all_devices_verbose >
save.txt
```

Next, open the file in a text editor, such as Notepad, and search the file for the device identifier. Finally, review the output for the device to determine its power capabilities and supported sleep states.

Maintaining Performance with Updates

Your computer's performance is tied directly to the Windows components, hardware devices, and applications that are installed. Poor programming and coding problems can keep your computer from performing optimally. You can ensure that the most recent updates and hot fixes are applied to your computer by using Windows Update.

Windows Update allows your computer to automatically download and update operating system components, device drives, optional components and related programs. To take this process a step further, you can configure your computer to use Microsoft Update, which ensures that updates for other Microsoft products are updated as well.

Many applications from third-party vendors have update features as well. Use these update features whenever possible to keep installed applications up to date and performing optimally.

Fine-tuning Automatic Updates

Windows Update integrates with Microsoft Update to ensure that the operating system and installed Microsoft applications stay up to date. You can determine whether your computer is using Microsoft Update by following these steps:

1. Click Start and then click Settings. In Settings, click Update & Security. In the left pane, the Windows Update option is selected by default.

2. In the main pane, scroll down and then click the Advanced Options link.

3. If your computer is using Microsoft Update, the Give Me Updates For Other Microsoft Products option is selected, as shown in Figure 9-4. If your computer isn't getting these updates and you want to get them, select the related checkbox.

Figure 9-4 Getting updates for other Microsoft products

While you are working with the Windows Update, you should optimize the update settings. Click Chose How Updates Are Installed List and then choose either Notify To Schedule Restart or Automatic.

With notification, you are notified to schedule a restart after Windows downloads updates that require a restart. You can then specify when the restart should occur or restart the computer manually. If there are updates that don't require a restart, you'll need to apply them manually. On Windows Update page, you'll see a message that there are updates ready to install. Click Next and follow the prompts. With some updates you may need to access license terms. If so, you'll need to click Accept And Install. Other times, you'll simply need to review the available updates and click Install.

Rather than constantly being notified about updates or having to check for updates that need to be applied, I prefer the Automatic option. With Automatic, Windows Update downloads and installed updates automatically. By default, your computer periodically checks for and downloads updates when you are connected to the Internet over wi-fi and doesn't download updates when you are using mobile data. If a restart is required to install the updates, Windows schedules the restart for a time when you aren't using the computer.

Scheduled restarts depend on you using the sleep mode rather than shutting down. If you try to shut down your computer after updates have been downloaded, you have the option of installing updates and then shutting down or shut down without installing updates.

By default, Windows schedules restarts at 3:30 AM on any day when a restart is needed. This time follows the Automatic Maintenance schedule, which is set to run daily at 2:00 AM. You can view available updates and determine whether a restarting is scheduled by following these steps:

1. Click Start and then click Settings. In Settings, click Update & Security. In the left pane, the Windows Update option is selected by default.
2. Available updates are listed in the main pane. Scroll up. If a restart is scheduled, this is stated, as shown in Figure 9-5.

3. You can restart immediately by clicking Restart Now. To change the restart schedule, choose Select A Restart Time. Next, specify a time and day for the restart, such as 8:00 AM, Tomorrow.

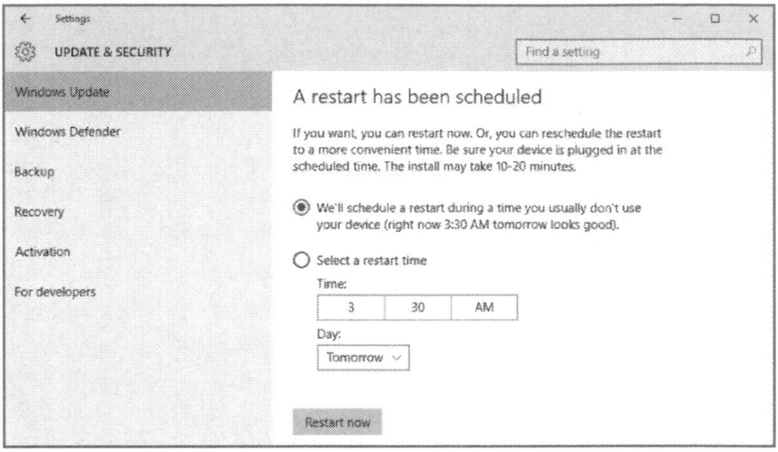

Figure 9-5 Getting information about a pending restart

Resolving Update Problems

Your computer may experience problems caused by installing updates. Although this happens rarely, it does happen. You can view a detailed update history and a list of successful, pending and failed updates by following these steps:

1. Click Start and then click Settings. In Settings, click Update & Security. In the left pane, the Windows Update option is selected by default.

2. In the main pane, scroll down and then click the Advanced Options link.

3. Click View Update History. On the View Update History page, updates listed with a Successful status were downloaded and installed. Updates listed with an Unsuccessful status were

downloaded but failed to install. Updates listed with the Requires A Restart status were downloaded and will be installed when the computer is restarted.

Some important changes to Windows Update that you should know about. Unlike early releases of Windows, Windows 10 gets updates for the operating system, device drivers and optional components automatically. You can't specify that you don't want these updates, nor can you decline installing these update. However, you can uninstall an optional update that proves problematic. If you are already on the View Your Update History page, click the Uninstall Updates link to open the Installed Updates page in Control Panel. Next, click the optional update to remove and then click Uninstall.

Optimizing Performance: Final Tune-up Suggestions

Throughout this book, and in this chapter particularly, I've discussed techniques for optimizing your computer's performance. If you've been following along, you've fine-tuned just about every aspect of your computer. Now let's look at a few additional areas for the final tune-up, including:

* Services and features
* Virtual memory
* Data execution prevention
* System cache
* Hard disk drives

The sections that follow discuss each in turn.

Disabling Unnecessary Services and Features

System services provide critical functions for your computer. However, unnecessary services use system resources and are a potential source of security problems. If your computer is running a service you don't need, such as Worldwide Web Publishing Service, you can disable the service or remove the related feature.

Typically, you should start by disabling services rather than uninstalling components. This way, if you disable a service that was actually needed, you can easily re-enable it if necessary. If you have local administrator privileges on your computer, you can disable a service by following these steps:

1. Type **Services** in the Search box, and then press Enter. This opens the Services console.

2. Right-click the service you want to configure, and then choose Properties. On the General tab, select Disabled in the Startup Type drop-down list.

3. Disabling a service doesn't stop a running service; it only prevents the service from being started the next time the computer is booted. As necessary, click Stop on the General tab in the Properties dialog box, and then click OK.

You can turn off Windows features by following these steps:

1. In the Search box, type **Windows Features**, and then press Enter. This opens the Windows Features dialog box.

2. Clear the check box for the feature you want to turn off, and then click OK. You may need to restart your computer. If prompted to do so, save your work and then click Restart.

Fine-Tuning Virtual Memory

Your computer uses virtual memory to extend the amount of available RAM. Virtual memory is written to disk through a process called paging. The operating system can access the paging file, Pagefile.sys, from disk when needed in place of physical memory. By default, Windows 10 creates an initial paging file automatically for the drive containing the operating system and does not use other drives for paging.

Typically, you don't need to put a paging file on multiple disks, because doing so won't necessarily boost performance, but you may want to put the paging file on your highest-performing drive. Windows 10 does a much better job than its predecessors do of automatically managing virtual memory. Typically, Windows 10 allocates virtual memory at least as large as the total physical memory installed on the computer. This approach reduces fragmentation of the paging file and helps to maintain overall read/write performance.

If you want to manually manage virtual memory, you'll typically want to use a fixed virtual memory size. You fix the size of the virtual memory by setting the initial size and the maximum size to the same value, and this in turn prevents fragmentation of the paging file. For most computers, I recommend setting the total paging file size so that it's at least as large as the physical RAM.

You can view the current virtual memory configuration by completing the following steps:

1. In the Search box, type **SystemPropertiesPerformance**, and then press Enter to open the Performance Options dialog box.

2. On the Advanced tab, click Change to display the Virtual Memory dialog box.

> **Note** You can get to the same dialog box through Control Panel as well. Click System And Security and then click System. In the left pane, click Advanced System Settings. In the Performance section, click Settings to open the Performance Options dialog box.

Figure 9-6 shows an automatically managed paging file configuration on the left and a manually set paging file configuration on the right. Note the following:

- **Automatically Manage Paging File Size For All Drives** Controls whether the operating system manages the paging file.
- **Drive [Volume Label] And Paging File Size (MB)** Shows the current configuration of virtual memory. Each disk volume is listed with its associated paging file (if any). The initial and maximum size values of the related paging file are shown as well.
- **Paging File Size For Each Drive** Provides information on the currently selected drive and allows you to set its paging file size. Space Available indicates how much space is available on the drive.
- **Total Paging File Size For All Drives** Shows the minimum, recommended, and currently allocated virtual memory.

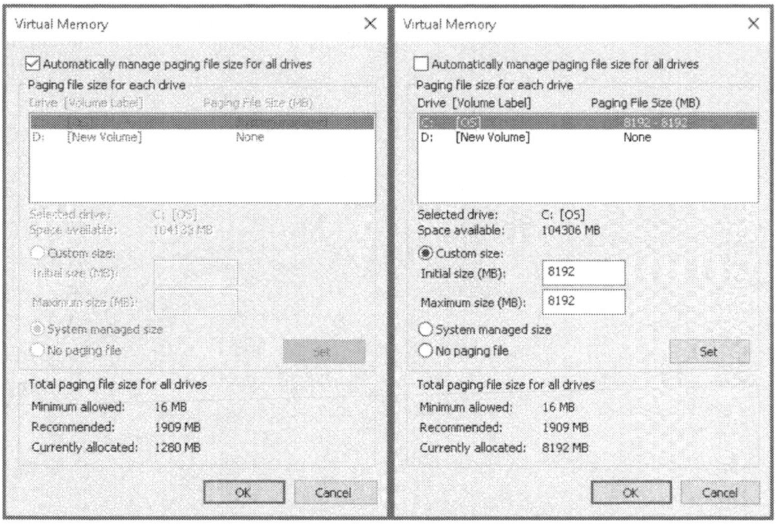

Figure 9-6 Checking your computer's virtual memory configuration

You can configure virtual memory by completing the following steps:

1. Open the Virtual Memory dialog box and do one of the following:

    *   If you want Windows to manage virtual memory, select Automatically Manage Paging File Size For All Drives, click OK, and skip steps 2–4.
    *   If you want to configure virtual memory manually, clear Automatically Manage Paging File Size For All Drives and continue with step 2.

2. In the Drive box, click the disk volume you want to work with, and then select Custom Size.

3. Enter an initial size and a maximum size for the paging file on the selected disk. Click Set to save the changes.

4. Repeat steps 2 and 3 for each disk volume you want to have a paging file.

5. Click OK. If prompted to overwrite an existing Pagefile.sys file, click Yes.

6. If you updated the settings for a paging file that is currently in use, you will be prompted that you need to restart the system for the changes to take effect. Click OK.

7. Click OK twice to close the open dialog boxes. A prompt asks if you want to restart the system. Click Restart.

Fine-Tuning Data Execution Prevention

Windows 10 uses Data Execution Prevention (DEP) to mark memory locations used by applications as nonexecutable unless the location explicitly contains executable code. If an application attempts to execute code from a memory page marked as nonexecutable, the processor can raise an exception and prevent it from executing. DEP is designed to thwart malware from inserting itself into areas of memory and in this way protects your computer.

DEP is implemented in hardware and software. Hardware-based DEP is the most effective because it encompasses any program or service running on the computer. Software-based DEP is less effective because it typically works best only when protecting Windows programs and services. Although DEP is designed to protect your computer, the feature can affect performance.

> **Real World** Windows 32-bit versions support DEP as implemented originally by Advanced Micro Devices Inc. (AMD) processors that provide the no-execute page-protection (NX) processor feature. Such processors support

the related instructions and must be running in Physical Address Extension (PAE) mode. Windows 64-bit versions also support the NX processor feature but do not need to be running in PAE mode.

You can determine whether your computer supports hardware-based DEP by completing the following steps:

1. In the Search box, type **SystemPropertiesPerformance**, and then press Enter to open the Performance Options dialog box.

2. If your computer supports hardware-based DEP, the lower portion of the Data Execution Prevention tab appears as shown in Figure 9-7.

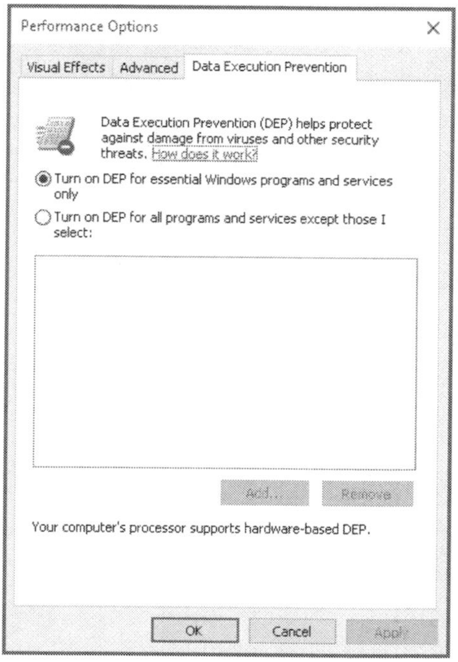

Figure 9-7 Checking for hardware-based DEP support

> **Note** You can get to the same dialog box through Control Panel as well. Click System And Security and then click System. In the left pane, click Advanced System Settings. In the Performance section, click Settings to open the Performance Options dialog box and then select the Data Execution Prevention tab.

After accessing the Data Execution Prevention tab, you can manage the way DEP works by using these options:

- **Turn On DEP For Essential Windows Programs And Services Only** Enables DEP only for services, programs, and components of the operating system. This is the default and recommended setting for computers that support execution protection and are configured appropriately.
- **Turn On DEP For All Programs And Services Except Those I Select** Enables DEP for services, programs, and components of the operating system and all other programs and services the computer is running.

Some programs won't work with or will become unstable with DEP, and you may find that you have to add exceptions when you enable DEP for all programs. Click Add to specify programs that should run without execution protection. Execution protection will work for all programs except those you have listed.

Enhancing Performance with ReadyBoost

Non-critical kernel memory is paged to virtual memory, as part of the system cache. Although virtual memory is useful, reading from and writing to a disk is significantly slower than reading from and writing to physical memory (RAM). To reduce the performance impact related to reading and writing the system cache from virtual memory, you can configure your computer to use Windows ReadyBoost.

Windows ReadyBoost lets you extend the disk-caching capabilities of the computer's main memory to a USB flash device that has at least 2 GB of high-speed flash memory. You cannot configure this feature on removable hard drives or USB flash devices with poorly performing flash memory.

The operating system uses the flash memory primarily for caching that uses random input/output and small, sequential input/output rather than large, sequential input/output. This is because the flash memory is better suited to random I/O and small, sequential input/output than large, sequential I/O. By caching data on the USB flash device instead of your computer's disk drives, Windows makes faster random reads, which boosts overall performance because it's up to 1,000 percent faster than reading from physical disk drives.

Real World   As a safeguard, Windows 10 adds protection to prevent the sudden removal of a USB flash device from crashing the computer and to prevent reading of any sensitive data written to the flash device. Windows 10 eliminates the potential for data loss when removing a flash device by writing to the paging file on disk first and then copying data to the flash device. Windows 10 encrypts all data written to a flash device to prevent reading of sensitive data on another computer.

To enable Windows ReadyBoost, insert a USB flash device into a USB 2.0 or higher port. Next, open File Explorer. In the left pane, you should see an entry for the flash device. The flash device will be assigned a drive letter, such as F:. If you don't see the device, select This PC and then look for the device in the main pane under Devices And Drives, as shown in Figure 9-8.

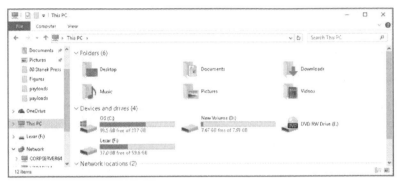

Figure 9-8 Locating the USB flash device in This PC

Next, right-click the device, and then select Properties. If the flash device is not compatible, you'll see a warning about this, as shown in the first example in Figure 9-9; you won't be able to turn on ReadyBoost. If the flash device is compatible, as shown in the second example in the figure, you can configure ReadyBoost.

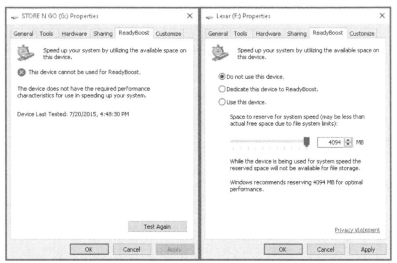

Figure 9-9 Enabling and configuring Windows ReadyBoost

You can reserve from 230 MB to 4094 MB of flash memory for
ReadyBoost. I recommend using as much as possible. To
automatically reserve the maximum amount of space for ReadyBoost,
select Dedicate This Device To ReadyBoost. Otherwise, select Use
This Device, and then use the Space To Reserve For System Speed
slider or combo box to set the amount of space to use with
ReadyBoost. When you click OK, Windows 10 extends the
computer's physical memory to the device.

> **Note**   Choosing either setting option doesn't prevent you
> from writing files to the device. Your choice simply
> determines the amount of space to reserve for ReadyBoost. If
> you reserve less than the total amount of space available, the
> free space can be used for files and data.

You can safely remove a USB flash device that uses ReadyBoost at any time. Simply right-click the USB flash device in the This PC window, and then choose Eject or Safely Remove.

Cleaning Up Your Disk Drives

Your computer may slow down as its disks fill to capacity, because it uses available space to write the paging file and other temporary files it needs to use. Ideally, you should ensure that any disk used by the operating system to write system files has at least 15 percent free space. Otherwise, you may start to notice that your computer is not as responsive as it should be.

You can clean up your computer's disks by using Disk Cleanup, which locates temporary files and allows you to remove them. Temporary files you can delete in this way include:

- Copies of network files designated for offline use.
- Dump files created because of STOP errors.
- Files that have been deleted from the computer but not yet purged from the Recycle Bin.
- Hibernation files used when your computer enters sleep mode.
- Log files and other temporary files that Office uses.
- Log files that Windows created during setup.
- Previous Windows installations saved under Windows.old.
- Programs downloaded for use by your browser.
- Temporary copies of recently used offline files
- Temporary files stored in the Temp folder by applications.
- Temporary files used for error reporting and checking for solutions to problems.

- Temporary Internet files stored to support browser caching of pages.
- Thumbnails of pictures, videos, and documents created by Windows.

Although you can delete most temporary files without hesitation, you may want to retain:

- Setup log files, if you are still configuring your computer after installation.
- Previous Windows installations, if you haven't saved user data or other necessary data they may contain.
- Dump files related to unresolved STOP errors, as they may be needed for troubleshooting.
- Thumbnails, because Windows would need to create them the next time you access folders.

Clean up your computer's disk by completing the following steps:

1. In the Search box, type **Disk Cleanup**, and then press Enter.
2. Select the disk that you want to clean up. When you click OK, Disk Cleanup examines the selected drive, looking for temporary files that can be deleted and files that are candidates for compression. The more files on the drive, the longer the search process takes.
3. When Disk Cleanup is complete, a list of temporary files that can be deleted appears as shown in Figure 9-10. Add system files to the cleanup list by clicking Clean Up System Files, selecting the primary system drive, and then clicking OK. The primary system disk is the disk with the Windows logo when you view it in File Explorer.

4. By default, only a few types of temporary files are selected. As appropriate, review the other types of temporary files that you can delete and mark them for deletion by selecting them.

5. Click OK. When prompted to confirm, click Yes.

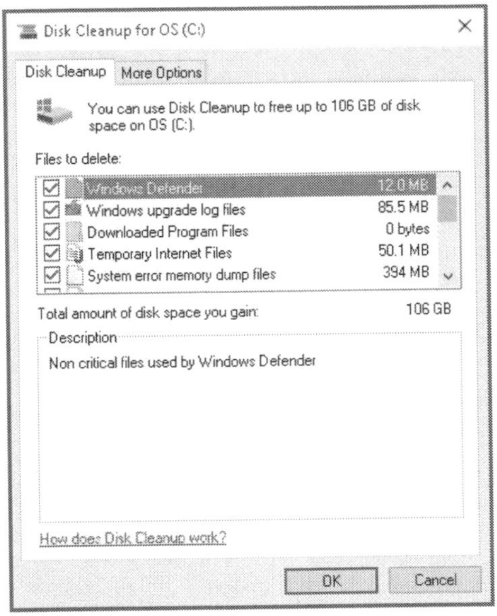

Figure 9-10 Reviewing files to delete using Disk Cleanup

Automating Maintenance

Windows 10 performs automated maintenance to help optimize your computer's performance. Unfortunately, while the idea of such of thing sounds terrific, the reality is a bit different.

Why Automated Maintenance Breaks

By default, automated maintenance occurs daily at 2:00 AM. If your computer is in sleep mode at this time, the computer wakes from sleep and resumes normal operations automatically so maintenance can be performed. Your computer will stay active during the maintenance schedule. By default, if your computer has updates that require a restart, your computer restarts at 3:30 AM. After the restart, if all goes well, your computer will resume any maintenance tasks that still need to be process or wait for the idle time to elapse and then re-enter sleep mode.

These automated processes work well, but are far from perfect. For starters, your computer must be plugged in and running on AC power for any automated maintenance to occur. Second, a user must also be logged in and the computer must be either idle or in sleep mode. If you logged out of your computer and no other user is logged in, automated maintenance won't occur, nor will it occur if you or someone else is using your computer during the maintenance window.

Starting to see a problem here? Yes? Well, there's more. If the maintenance window is missed, Windows won't try again until the next day at the scheduled maintenance time. Additionally, the housekeeping tasks don't follow these same rules. Once a disk check or disk defrag start, they will continue until they are finished, regardless of whether a user is logged on—and both of these tasks will continue running off and on for up to 3 days if necessary.

Optimizing the Maintenance Window

Personally, I don't want my computer to wake at 2:00 AM, nor do I want it to restart at 3:30 AM. I'm often going into the office and finding the computer running when I arrive for work in the morning—hours after it should have reentered sleep mode. There are many reasons this can happen. The two most common: A pending action or power options that prevent sleep mode when idle.

Because I don't want my computer running for 5, 6, 7 or 8 hours before I get to the office, I configure automated maintenance to start about 2 and a half hours beforehand and I schedule restarts to occur about an hour and a half later.

You can change the maintenance start time by following these steps:

1. Type Security And Maintenance in the Search box and press Enter.

2. In Security And Maintenance, expand the Maintenance panel and then click Change Maintenance Settings.

3. On the Automatic Maintenance page, shown in Figure 9-11, use the Run Maintenance Tasks lists to set the desired start time, such as 6:00 AM.

4. Optionally, if you don't want Windows to wake your computer to perform automated maintenance, clear the Allow Scheduled Maintenance... checkbox.

5. Click OK to save your settings.

Figure 9-11 Setting the maintenance start time

Running Maintenance Manually

Of the many housekeeping tasks performed during automated maintenance, these are the most important:

- Check Disk
- Disk Defragment
- Problem Reporting

Your computer is constantly reading from and writing to its primary disk. If a particular sector or cluster on a disk is damaged or otherwise cannot be written to, your computer will experience problems whenever it tries to read from or write to this sector or cluster. Although the operating system and drive controllers help to mitigate and correct disk problems, they can't prevent and correct all disk problems. Occasionally errors occur, and Check Disk can correct these errors.

Another problem that causes disk drives to perform poorly is fragmentation. Fragmentation occurs when a file can't be written to a single contiguous area on the disk and the operating system must write a single file to several areas on the disk. Not only does this slow down the write process, it also slows down the read process. To reduce fragmentation, Windows 10 uses Disk Defragmenter to defragment disks automatically.

Other types of problems that occur on your computer may be detected by automated problem reporting and diagnostics, which were discussed in "Checking for Problems That Are Affecting Performance" in Chapter 8.

You can initiate these and other maintenance tasks at any time by following these steps:

1. Type Security And Maintenance in the Search box and press Enter.

2. In Security And Maintenance, expand the Maintenance panel and then click Start Maintenance.

About the Author

William R. Stanek (http://www.williamstanek.com/) has more than 20 years of hands-on experience with advanced programming and development. He is a leading technology expert, an award-winning author, and a pretty-darn-good instructional trainer. Over the years, his practical advice has helped millions of programmers, developers, and network engineers all over the world. His current and books include *Windows 8.1 Administration Pocket Consultant, Windows Server 2012 R2 Pocket Consultant* and *Windows Server 2012 R2 Inside Out.*

William has been involved in the commercial Internet community since 1991. His core business and technology experience comes from more than 11 years of military service. He has substantial experience in developing server technology, encryption, and Internet solutions. He has written many technical white papers and training courses on a wide variety of topics. He frequently serves as a subject matter expert and consultant.

William has an MS with distinction in information systems and a BS in computer science, magna cum laude. He is proud to have served in the Persian Gulf War as a combat crewmember on an electronic warfare aircraft. He flew on numerous combat missions into Iraq and was awarded nine medals for his wartime service, including one of the United States of America's highest flying honors, the Air Force Distinguished Flying Cross. Currently, he resides in the Pacific Northwest with his wife and children.

William recently rediscovered his love of the great outdoors. When he's not writing, he can be found hiking, biking, backpacking, traveling, or trekking in search of adventure with his family!

Find William on Twitter at www.twitter.com/WilliamStanek and on Facebook at www.facebook.com/William.Stanek.Author.

Windows PowerShell 3.0 and Windows PowerShell 4.0

THE PERSONAL TRAINER™

Windows PowerShell

WILLIAM STANEK
Award-winning technology expert